MODERN HUMANITIES RESEARCH ASSOCIATION

CRITICAL TEXTS

VOLUME 14

Editor
MALCOLM COOK
(*French*)

LA MILIADE

LE GOUVERNEMENT PRESENT

OU

ELOGE DE SON EMINENCE,

SATYRE OU LA MILIADE

Edited by

Paul Scott

MODERN HUMANITIES RESEARCH ASSOCIATION
2010

Published by

The Modern Humanities Research Association,
1 Carlton House Terrace
London SW1Y 5AF

© The Modern Humanities Research Association, 2010

Paul Scott has asserted his right under the Copyright, Designs and Patents Act 1988 to be identified as the author of this work.

Parts of this work may be reproduced as permitted under legal provisions for fair dealing (or fair use) for the purposes of research, private study, criticism, or review, or when a relevant collective licensing agreement is in place. All other reproduction requires the written permission of the copyright holder who may be contacted at rights@mhra.org.uk

First published 2010

ISBN 978 0 947623 77 7

ISSN 1746-1642

Copies may be ordered from www.criticaltexts.mhra.org.uk

Table of Contents

List of Illustrations 1
Acknowledgements 2
Abbreviations 4
Introduction 7
Date and Place of Publication 8
Authorship 13
    Charles de Beys 14
    Comte d'Ételan 16
    Bruc de Montplaisir 23
    Girou 25
    Jacques Favereau 27
    Bussy Pasquier 37
    Other Contenders 38
Publication History 41
    The Octavo Edition 42
    The Quarto Edition 48
    Anthology 51
    Manuscripts 53
The *Miliade* as Political Satire 54
Satirical Targets 63
Techniques of Discontent 70
The *Miliade*'s Legacy 85
Establishment of the Text and
    Editorial Practice 89
LA MILIADE 91
Notes to the Text 123
Appendix 157
Bibliography 167

LE GOUVERNEMENT PRESENT

Rés	Bibliothèque nationale de France réserve copy (Rés Ye 4086)
Rich	Bibliothèque nationale de France, Département des manuscrits, Richelieu site copy (1518.72.30)
RMS	Bibliothèque nationale de France, MS fonds français 22579
Tab (1649)	*Le Tableau du gouvernement present, ou eloge de son Eminence. Satyre de mille vers. Nouvelle edition reveuë, et exactement corrigée* (Paris: [n.pub.], 1649)
Tall	In the footnotes to the edition this refers to 'Le Tableau du gouvernement present ou eloge de Monsieur le Cardinal de Richelieu', Bibliothèque nationale, MS fonds français 19145; in the introduction and endnotes it refers to Gédéon Tallemant de Réaux's marginal annotations to this manuscript.

Le Gouvernement Present

INTRODUCTION

The *Miliade* is already quite well known to scholars by reputation, but less so in its detail. The work has only been edited once since the seventeenth century, a mid-nineteenth-century edition by Édouard Fournier which does not adequately tackle many unresolved questions surrounding the work, unsurprisingly given that Fournier published the edition as part of a multi-volume collection of interesting historical documents, situating it within the context of neglected curiosa rather than standing in its own right.[1] The *Miliade* held a legendary status among its contemporaries and this was consolidated by the uncertainty surrounding its production, which includes the unidentified authorship, the date of its appearance, and the trajectory of the various reprints of the first edition. The work stands as one of the few remaining literary mysteries of early modern France, and this edition aims to resolve these open-ended questions. I believe that I have satisfactorily settled the question of authorship using both the internal evidence of particular stylistic traits as well as a series of circumstantial proofs which point to a particular candidate. Moreover, the same criteria have allowed for the claims of other potential authors to be discounted. This edition therefore decodes a public puzzle that not even Richelieu, with his far-reaching intelligence network, was able to solve, notwithstanding his implacable determination to do so.

The poem deserves to be better known for several reasons. Firstly, in terms of its content as a parody of Cardinal Richelieu and the members of his government, it makes a valuable contribution to satirical literature during the reign of Louis XIII. Secondly, in view of the fact that the minister took the unprecedented action of having as many as five writers imprisoned on suspicion of having written it, without ever satisfactorily finding out who was its creator, the chequered success of the pamphlet marks a crucial moment in the history of censorship during the Ancien Régime. Finally, I will argue that the work had far-reaching effects in the format of anti-

---

[1] Édouard Fournier, *Variétés historiques et littéraires: recueil de pièces volantes rares et curieuses en prose et en vers*, 10 vols (Paris: Pagnerre, 1855-63), IX (1859), 5-46.

government discourse and would play a major part in inspiring the Mazarinades that would crystallize public opinion during the Fronde.

The poem has all too often been categorized and ultimately dismissed as a vulgar and partisan diatribe, which certainly, in places, it is, making it all the more agreeable to read. However, some sophisticated techniques and tropes underpin the *Miliade* and it accordingly deserves closer attention as a literary work of some merit.

DATE AND PLACE OF PUBLICATION

Several dates have been proposed for the work, ranging from 1633 to 1638. Barbier mentions 1633 whereas Brunet opts for 1635.[2] Moreau, when dealing with the pseudo-Mazarinade versions of the *Miliade*, states that: 'On sait que l'édition originale de ce pamphlet est de 1635'.[3] In following the suggested date of 1633, one editor proceeds to conjecture that a poem sent to the scholar Nicolas-Claude de Pereisc in that year was in fact the *Miliade*.[4] Following these authorities, the catalogue of the Bibliothèque nationale de France currently provides either date, that is to say 1633 or 1635 depending on the copy. More recently, Antoine Adam believes that

---

[2] Alexandre-Antoine Barbier, *Dictionnaire des ouvrages anonymes*, 2 vols (Paris: Daffis, 1874), II, col. 551; Jacques-Charles Brunet, *Manuel du libraire et de l'amateur de livres*, 2 vols (Paris: Didot, 1861), II, col. 1684.

[3] Célestin Moreau, *Bibliographie des Mazarinades publiée pour la Société de l'Histoire de France*, 3 vols (Paris: Renouard, 1850–51), II (1851), 11–12.

[4] The editor comments on a letter sent from Samuel Petit to Pereisc dated 16 September 1633 in which he notes: 'Je vous envoye le Cæsar, manuscrit que vous désiriés de voir, avec un autre manuscrit françois que je viens de recouvrer et le poème de Monsieur Favereau dont je vous parlay' In his note, Larroque comments 'Le poème envoyé à Peiresc était-il: *Icon Ludovici XIII, Franciæ et Navarræ regis christianissimi* (Paris, 1633, in f°)? N'était il pas plutôt un autre poème plus fameux que l'on a parfois attribué au spirituel magistrat et qui semble bien avoir été imprimé pour la première fois en 1633, comme l'a cru le savant bibliographe Weiss (*Bibliographie universelle*): *Le Gouvernement présent, ou Eloge de Son Eminence. Satyre, ou La Miliade*, petit in-12?', in *Les Correspondants de Peiresc: lettres inédites*, ed. by Philippe Tamizey de Larroque, 2 vols (Paris, 1879–97; Geneva: Slatkine, 1972), II, 164–65.

it was distributed in 1638.⁵ In fact, the date of the composition of the work may be inferred from pieces of internal evidence. François Sublets de Noyers is termed a 'nouveau secretaire' in line 483; since he was named *sécretaire d'État à la guerre* on 17 February 1636 and had held a post of *intendant* before then, the poem was demonstrably created within a few months of this promotion. The author refers to the taking of La Capelle (l. 232), which was seized by Spanish troops on 9 July 1636. However, there is no mention of Corbie whatsoever in a satire which makes much capital of recent events, and it is therefore evident that the capture of Corbie on 14 August in the same year postdates the work. It is inconceivable that Corbie would not have been mentioned had it occurred since this military development left a deep impression on the populace with 1636 becoming known simply as *l'année de Corbie*. This town near Amiens was within fifty miles of the capital and an invasion of Paris not only appeared to be a real prospect but also an inevitable one.

The psychological impact of this humiliating event cannot be understated and should not be underestimated. Vincent Voiture captures a collective apprehension when, in a letter dispatched in December 1636 to Richelieu, he writes how, during that dark period, he visualized Spanish troops milling around Notre-Dame cathedral as conquerors and possessors, in an imagined, though somewhat masochistic, vision of alien penetration of the historical heart of the nation.⁶ The Cardinal himself seems to have been in extremely low spirits during this uncertain period. While Louis XIII took steps to ensure he was accessible and, more importantly, visible to his people, opting to travel on horseback rather than in the customary carriage, such steps were impossible to his minister who became the focus of public discontent.⁷ The personal panic of Richelieu might perhaps be best seen in two instances of recourse to spiritual arms during this time. He suggested to Louis XIII the idea of solemnly

---

⁵ Antoine Adam, *Histoire de la littérature française au XVIIᵉ siècle*, 5 vols (Paris: Domat, 1948–56), II (1951), 1.

⁶ *Lettres de Vincent Voiture*, ed. by Octave Uzanne (Paris: Librairie des Bibliophiles, 1880), pp. 223–36 (p. 225); letter dated 14 December 1636.

⁷ 'L'esprit de sédition se renforçait. Le people rejetait toute la faute sur le cardinal de Richelieu parce qu'il avait fait déclarer la guerre. Grands et petits parlaient ouvertement contre Richelieu dans les compagnies souveraines, au parlement, à la chambre des comptes, à la cour des aides, dans les rues où le peuple s'assemblait par troupes. Ce pouvait être la révolte et la débâcle', Roland Mousnier, *L'Homme rouge ou la vie du Cardinal de Richelieu (1585–1642)* (Paris: Laffont, 1992), p. 587.

consecrating the kingdom to the protection of the Virgin Mary. This was only to be accomplished the following year and was subsequently ordained to be renewed annually throughout France in thanksgiving for the birth of an heir, the original motivation being subsumed into an event with more positive connotations, a reinvention with a complete disassociation from the circumstances of anxiety which had inspired it.[8] Richelieu also asked his close associate, Père Joseph, to have the Filles du Calvaire pray for the nation to be saved; the priest had founded this order of enclosed nuns. One of these religious, Anne-Marie de Goulaine, had an apparition which foretold that the French would retake the town, which was passed on to the prelate. A grateful Richelieu donated the substantial sum of 30,000 *livres* to the convent.[9]

The Cardinal was desperate for any assistance and it seemed that, having weathered the machinations of royal favorites, the combined resistance of the King's mother and brother, and survived several plots to oust or even assassinate him, Richelieu was finally on the verge of being toppled. Little wonder that the *Miliade* hit close to the bone; it seemed that a poem might be the catalyst to unravelling his entire ministry. Richelieu's aggravation and the stern measures he took to punish the supposed author are more readily understood within this context. One contemporary source paints a vivid picture of this threat to the prelate's position:

> Sur quoy il y en a qui se voudroient persuader, qu'une grande partie de cette peur fut artificielle, et que la Cour fut bien ayse d'alarmer extraordinairement le peuple de Paris, afin d'en tirer plus promptement le grand secours d'argent et d'hommes, que la crainte du danger present leur fit consentir. Mais ils auront de la peine à le persuader à ceux qui feront reflexion sur les mauvais effets de cette epouvante, et le licence que jusqu'aux moindres artisans se donnerent de sindiquer le Gouvernement de l'Estat, et declamer contre le PREMIER MINISTRE. Ils ne l'acusoient pas de moins que de trahison, et se plaignoient hautement, que sous pretexte d'agrandir Paris du costé du faux-bourg Saint-Honoré, il en avoit fait abatre les rempars et les murs afin d'exposer la Ville, qui restoit sans defenses aussi bien que sans munitions, à la mercy des Espagnols et au pillage. Et quoy que ces bruits, destituez non moins de vray-semblance que de raison, ne fussent nullement considerables; toutefois les mal-intentionnez ne laisserent pas de se prevaloir des murmures du peuple,

---

[8] René Laurentin, *Le Vœu de Louis XIII: passé ou avenir de France, 1638–1988, 350ᵉ anniversaire* (Paris: L'Œil, 1988), pp. 29–36.

[9] Mousnier, *L'Homme rouge*, p. 304.

aussi bien que du chagrin qu'avoit le Roy de la desolation de son Royaume et de l'oppression de ses Sujets, pour decrier la conduite du CARDINAL, et faire comprendre à sa Majesté meme qu'il n'estoit pas si digne qu'on l'avoit creu jusques-là, de l'honneur de ses bonnes graces et de la premiere place. Ce qui embarassoit extremement NOSTRE PREMIER MINISTRE, et luy causoit souvent de cuisans déplaisirs et les dernieres inquietudes.[10]

Another source underlines the precariousness of the Cardinal's standing in the wake of the fall of Corbie:

> Les opinions furent partagées; les uns estoient d'advis que par des intrigues du Cabinet l'on fist connoistre au Roy, que le Malheur de la guerre avoit esté attire à son Royaume par l'ambition du Cardinal; que pour se rendre necessaire, avoit voulu embarquer sa Majesté dans ses affaires, qu'il estimoit seul capable de conduire, et que cette guerre estrangere, qui avoit des suittes considerables, et selon les evenemens des consequences tres-dangereuses, feroient naistres des factions, qui porteroient les Princes, et grands Seigneurs à former un party, qui causeroit une guerre Civile, qui ruineroit l'Estat. A cette sorte d'opinions ils joignirent celles de s'asseurer de ceux, qui avoient le principal commandement dans l'armée, et des Gouverneurs des places et des provinces, qui n'avoient pas sujet de desirer la durée de son authorité. Plusieurs ne s'en esloignoient pas pourveu que sans differer advantage l'on commençast d'entreprendre couvertement la perte du Cardinal.[11]

Even more damaging for the prelate was the revelation that the governor of Corbie, Maximilien de Belleforière, had written on 21 July 1636 to Chavigny, *sécretaire d'État* with a portofolio covering foreign affairs and diplomacy, stressing how vulnerable the garrison was and how desperately in need of funds his soldiers were; revenues had been appropriated for the war effort and the fall of the city and other Spanish victories reflect 'the progressive failure of financial support based on poor-quality assignations'.[12] The government had been forewarned and yet was not forearmed. It is not difficult to conclude that it was during this unsettled climate in the capital that the *Miliade* was produced and diffused; indeed, the

---

[10] Antoine Aubery, *Histoire du Cardinal duc de Richelieu* (Paris: Antoine Bertier, 1660), pp. 228–29.

[11] Claude de Bourdeille, comte de Montrésor, *Mémoires de Monsieur de Montresor. Diverse Pieces durant le Ministere du Cardinal de Richelieu*, 2 vols (Cologne: Jean Sambix le jeune, 1663), I, 83–84.

[12] David Parrott, *Richelieu's Army: War, Government and Society in France, 1624–1642* (Cambridge: Cambridge University Press, 2001), pp. 265–66 (p. 266)

poem is saturated wth immediacy. The work, then, was almost certainly composed during mid-July to mid-August. One manuscript version in the hand of Valentin Conrart includes the date 'Aoust 1636' immediately after the text.[13] Other authorities also corroborate 1636 as the authentic publication date.[14] If it had circulated in a manuscript version and subsequently been published following the taking of Corbie, it is surprising that there is no mention about this event; such an addition would have been a relatively straightforward one involving adding a couplet or even completing a minor modification of words (for example, reworking line 234 'Quand une Province se pert' to include Corbie instead of 'une Province'). This suggests that the satire came off the press during this period rather than being surreptitiously passed around among like-minded critics of the government at this juncture.

At the end of the octavo edition of the poem, which I will argue to be the first edition, there is the mention 'Imprimé à Envers. Fin.' This place of publication has long been taken at face value, and certainly many contentious tracts were printed in the Low Countries, not least of which were those of Mathieu de Morgues. However, it is also feasible to suppose that the work might have come off a clandestine Parisian press. It is interesting that the supposed place of publication is prominently displayed at the end, rather than the beginning of the work, as is usual, while at the same time no date or publisher are supplied. Moreover, the city's name is misspelt as the homophonic 'Envers' a curious error that cannot be readily assigned to a Flemish compositor ignorant of French who would be unaware that 'en' and 'an' represent the same nasal vowel [ã]. I would suggest that this mistake is purposeful and subtly advertises the phoniness of the city of origin, much in the same way as early modern fictitious publishers such as Pierre Marteau of Cologne which acted as accommodation addresses for radical or pirated works. The only other examples of the use of this misspelled version of Anvers that I have been able to locate during the seventeenth

---

[13] Paris, Bibliothèque de l'Arsenal (Ars), MS 3135, fols 1115–41 (fol. 1141). This replaces the usual 'Imprimé à Envers. Fin'. I am grateful to Mme Claire Lesage at the Arsenal for confirming that this hand is indeed that of the *académicien*.

[14] See *Naudæana et Patiana, ou singularitez remarquables prises des conversations de Mess. Naudé et Patin* (Paris: Florentin and Pierre Delaulne, 1701), p. 77. Also Gédéon Tallemant des Réaux affirms that 'Cette pièce fut terminée en 1636 sur la fin de l'esté', *Hist*, I, 922n.

century all concern subversive pamphlets.[15] Moreover, it might also represent a closing pun since the satire is, after all, 'en vers'. The reader is invited not to take the close of the poem at face value, just as the 'Éloge de son Éminence' contained within the title is unequivocally ironic.

AUTHORSHIP

Unlike dating the work, the authorship is decidedly more problematic. I will list the possible candidates and evaluate the validity of each one's claim to having authored the work, as well as considering the possibility of a collaborative effort. In the manuscript known as the *Recueil de grand papier*, which I discuss later, Tallemant conjectures about the authorship in a lengthy annotation situated at the end of his copy of the *Miliade*:

> Cette pièce fut terminée en 1636 sur la fin de l'Esté. Plusieurs furent mis dans la bastille pour cela mais on n'a jamais sceû qui l'avoit faitte. Un nommé Beys y fut mis et un nommé Girou qui est à M^r le Coad. Paul-Francois de Gondy. On en soupçonna le C. d'Etlan. Il s'en justifia. En effet il l'auroit mieux faitte, et j'ay veu une piece de luy sur le mesme sujet qui n'est pas achevée, qui est sans comparaison meilleure. Son frère l'a, mais ne la montre qu'a ses intimes. Ce n'est point St Amant nomplus, mais J'y reconnois le stile de Mr de Montplaisir.[16]

Of these suspected authors, we know for a fact that Beys, Ételan, and Montplaisir were imprisoned in the Bastille since these three writers composed poems defending their innocence (the poems are provided in the Appendix).

---

[15] To give only two examples: *Sur L'Enlevement des reliques de sainct Fiacre, apportées de la ville de Meaux, pour la guerison du cul de M^r le Cardinal de Richelieu* ('En Envers': [n.pub.], 1643); *Le créve coeur, et les sanglots de Monsieur le Prince. Addressez à la France* ('A Envers': [n.pub.], 1649?).

[16] Paris, Bibliothèque nationale (BN), MS fonds français 19145, fol. 37^r. This is given as the original though I have added punctuation, which is largely absent in Tallemant's annotations.

Charles de Beys

The most prominent detainee was Charles de Beys (1610–1659), a playwright whose recent comedy *L'Hôpital des fous*, performed from 1634 and published in 1636, was an overwhelming success going through several subsequent re-editions and revitalising the sub-genre of madhouse comedies.[17] By all accounts he was a lively figure and lost his right eye in a tavern brawl, later addressing a poem to the missing organ and another one to his glass eye.[18] Notwithstanding his reputation as a 'Poëte sans soucy',[19] the experience of at least six month's confinement left a lasting impression on Beys: when he came to rework the asylum-themed comedy in 1653, which he re-titled *Les Illustres fous*, he accentuated the capacity for authority to become abusive, particularly in the person of the *concierge* who is metamorphosed from a benign overseer in the original version to a tyrant in the later one.[20] Beys was released from incarceration in the Bastille when a poem defending himself against having authored the *Miliade* was discovered among his affairs. This was taken at face value yet this apparent apologia is saturated with the type of studied irony at which Beys excelled. I have commented elsewhere on how, at the close of the Fronde, he produced a highly ambivalent dedication to a minor royalist leader, the duc d'Arpajon, in his *Illustres fous*, despite having written verse in favour of the prince de Condé earlier in the civil war when he was arrested in 1650 on the orders of the regent, Anne of Austria (see 'A Monseigneur le Prince, sur sa Prison. Sonnet' in the Appendix, p. 162). In this dedication, 'Beys attains the requisite level of acquiescence in the newly victorious political

---

[17] Charles de Beys, *L'Hospital des fous, tragi-comédie* (Paris: Thomas Quinet, 1636).

[18] 'Epigramme, sur un œil perdu' and 'Epigramme sur un œil droit artificiel', in *Les Œuvres poétiques de Beys* (Paris: Toussainct Quinet, 1651), pp. 64 and 199 respectively.

[19] François Colletet, 'Beys au tombeau', in *La Muse coquette; ou, les delices de l'honneste Amour et de la belle Galanterie*, 3 vols (Paris: Jean-Baptiste Loyson, 1665), III, 220–21 (p. 220).

[20] For a fuller consideration of the differences between the two plays and the dramatist's radical agenda, see Paul Scott, 'Subversive Revisions in the Work of Charles de Beys', *French Studies*, 60 (2006), 177–90.

establishment, while at the same time including a subtle, barely discernible, element of dissent'.[21]

The author engages in a similar display of irony with his 'Stances, contre l'autheur inconnu d'un libelle dont je fus soupçonné', commenting how 'Plus on est Eminent, plus elle est outragée' and condemning the author as a 'Monstre qui t'eslanças des gouffres de la Terre', markedly hyberbolic sentiments even when considered within the context of the laudatory register of the poem.[22] Beys seems to be signalling his personal opinions through a barely veiled smokescreen of polarity. It is worth citing one stanza, the eighth one out of ten, which illustrates Beys's audacious strategy:

> FRANCE, leve tes yeux vers ce puissant Genie,
> Qui durant le grand bruit qu'a fait cette manie,
> Ne s'est pas detourné de l'oreille du Roy;
> Voy comme cette haute et pure Intelligence
> Montre sans s'émouvoir la mesme diligence,
> A gouverner toûjours les Astres dessus toy.

Here, the outward and customary markers of respect are present. At the same time, the archetype of the iniquitous counselor stationed at the ear of the King is posited, and the prelate is described in amplified terms that sit uneasily next to the mention of the monarch, introducing an element of inappropriateness. Indeed, this was an obvious and common contemporary criticism; Cardinal de Retz opined that the minister 'anéantissait par son pouvoir et par son faste royal la majesté personnelle du Roi'.[23] Strikingly, Richelieu is described as being impervious to the *Miliade* and 'le grand bruit' that it generated, when patently this is not the case: it was a matter of public record that the minister was enraged by the poem and was determined to punish anyone who fell under even the slightest suspicion of being involved in its appearance. At the same time, if Richelieu did not leave Louis's side and was monopolising his attention, then the King remains sheltered from the *Miliade*'s message, in particular the appeal addressed to him in the closing section (ll. 937–54). The poem echoes the language of the *Miliade* in a noticeable manner. From the stanza cited above, we find similar

---

[21] Scott, 'Subversive Revisions', p. 188.

[22] 'Stances, contre l'autheur inconnu d'un libelle dont je fus soupçonné', in Les Œuvres poétiques de Beys, pp. 177–86 (pp. 181 and 177).

[23] Jean-François Paul de Gondi, Cardinal de Retz, Œuvres, ed. by Marie-Thérèse Hipp and Michel Pernot (Paris: Gallimard, 1984), p. 196.

vocabulary in the satire; for example, 'genie' (ll. 244 and 507). There is a striking parallel between this stanza and the opening of the *Miliade* where the Cardinal is termed 'la premiere intelligence' (l. 3) and whose countenance resembles 'Le Globe de l'Astre des Cieux' (l. 9) just as he governs the heavens in Beys's apologia. Another way in which the *stances* possess resonances with the *Miliade* is with the inclusion of either alliteration or anaphora at the beginning of lines, such as the thrice repeated 'Qui' in the fourth stanza.

This naturally begs the question: do the similarities between the two works point to an assertion of authorship on the part of Beys? Given that some of the techniques used in the satire are not typical of the poet, namely the unusually rich vein of anaphora and the use of octosyllabic verse, which Beys otherwise eschewed for the alexandrine in the majority of his other dramatic and poetic verse, this is a conclusion that should be resisted. I propose that, by using a selection of terminology and employing techniques which are solidly reminiscent of the *Miliade*, the poet is rather demonstrating both his familiarity with, as well as his solidarity towards, the infamous work. It might be noted that this poem was first published in the edition of Beys's collected works in 1651, at the height of the Fronde. Since this poem had never hitherto been published, Beys could easily have exercised editorial discretion in omitting an unknown poem written fifteen years earlier. However, releasing this work to the public domain reminded his readership of his subversive credentials and that Beys was a veteran, subtle agitator who had suffered for his opinions. In short, while this figure belonged to a liberal-minded milieu from which the *Miliade* might reasonably be supposed to emanate, it is revealing that commentators such as Tallemant des Réaux do not accept that Beys created it. Most of all, Richelieu himself reached this conclusion for he would never have released the poet from internment after a matter of months had he believed otherwise.

Comte d'Ételan

Another writer consigned to a spell in the Bastille and who also penned a poem protesting his innocence was Louis d'Espinay de Saint-Luc, abbé de Redon and abbé de Chartrice, comte d'Ételan (1605–1640), son of the Maréchal de Saint-Luc and nephew of the Maréchal de Bassompierre. Pierre de La Porte, a favourite of Anne of Austria and who was held in the Bastille in 1637 by order of

Richelieu because of his involvement in court intrigues,[24] relates how his personal effects were subject to a thorough search upon arrival in the fortress:

> Après cela, il commença à faire mine de tirer de son sac quelques papiers de conséquence, et en mêmes-tems il me regardoit fort fixément. J'avoue que d'abord j'eu peur que ce ne fussent les papiers du trou, et je ne sçais s'ils s'apperçut de ma peur, mais je la sentois bien, et j'étois fort en colere contre moi de ma foiblesse; enfin ce ne fut rien que des vers à la louange de S.E. qui s'étoient trouvés dans mon coffre, avec ceux que Barault avoit faits pour la Reine, sur le déluge de Narbonne; ils les remit aussitôt faisant semblant d'en chercher d'autres, afin de voir ma contenance, qui fût toujours la même quoique le dedans fut fort ému toutes les fois que je voyois sortir un papier du sac, craignant toujours que ce ne fussent ceux du trou, où il y avoit un magasin de toutes les pièces du tems contre S.E. et même la Milliade de l'Abbé d'Estelan, pour laquelle il y avoit alors quatre ou cinq prisonniers à la Bastille.[25]

This is a valuable source testifying not only to how dangerous it was even to possess a copy of the satire, but also to the fact that some contemporaries believed Ételan was behind the libel. He was known to be responsible for a pamphlet targeting Richelieu known as *Le Passage de Somme* which was circulated but never printed. Two copies of this unfinished poem exist, one which is complete and in the careful hand of the seventeenth-century *académicien* and bibliophile Valentin Conrart and another incomplete version in Tallemant des Réaux's script lacking several sections.[26] This work shared a common target with the *Miliade* and covers some of the same type of criticisms, but concentrates firmly on 1636 and in particular the European military situation. Estimates of the date of its creation range from 1636 to 1639.[27] This writer was therefore in the

---

[24] Hans-Jürgen Lüsebrink and Rolf Reichardt, *The Bastille: A History of a Symbol of Despotism and Freedom*, trans. Norbert Schürer (Durham, NC: Duke University Press, 1997), p. 15.

[25] Pierre de La Porte, *Mémoires de M. de La Porte, premier valet de chambre de Louis XIV* (Paris: Volland, 1791), pp. 129–30.

[26] Paris, Bibliothèque de l'Arsenal (Ars), MS 4145, fols 545–54 and Paris, Bibliothèque nationale (BN), MS fonds français 19115, fols a–b, hereafter 'Passage de Somme'.

[27] Antoine Adam opts for 1636, *Hist*, II, 1014–15n, whereas N. N. Condeescu makes the case for a later composition of 1638 or early 1639, 'Étlan contre Richelieu: à propos d'un pamphlet inédit "Le Passage de Somme" ou "Vers

business of agitating against the prime minister and little wonder that he fell under suspicion of its authorship. Moreover, since his uncle, Bassompierre, was disgraced and held at the Bastille from 1631 until his release after Richelieu's death in 1643, coupled with familial connections to the circle of Gaston d'Orléans, there was every reason to suspect this character of harbouring anti-Richelieu sympathies.

Like Beys, Ételan is an intriguing character. He became addicted to sleeping medication though the influence of his stepmother, Marie de Chazeron, and penned a sonnet 'Sur l'oppium', the early modern equivalent of Ambien.[28] He collaborated with Saint-Évremond on the *Comédie des Académistes* (1638) and dedicated a novel to the Marquise de Sablé which has sadly not survived.[29] An abbé who flirted with libertinage, he frequented leading salons such as those of the Marquise de Sablé and Mme de Rambouillet. Something of his bawdy reputation may be gleaned in the fact that Jean L'Ange initially claimed that Ételan had written the licentious *L'École des filles* during his interrogation by the authorities in 1655.[30] As the eldest son of a noble family, it is astonishing that he took Holy Orders, a rare step for someone in his position that remains inexplicable but surely implies that there was a heterodox attitude to social conventions within the family. He often visited his uncle in the Bastille before his own confinement there.[31] Any advancement for which he could have hoped in the Church was all but closed off

---

héroïques"', *Revue des Sciences Humaines*, 137 (1970), 15–26 (p. 22). Contemporary variants of Ételan's name include Étlan and Estelan.

[28] Condeescu, 'Étlan contre Richelieu', p. 23. The sonnet exists in Conrart's transcription: Paris, Bibliothèque de l'Arsenal, MS 4126, fol. 1086.

[29] Ételan alludes to this lost work in his 'Stances de Monsieur le Comte d'Estelan pour Madame la Marquise de Sablé en lui envoyant son Roman de l'Inconnu', Paris, Bibliothèque nationale, MS fonds français 6712, fols 53ᵛ–54ʳ. He tantalisingly offers the novel to his hostess with the plea: 'Ce que vous verrez dans ce Livre, / Lisez le au coeur de votre amant' (fol. 54ʳ).

[30] Patrick J. Kearney, *A History of Erotic Literature* (London: Macmillan, 1982), p. 31.

[31] François de Bassompierre, *Journal de ma vie: memoires du maréchal de Bassompierre. Première édition conforme au manuscrit original*, ed. by Audoin de Chantérac, 4 vols (Paris: Renouaurd, 1870–77), IV (1877), 317.

in the wake of such a public family disgrace.[32] All in all, he seems a likely candidate, then, for producing the *Miliade*. However, the *Passage de Somme* is manifestly dissimilar in its register from the *Miliade*, even if it shares its satirical verve. The air of careful and contained elegance of the *Passage* is a world away from the *Miliade*, and Ételan's pamphlet, in the words of one critic, 'conserve une tenue littéraire. Son vocabulaire est toujours celui des honnêtes gens. Ses alexandrins sont toujours corrects, aux accents bien distribués et aux rimes contamment riches'.[33] The Cardinal's well-documented discomfort caused by his recurring haemorrhoids merits two mentions in the *Miliade* (ll. 331–32 and 534) but is accordingly absent from *Le Passage*.

Since we possess a text by Ételan written during the same period as the *Miliade* or shortly thereafter, and sharing corresponding satirical aims, it is worth citing the author directly in order to draw comparisons from the respective treatment of the same targets. Like the *Miliade*, Père Joseph is a primary object of derision, a confidant who facilitates Richelieu's excesses:

> Il demeure tout seul et soudain, il appelle
> Joseph le capuchin son conseilleur fidelle,
> Ce fils de St François, qu'un zèle immodéré
> De servir au Public, a du convent tiré,
> Et qui dans les grandeurs dont son esprit se flate,
> Ne pense qu'à changer la Grise en écarlatte.
> Du mesme esprit de Dieu dont il parle aux bigots,
> Il traitte avec les Turcs, les Danois, et les Gots;
> Comme un nouveau St Paul, de son siècle l'Apostre
> Se fait Juif, et Gentil, pour gagner l'un et l'autre.
> Il s'accorde à Luther parmy les Protestans,
> Révére Mahomet chez les Mahometans,
> Et broüillant tout-ensemble, enferme en son capuce
> L'Alcoran, l'Evangile, et la Loy du Prépuce,
> Sans avoir autre objet que la gloire de Dieu,
> Le salut de l'Estat, l'honneur de Richelieu.[34]

---

[32] His uncle, Timoléon d'Espinay, marquis de Saint-Luc (1580–1644), chose to serve the Cardinal and carried out spying missions for him. In a letter dated 6 January 1632, he assures the Cardinal of his unconditional loyalty, notwithstanding the situation of other family members, by which he means his brother-in-law, Bassompierre: *La Correspondance du cardinal de Richelieu: au faîte du pouvoir, l'année 1632*, ed. by Marie-Catherine Vignal Souleyreau (Paris: L'Harmattan, 2007), pp. 60–61.

[33] Condeescu, 'Étlan contre Richelieu', p. 20.

[34] Paris, Bibliothèque de l'Arsenal, MS 4124, fols 545–54 (fol. 547).

This section may be compared with the *Miliade*'s analogous digression about the religious:

> Le Moyne imite S. François,
> Il protege les Suedois,
> Il a le Zele Seraphique,
> Il travaille pour l'heretique,
> Il est percé du divin traict,
> Mais non encor tout a faict,
> Car il porte bien les stigmates,
> Mais non les marques d'escarlates,
> Son Capuchon Piramidal,
> Ne luy plaist qu'estant a cheval,
> Sur la beste luxurieuse,
> Qui prend la posture amoureuse. (ll. 357–68)

Certainly these two extracts hold many elements in common, such as the disparagement of the friar's alliance with Scandinavian nations and his alleged ambition to be raised to the cardinalatial dignity. The two texts also contain jokes at the expense of the conspicuous hood of the Franciscan habit, which was already a commonplace in works attacking the Capuchin branch of the Franciscans who suffered from a long-standing and popular prejudice as seen in authors from Marguerite de Navarre to La Fontaine.[35] Despite these communal preoccupations and affinities, the style of each text is distinctly different. Ételan employs a narration that unfolds like a play: Richelieu interacts with Père Joseph, summoning him in order to seek his counsel, whereas the narrative of the *Miliade* provides an overview of the figures in Richelieu's government, more within the framework of a succession of *tableaux* than a drama. Whereas the *Miliade* contains a concise critique ('Il protege les Suedois'), that of Ételan is sustained (he specifies 'les Turcs, les Danois, et les Gots'). It is evident that this is not related to any economy of verse since the *Miliade* is twice as long as the surviving fragment of *Le Passage*. Ételan takes his comments further, amplifies them, and unfolds an underlying trope:

---

[35] They were known as Cordeliers in France. The unfavourable opinion many held about the order may have arisen because of their itinerant status. The episodes in the two authors I mentioned are as follows, but there are certainly many more such adverse depictions to be found: Marguerite de Navarre, *Heptaméron*, ed. by Simone de Reyff (Paris: Garnier Flammarion, 1982), pp. 73–77 (nouvelle 5 in which the boatkeeper outwits two friars attempting to rape her) and Jean de La Fontaine, 'Les Frères de Catalogne' (first published in 1666), in *Contes et nouvelles érotiques*, ed. by Jean-Paul Morel (Paris: Séguier, 1995), pp. 60–66.

for the abbé, Richelieu's confidant is to be seen as a perverted example of the Pauline admonition to be all things to all men (I Corinthians 9.22).

The register of the *Miliade* is more immediate, more burlesque, and conforms to the tone of popular *chansons* whereas Ételan's narrative suggests the cadences of the classical stage. The *Miliade* employs words which are decidedly proverbial such as 'triboulet' (l. 486) which would not be formally recognized by dictionaries until almost a century later in 1727. It is to be noted that, in the two selected passages, the *Miliade* has four lines beginning with 'Il', a use of initial alliteration that is predominant in the satire. Ételan, on the other hand, uses any form of anaphora extremely sparingly throughout this and, indeed, all of his poetic output. The word 'bien' occurs fifteen times in the *Miliade*, either adjectivally or adverbally.[36] Since the word is used so frequently in the *Miliade*, Ételan's minimal use of it is striking; in fact, there is a sole occurrence of the word throughout all of his verse.[37] The author of the *Miliade* uses the Cardinal's first name, Armand, a total of twelve times, all of which occur either at the beginning of the line (in nine cases) or else in the middle of the line.[38] Ételan, on the other hand, uses Armand on only three occasions with which to refer to the prelate, but in two of these it is positioned as the very last word of the line.[39] Ételan refers to Richelieu as 'Prince' a total of four times and once as 'prélat', titles that are not employed at all by the author of the *Miliade*.[40] These incidents of vocabulary further weigh against his candicacy.

Ételan's pedigree provided enough doubt for his contemporaries and, indeed, the Cardinal, to deduce he had played some part in the *Miliade*, but closer inspection of his works readily eliminates his alleged collaboration. His writings remained inaccessible outside of

---

[36] The other fourteen occurrences are in lines 195, 197, 304, 363, 377, 432, 475, 484, 493, 639, 713 (twice), 724, 850, 931.

[37] Ételan, 'Le Passage de Somme', fol. 546.

[38] Armand is to be found in lines 111, 123, 239, 265, 289, 525, 547, 607, 750, 791, 831, 915.

[39] Ételan, 'Le Passage de Somme', fols 546 and 552.

[40] Ételan, 'Le Passage de Somme', fols 545, 546, 548, 553. On fol. 549, Richelieu seeks Joseph's help after the taking of La Capelle and is a desperate state: 'Il s'agit de sauver le Prince, et la Patrie', which remains ambiguous as to whether it refers to Richelieu or Louis XIII. 'Prélat' occurs once on fol. 548.

a narrow circle of intimates since, as a *salonnier*, he chose not to sully himself with seeing his works into print under his name and during his lifetime, and he did not benefit from a posthumous edition of his collected works, meaning that his reputation has remained the sole element perpetuating his association with the *Miliade*.[41] In the *Stances* he produced to aid his departure from the Bastille, Ételan employs a nautical allegory, that of Richelieu guiding the ship of state. Ételan depicts the minister navigating the ship through turbulent waters whereas the *Miliade* portrays a violent tempest affecting the boat. Both writers use this imagery to great effect to underline the strength of the opposition to the Cardinal, a factor which is most explicit in Ételan ('soubs son vaisseau toute la mer s'irrite'), and both mention the Cardinal's apparent mastery of the elements. For the cleric, Jupiter is not able to trouble the prelate's spirit: 'desbranler sa constance il n'a pas le pouvoir', whereas the *Miliade* claims that 'Luy seul bride le fier Neptune' (l. 271). The poems' similar concerns but differing emphases point to a shared ideology of hosility but do not denote a common authorship.

Finally, it should be remembered that Tallemant des Réaux was close to the Ételan family. His portrait of the abbé, his father, and his uncles is one of the most flattering to be found in the *Historiettes*, which is not always so merciful to its subjects. Tallemant was on familiar enough terms to be allowed to look at and, indeed, copy the *Passage de Somme* by Ételan's sister, Henriette, who was a nun at Reims.[42] The fact that she allowed him access to a highly incriminating document testifies to links that far surpassed social acquaintanceship, involving as it did real risk to both sides. Tallemant would have been well-placed, then, to receive confirmation of Ételan's authorship yet not only does he fail to mention it but he also dismisses it in his annotations to his copy of the *Miliade*. This definitive conclusion made by an individual on intimate terms with the family is perhaps the most forceful piece of evidence indicating that the abbé did not write the piece.

---

[41] The scholar who was the most acquainted with Ételan's *œuvre*, Nicolae Condeescu, adamantly dismissed his subject's purported attribution of the libel: 'Les *Mil vers* n'étaient pas de lui; la voix publique les attribuait à d'autres ennemis du Cardinal: Favereau, Bussy-Pasquier, Bruc de Montplaisir', 'Étlan contre Richelieu', p. 25. This does contradict La Porte's comments, quoted earlier, in which he refers to Ételan's authorship as a given fact.

[42] See *Hist*, I, 116. The *Historiette* dealing with the family is on pp. 113–17.

Bruc de Montplaisir

René de Bruc, marquis de La Guerche et de Montplaisir (1610–1673) is another writer documented to have endured some time in the Bastille in the aftermath of the satire's publication. Hailing from a noble Breton family he had a distinguished military career during the Thirty Years War fighting the Spanish, a fact which is enough in itself to cast doubt on attributing the *Miliade*: the poem unabashedly gloats about the Cardinal's failure in the war, sentiments that sit uneasily with a soldier's sense of loyalty. He styled himself as a marquis for all of his adult life until the title was finally confirmed by Louis XIV erecting his property into a marquisate shortly before his death.[43]

He came under suspicion for authoring the *Miliade* and, in the judgement cited earlier, Tallemant was confident that he recognized Montplaisir's handiwork in the satire's verses. From a technical perspective, Montplaisir uses initial alliteration or anaphora frugally, and when he does, it rarely involves more than a pair of lines. As I have already pointed out, the *Miliade* uses this technique liberally. In fact, alliterative or anaphoric devices at the start of lines are easily the overwhelming stylistic feature of the entire poem, ranging from one letter or an entire syllable to two whole words. It also often goes further than couplets, as with the fourfold repetition of 'Les' in lines 41–44, or the initial 'En' being repeated thirteen times (see Figure 3), which creates an arresting visual and audial parison. Indeed, there are 118 occurrences of initial anaphora or alliteration involving 287 lines of the text, with a further 48 cases of indirect initial alliterative letters or syllables where the two alliterative lines are separated by a line in between them which does not carry the same initial syllable or word; this concerns a total of 88 lines. In short, 375 lines of the 956-line poem employ this technique, just under 40% of the entire work's content, and it is sustained throughout every part of the poem, signalling a sole author and one who was somewhat partial to this technique and uses it unsparingly and abundantly. Such a liberal use of the device is not discernible in Montplaisir, most of whose poetry was collected in the mid-eighteenth century, together with the verse of his contemporary and associate, Pierre de Lalanne.[44] A

---

[43] Daniel Russell, 'M. de Montplaisir and His Emblems', *Neophilologus*, 67 (1983), 503–16 (p. 503).

[44] *Poesies de Lalanne et du marquis de Montplaisir*, ed. by Charles Hugues Lefebvre de Saint-Marc (Amsterdam and Paris: Pierre Alexandre Leprieur, 1759).

sizeable proportion of his poems does not contain any initial alliteration, and the few pieces that do tend to rely on alliteration as opposed to anaphora which, when it does occur in Montplaisir's output, involves only a monosyllabic word such as 'Il' (pp. 11, 47, 64, and 80) or 'Et' (pp. 14, 17, 55, and 91). On only two occasions within the 115-page collection does Montplaisir use a direct anaphora involving more than single syllable with 'Ombre vaine' (p. 50) and 'Tous ceux' (p. 91). Anaphoric incidents of more than one syllable appear 24 times in the *Miliade* and this figure does not include initial lines separated by another nor cases such as the multiple repetition of the strong nasal vowel [ã] in the sequence beginning with 'En destruisant son abondance' (ll. 206–21), a repetition that is further bolstered by 28 internal occurrences of the same nasal vowel within this section. It is not entirely conclusive, but Montplaisir's reliance on this type of rhetorical repetition is indisputably not as perceptible as that of the *Miliade*'s author.

Tallemant provides an example to substantiate his verdict that Montplaisir's style could be detected:

> Il est aisé de le voir par la comparison qu'il met Icy: 'Ainsi l'Astre par sa lumiere' etc., et par celle qui est a la fin d'un sonnet pour le C. de Richelieu qui finit ainsy: 'Elle s'aveugle seule en cachant ce bel œil' etc. Et qu'on ne dit point que cette piece Icy et ce sonnet la dissent tout le contraire l'un de l'autre, car je croy qu'il le fit pour empescher qu'on ne le souçonnast d'Estre l'Autheur de la satyre, puis il a de l'attachement pour la maison de Retz.[45]

It is expedient to quote the two sections to which he refers in order to furnish a direct comparison. From the *Miliade*, the section mentioned by Tallemant continues over eight lines:

> Ainsi lastre par la lumiere,
> Esclatte une vapeur grossiere,
> Qui ternist toute la clarté,
> Et qui nous cache sa bauté.
> Que si le Soleil chasse l'ombre:
> S'il perce le nuage sombre
> Espere que les envieux;
> Te verront un jour glorieux. (ll. 511–18)

The line from Montplaisir occurs in the last tercet of his 'Contre la satyre Qu'on appelle vulgairement la piece de mille vers' (a fully transcribed version of which is provided in the Appendix, p. 165):

---

[45] Tall, fol. 37ʳ.

> Ainsi la terre en vain escale en divers lieux,
> Ses nuages espais vers le flambeau des Cieux,
> Et jamais ne ternit l'Esclat de sa lumiere.
> Elle saveugle seule en cachant ce bel œil,
> Et ses noires vapeurs fournissent la matiere
> Des foudres dont le Ciel doit punir son orgueil.[46]

While the tropes of sight, light, and darkness are explored in both extracts, it is difficult to maintain that these two extracts share perceptible stylistic features. Montplaisir uses a single eye in his allegory of vision whereas this organ always occurs in the plural in the five times that it is invoked in the *Miliade* (ll. 18, 121, 504, 925, 943). Furthermore, 'Cieux' is never rhymed with 'lieux' in the *Miliade* in the five times it occurs in the satire (ll. 9, 293, 782, 814, 874); in fact, 'lieu', either in the singular or pluralized forms, does not feature at the end of any line throughout the whole of the *Miliade*. The obvious exception is the Cardinal's surname, but even this is never rhymed with 'Cieux' as it almost ubiquitously is in verse. There are two words that occur in both extracts, *nuage* and *vapeur*, though Montplaisir uses these in the plural, unlike the single form in which they appear in the *Miliade*. Despite the superficial affinities that so obviously caught Tallemant's eye, there are enough distinguishable disparities in vocabulary and versification to cast serious doubts on his findings. It should be added that Montplaisir's published poetry is overwhelmingly *galant* and there is no satirical verse with which to allow a direct textual comparison as is the case with Ételan.

Girou

Tallemant mentions that an individual named Girou, of Abbé (later Cardinal) de Retz's household, was the identity of the other person detained. Contemporary sources do not specify any other names in connection with the *Miliade*, and the only four about which we may entertain any degree of certainty as to their imprisonment are Girou, Beys, Ételan, and Montplaisir. Another name that Tallemant proposes is that of the poet Marc-Antoine Gérard de Saint-Amant, who was, like Girou, a member of Retz's circle. It has been argued that the experience of being suspected of writing the *Miliade*, even

---

[46] Paris, Bibliothèque de l'Arsenal, MS 4129, fol. 724.

though it did not lead to reprisals, made Saint-Amant more prudent.[47] The figure of four might even represent the total amount of suspects who were rounded up by Richelieu since La Porte discloses that there were 'quatre ou cinq prisonniers à la Bastille' at the time he was himself held there. It is difficult to assess Girou's potential authorship since we do not possess any of his works and there are only a few scraps of biographical information about this figure. Nonetheless, it is perhaps telling that Tallemant does not entertain his claim seriously; the diarist had a long-standing friendship with Retz and being as finely attuned as he was to gossip, would have been well placed to pick up on any hint authenticating Girou. He does go some way in answering why this individual might have raised doubts: 'vous voyez aussy que Girou a cette piece des premiers. Et pour ce qui est de son particulier a luy, le Grand Maistre de la Meilleraye auroit osté a son pere, un gentilhomme de Bretagne, la charge de procureur des Estats qui luy valoit beaucoup'.[48] The marquis de La Meilleraye was Richelieu's cousin and held the office of *grand maître de l'artillerie*. Girou had every reason to bear a grudge given that his father had been humiliatingly side-lined by La Meilleraye; if he did create the *Miliade* it would be surprising that he did not allocate more space to parodying the official who had cost his father his livelihood and position other than the most fleeting of mentions provided in line 563. Here, La Meilleraye is named as an example, together with Urbain de Maillé-Brézé, of the mediocre quality of administrators working for Richelieu, as well as furnishing a snipe at the Cardinal's nepotism (the latter was his brother-in-law). There is nothing vindictive or detailed in this passing generalized reference in a poem which dedicates many vindictive and detailed comments to other governmental officials.

Above all, other than Tallemant's mention of his arrest, there is no contemporary documentary evidence to substantiate Girou possible authorship. There was certainly no love lost between Retz and Richelieu, and Retz had close ties to the Marillac family and the Queen Mother. In fact, one biographer indicates that all of Retz's intimates were known for their unreconstructed hostility to

---

[47] Jean Lagny, *Le Poète Saint-Amant (1594–1661): essai sur sa vie et ses œuvres* (Paris: Nizet, 1964), p. 246.

[48] Tall, fol. 37^r.

Richelieu's administration.[49] Given this public stance, it could well be that Richelieu selected Girou as well as Montplaisir as an overt warning to Retz and his circle, *pour décourager les autres*.[50] That three members of Retz's coterie came under suspicion, counting Saint-Amant, confirms that the young cleric's entourage of writers exerted political significance in the years leading up to the Fronde.[51] Beys could well have been selected in the same spirit, a token victim from his artistic milieu; his prominence certainly ensured maximal exposure of publicity and no one who followed current events in the 1630s could have been unaware of the Cardinal's determination not to tolerate any tract sharing the *Miliade*'s sardonic spirit.

Jacques Favereau

This brings us to another possible contender, a writer who was fortunate enough to escape both scrutiny and internment on suspicion of the satire's genesis: Jacques de Favereau (1590–1638). Tallemant does not even consider him and his candidacy might otherwise have never been taken into account were it not for an observation made by Guy Patin and committed to print several decades later:

> Le vrai Auteur des Milles vers qui est une satyre tres-violente contre le Cardinal de Richelieu et ses adherans faite l'an 1636. laquelle commence ainsi:
>
> *Peuple élevez des Autels,*
> *Au plus éminent des mortels,*
>
> est, selon quelques-uns M. Favereau Conseiller en la Cour des Aides qui mourut l'an 1638. D'autres disent que c'est M. d'Estelan fils du Marêchal de S. Luc, mais il n'est pas vrai. Je vous prie de croire que c'est ce M. Favereau, qui de peur d'en être soupçonné l'Auteur fit en même têms imprimer un Poëme Latin à l'honneur du Cardinal de

---

[49] 'Tous ceux qu'il fréquente professent la même opposition aux options fondamentales de Richelieu', Simone Bertière, *La Vie du cardinal de Retz* (Paris: Fallois, 1990), p. 58.

[50] No one of this name or any variants of it is afforded a reference in the Retz's memoirs, which does not imply any degree of familiarity between him and the prelate.

[51] Sylvia P. Vance, *The Memoirs of the Cardinal de Retz*, Biblio 17, 158 (Tübingen: Narr, 2005), p. 29.

Richelieu. Ce M. Favereau estoit un bon et sçavant Poëte et fort honnête homme, qui haïssoit horriblement le Cardinal.[52]

This assertion is made in an assured fashion, and Patin flatly negates Ételan's authorship; Favereau has been listed as a possible author ever since.[53] He also states that Favereau was vigilant in concealing his dissent; the poem alluded to by Patin appeared in a collection published in 1635.[54] Favereau possessed impeccable credentials as a supporter of Richelieu's ministry. In 1626, he had denounced the Jesuit scholar François Garasse as the author of a subversive satire, *Questiones politicæ quod libelicæ*, which initiated his ties with Isaac de Laffemas, whose role as *conseiller d'État* and *lieutenant civil au Châtelet* coupled with his close association with Richelieu, meant that he was widely seen as the minister's enforcer.[55] Garasse surmised that Favereau was his principal accuser and records that he and Laffemas 'faisaient publiquement des assemblées dans la maison de Saint-Germain, auxquelles on examinait tous mes livres pour en tirer quelque conformité du style'.[56] It is tempting to think that Favereau may have used these exegetical skills to disguise his own work a decade later. Perhaps he became disillusioned, as many did, after the Day of Dupes or as a result of the losses suffered by France following its entry into the Thirty Years War in 1635, or perhaps he practised dissimulation from the outset, cultivating an outwardly conformist personality while discreetly entertaining serious doubts about the government and its policies in private. We will never know, yet the hypothesis of Favereau's authorship would

---

[52] *Naudæana et Patiana*, pp. 77–78.

[53] 'On n'est pas encore bien certain du nom de l'Auteur de cette Satyre; les uns l'attribuent à M. FAVEREAU, Conseiller en la Cour des Aides, fort honnête homme, mais grand ennemi du Cardinal; les autres à M. D'ESTELAN, fils du Maréchal de Saint-Luc', Jacques Lelong, *Bibliothèque historique de la France, contenant Le Catalogue des Ouvrages, imprimées et manuscrits, qui traitent de l'Histoire de ce Royaume, ou qui y ont rapport*, rev. ed. by Fevret de Fontette, 5 vols (Paris: Jean-Thomas Herissant, 1759), II, 487, no. 22095.

[54] 'Excerptum è poëmate cui nomen ICON', in *Le Sacrifice des Muses, au grand cardinal de Richelieu* (Paris: Sebastien Cramoisy, 1635), pp. 208–10.

[55] Georges Mongrédien, *Isaac de Laffemas: le bourreau de Richelieu (documents inédits)* (Paris: Brossard, 1929), p. 56.

[56] François Garasse, *Mémoires de Garasse (François) de la Compagnie de Jésus*, ed. by Charles Nisard (Paris: Amyot, 1860), p. 180. The priest escaped punishment after solemning swearing on the Canon of the Mass before the Jesuit provincial of France, Pierre Coton (p. 181).

go far in explaining why the identity of the satire's creator was never uncovered and why Favereau remained outside of the Cardinal's probing enquiries. One critic has picked out 'une indépendance de ton' as a defining feature of Favereau's work, and there is certainly more to this apparently unassuming pillar of the establishment than meets the eye.[57]

Favereau's authorship is supported by a number of factors. The most convincing evidence is on a stylistic level: he was extremely partial to employing anaphora or initial alliteration in his poetry, both in the vernacular and in Latin. It occurs so abundantly that is manifestly a feature on which Favereau relied; the only other poet from the first half of the seventeenth century in whose work I have detected such a recurrent application of this trait is Antoine Godeau.[58] Since this feature stands out as a distinctive poetic hallmark, it is worth considering some examples of this technique in Favereau's poetry:

> Et aux douloureux cris des peuples qui perissent,
> Aux animeux accents des Chevaux qui hansent,
> Aux fanfares des Clairons,
> Aux chamades des Trompettes,
> Aux salues des Escoupettes,
> Au bruit des Canons ronnants.
> Et au dur battement des Tambours resonnants,
> Les Cieux meuglent, les Airs crissent,
> La Terre tremble, et les Ondes gemissent.[59]

The insistant repetition of [o] together with it occurring in the first and seventh quoted lines after 'Et', as well as the presence of internal alliteration such as 'des' consolidating the repetitive effect, possesses great kinship to the manner in which this practice occurs in the *Miliade*, for example in the following portion:

---

[57] Giambattista Guarini, *Il compendio della poesia tragicomica / De la poésie tragicomique*, ed. by Laurence Giavarini, Textes de la Renaissance, 140 (Paris: Champion, 2008), p. 148.

[58] As an example chosen at random, the poet uses an initial 'Il' seven times, five of which are followed by 'ne', one one page of a twenty-eight-page poem extolling the Sorbonne, an anaphoric fecundity that is reminiscent of Favereau and the *Miliade*; Antoine Godeau, *La Sorbonne, poëme* (Paris: Pierre Le Petit, 1653), p. 6.

[59] Jacques Favereau, *La France consolée, epithalame pour les nopces du tres chrestien Louys XIII Roy de France et de Navarre et d'Anne d'Autriche Infante d'Espagne* (Paris: Jean Petit Pas, 1625), pp. 57–58.

> En nous livrant aux estrangers,
> En mesprisant les grands dangers,
> En desgarnissant les frontieres
> En n'assurant point les rivieres,
> Bref en abandonnant les Lys,
> A la fureur des ennemis,
> Au sort des armes si funestes,
> A la faim la guerre la peste. (ll. 217–24)

The two poems are radically different in their purpose, the former designed to mark a significant royal event and constituting an original attempt 'to acclimatize Italian *versi sciolti* in France', the application of which marked a 'revolutionary departure from Malherbe'.[60] One work by Favereau that does parallel the satirical spirit of the *Miliade* is an unpublished poem entitled 'La satyre Ménippée de Caresme prenant Autrement les Visions Amoureuses du Berger Amynthe, surnommé le Pasteur fidèle'.[61] This piece, written in the first person, surveys Favereau's circle of family, friends, and acquaintances, elliptically identifying each character using wordplay and contributing a stanza-length portrait of each of these, some of which are positive whereas others are positively mordant. These sketches *à clef* have been rendered more identifiable by annotations added in the right-hand margin of the sole surviving manuscript in what is almost certainly another hand. The poem testifies not only to an aptitude for satire on Favereau's part but also to a fondness for a particular type of pun that runs throughout the *Miliade*. One stanza begins 'Je voy un grand Mont assez Clair' which is elucidated by a marginal annotation: 'M^r de clairmont, tresorier de France'.[62] This is not unlike line 386 of the *Miliade* which evokes 'Un Ange les escrit tousjours' which refers to Père Ange de Mortagne, the secretary of and companion to Père Joseph or the 'Le gros coquet' mentioned in line 625, which denotes Jacques Coquet, who presumably was of substantial girth.[63] As well as a

---

[60] Renee Winegarten, 'A Neglected Critic of Malherbe: Jacques Favereau', *French Studies*, 6 (1952), 29–34 (p. 30 and 32).

[61] Paris, Bibliothèque nationale, MS fonds français 19142, fol. 120^r–25^v.

[62] BN, MS f. fr. 19142, fol. 121^v.

[63] This comic device tends to flatter the reader's intelligence in recognising the veiled allusions and necessitates an engagement on their part. As Walter Redfern asserts, '[t]he pun demands a close collaboration or complicity between reader and author', *Puns* (Oxford: Blackwell, 1984), p. 180.

penchant for paronomasia, Favereau also displays a taste for salacious tittle-tattle in this poem:

> Je vois tout plein d'autres familles
> Où le clerc avecque les filles
> La femme aveque les garçons
> Le Maistre aveque la chambriere
> Accouplez comme hanetons
> Se tenoient tous par le derriere.[64]

This reiterates the gleeful delight the *Miliade*'s author takes in divulging Mme Séguier's purported affair with a canon of Notre-Dame (l. 480) or irreverently mocking the idea that Combalet was a virgin at the time of her betrothal (l. 869). This poem attests to an aptitude for vituperative commentary, which may also be found in Favereau's 'Lettre to Malherbe', all of which is greatly analagous to the *Miliade*.[65]

There are some minor pieces of evidence, which if considered together, add further weight to the case of Favereau's authorship. Firstly, Favereau was inordinately partial to numbers. His friend Michel de Marolles edited the *Tableaux du Temple des Muses*, a collection of emblems in which each one is accompanied by an explanatory commentary and sonnet. Favereau was a passionate and serious art-collector and had commissioned the engravings for the projected volume at great expense.[66] Marolles carried this project to completion seventeen years after his friend's death. Marolles was clearly fond of Favereau yet betrays a note of exasperation when alluding to, and refusing, his companion's choice of the number of engravings that the work should encompass: 'lesquels il vouloit porter jusqu'au nombre de cent, pour appeler son Livre *l'Ouvrage de cent Sonnets*, faisant allusion au mot *Sansonnets*; je ne sais pourquoi:

---

[64] BN, MS f. fr. 19142, fol. 125^r.

[65] In this document, Favereau takes aim at Malherbe through some vindictive swipes at *malherbiens*: 'Mais qu'à vostre exemple, ou plutost à votre prejudice, une infinite de gens, que les Muses chassent du mont Pimplée, comme dit le Poëte, à coups de fourche, se licentient, sous ombre de quelque prose qu'ils ont rime, de trancher les Musagetes, et d'establir sans aucun fondement des maxims et des regles pour donner la loy à tout le reste de la France, c'est un abus qu'il faut donner à la corruption du Siecle', 'Lettre au sieur de Malherbe, pour servir d'advertisement au Lecteur, sur la nouvelle sorte de Vers, dont ce Poëme est composé', in Favereau, *La France consolée*, sig. ẽ^r–ĩ^r (sig. ẽ^v).

[66] Alexis Merle du Bourg, *Peter Paul Rubens et la France* (Lille: Presses Universitaires du Septentrion, 2004), p. 133.

car enfin M. Favereau montroit de l'esprit en tout ce qu'il faisoit'.[67] It would appear that Favereau suffered from an obsessive compulsive disorder *avant la lettre*, and this fascination with numbers might manifest itself in writing a thousand-line poem. Moreover, the type of pun to which Favereau was so plainly attached recalls the play of words on 'Envers' at the end of the *Miliade*.

Finally, the treatment of two particular individuals in the *Miliade* reveals an emphasis that reflects Favereau's personal and professional alliances, the first of whom stands out through his omission from the satire. In a poem which mercilessly disparages the literary establishment and specific writers, with scathing jibes made at the expense of the Cinq Auteurs (l. 12), Boisrobert and the capital's theatrical milieu (ll. 225–34), and the Sorbonne (l. 934), there is one glaring oversight: the Académie française. The *Miliade*'s author might have been expected to make some capital out of this recently founded institution, the Cardinal's pet project which benefitted from his personal protection, but there is not the slightest insinuation in this direction.[68] Three of the Cardinal's greatest publicists were part of the institution, namely Paul Hay du Chastelet, François Le Métel de Boisrobert, and Jean Chapelain. Favereau seems to have inspired sentiments of loyalty among his friends as seen with Marolles's determination to realize his iconographical project. Following Favereau's death in 1638, Chapelain wrote to Guez de Balzac (who had, himself, corresponded with Favereau several weeks before his death) lamenting his loss, rejoicing in the fact that he had been prepared for death and fortified with the last sacraments, and stating he had been a true friend.[69] Theirs was a long-standing friendship and they were regular correspondents who respected each other's literary judgements.[70] In omitting to denigrate

---

[67] *Mémoires de Michel de Marolles, abbé de Villeloin*, ed. by Claude Pierre Goujet, 3 vols (Amsterdam: [n.pub.], 1755), III, 275.

[68] An example of this is to be found with the solar trope used in the first few lines and discussed earlier. While the Cardinal's rays produce thirty authors, alluding to the Cinq Auteurs, a possible prototype for this image related to the Académie: 'Une espece de fou, nommé la Peyre, s'advisa de mettre au-devant d'un livre un grand soleil, dans le milieu duquel le Cardinal estoit représenté. Il en sortoit quarante rayons, au bout desquels estoient les noms des quarante académiciens', *Hist*, I, 272.

[69] *Lettres de Jean Chapelain, de l'Académie française*, ed. by Philippe Tamizey de Larroque, 2 vols (Paris: Imprimerie Nationale, 1880), I, 256–59 (Lettre CLXXV).

[70] This is demonstrated in the 'Lettre ou discours de M. Chapelain, en forme de poëme, à M. Favereau, Conseiller du Roy en sa Cour des Aydes, portant son opinion

the organization with which his friend was so intimately associated, Favereau may well have unwittingly left a significant clue indicating his authorship. A similar amnesty is accorded to Chapelain himself, who is entirely absent from the *Miliade*.[71] This is surprising, to say the least, since he was on very familiar and trusted terms with the Cardinal. In addition to this, he was a caricaturist's dream subject: his avarice was proverbial in Parisian circles and he always wore unfashionable, threadbare clothes, an outfit that was completed by a visibly dog-eared wig and hat.[72] Yet there is not a word in the poem about this easy target, even though Séguier's weather-beaten wig and parsimony are denounced. If Favereau shows leniency towards a friend in an anonymous work, then it testifies to a high level of solicitude towards those he knew, and thus we should not be too surprised that Favereau's secret was not betrayed to Richelieu or his agents. As Chapelain makes a point of noting: 'C'estoit un bon homme et de service quand il aimoit quelqu'un'.[73] Affording both Chapelain and the Académie Française such consideration certainly does not sound like Ételan, whose *Comédie des Académistes* ruthlessly pillories both and was composed only a matter of months following the *Miliade*.[74]

---

sur le poëme d'Adonis du Cavalier Marino' in Giambattista Marino, *L'Adone* (Venice: Oliviero di Varano, 1623), pp. i–xvi. Chapelain states 'Telle est donc l'opinion que vous avez voulu avoir de moy touchant l'ouvrage de nostre amy, pour laquelle appuyer d'avantage j'eusse peu estendre plus au long ce que j'en ay dit en peu de mots, et aurois encore tout plein de choses à dire si je parlois à une personne moins entenduë, ou moins affectionnée à l'honneur du Chevalier Marin, c'est à dire à la verité' (pp. xv–xvi).

[71] Carl J. Burckhardt considers Chapelain as important to the Cardinal as Boisrobert in maintaining his hold over the literary establishment, seen in his being commissioned to write his 'Lettre à Antoine Godeau sur la règle de vingt-quatre heures' (1630); *Richelieu and His Age*, trans. Bernard Hoy, 3 vols (New York: Jovanovitch, 1970), III, 373. He was also responsible for drawing up the Académie Française's response to Corneille's *Le Cid* at Richelieu's behest.

[72] François Charpentier, *Carpentariana ou remarques d'histoire, de morale, de critique, d'érudition, et de bons mots de M. Charpentier, De l'Academie Françoise*, ed. by M. Boscheron (Paris: Nicolas Le Breton, 1724), pp. 127–29.

[73] *Lettres de Jean Chapelain*, I, 258. In the same letter, Chapelain discusses the need to censor Mathieu de Morgues's latest anti-Richelieu tract that has filtered to Paris from the Low Countries.

[74] Ételan also makes capital out of the Académie française in 'Le Passage de Somme', remarking 'Dont on voit bien-souvent un autheur accablé', fol. 545. Paolo Carile has argued that Ételan made a larger contribution to the work's production

With the second individual in question, it is more a question of what is said than what is left out, unlike the case of Chapelain. When it comes to Nicolas Le Jay, who presided over the Parlement de Paris, the portrait we are given is remorselessly vitriolic to a degree that makes it conspicuously so in a satire which is never reticent in its vilification of pillars of the regime. His private life is dealt with at length: the poem provides a detailed exposition of his unbridled libido, sketching a man devoid of any moral compass, whose excess in the bedroom is matched only by the betrayal of his office in his disobedience to the Parlement and monarch to whom he was sworn to serve. In fact, what is quite possibly the *Miliade*'s strongest accusatory term is applied to him: 'Cet Athée ennemy de Dieu' (l. 729). The *tableau* dedicated to Le Jay is also remarkable because of its length, reaching over a hundred lines, that is to say more than a tenth of the satire (ll. 652–750). The office of *premier président* was an ancient and symbolic one, and unlike the other important offices of state, was conferred for life in the gift of the sovereign as a non-venal post.[75] In the *Catolicon françois*, published in the same year as our satire, there is a damning evaluation of Le Jay's interactions with Richelieu. After having coerced the Parlement to levy further taxes to fund the war effort, some notable Parlementarians come to the prelate's cabinet in order to plead with him, but Père Joseph slams the door in their face: 'Le President le Jay est bien plus sage que vous, et ne parle jamais des miseres du peuple n'y du gouvernement des Ministres, allez à son Escole, et quand vous aurez apris son ramage l'on vous ouvrira la porte'.[76] It would seem that this sycophancy was not far off the mark. On the occasion of the *lit de justice* of 12 August 1632, where the Parlement was to ratify the declaration of *lèse-majesté* against Gaston d'Orléans and his supporters, Le Jay did not speak for the many voices of discontent within the body he led, but rather sought to stifle this dissent and urged their acquience to the the ministry's wishes. After the King

---

than Saint-Évremond, see *Saint-Évremond et comte d'Ételan, La Comédie des Académistes et Saint-Évremond, Les Académiciens*, ed. by Paolo Carile (Milan: Cisalpino-Goliardica; Paris: Nizet, 1976), p. 57.

[75] Charles Desmaze, *Le Parlement de Paris: son organisation, ses premiers presidents et procureurs généraux* (Paris: Lévy, 1859), p. 137.

[76] [Mathieu de Morgues], *Catolicon François, ou plainctes de deux chasteaux, rapportées par Renaudot, maistre du bureau d'adresses* ([Antwerp?]: [n.pub.], 1636), p. 28.

had spoken 'M. le premier président a seulement répliqué que cette parole leur fermoit la bouche; qu'ils obéiroient, puisqu'il lui plaisot, à un commandement si absolu'.[77] The 1630s, in particular, were marked by increasing tension between the King – and therefore Richelieu – and the Parlement.[78] Matters came to a head at the beginning of 1636 when Louis created twenty-four new positions within the Parlement, an effective way of curtailing its authority. After the imprisonment of six members of the Parlement because of their vocal opposition to this measure, an episode mentioned in line 737 of the *Miliade*, Le Jay did all he could to support the government and force the Parlement to accept this *fait accompli*:

> Le premier président rendit compte de son entrevue avec le roi et déclara qu'on ne devait pas délibérer sur la proposition précédemment faite à cause de la défense du roi. Les présidents des Enquêtes insistèrent pour que la délibération s'ouvrît, mais le premier président résista jusqu'à la fin de l'audience, de sorte que rien ne fut fait. Pendant les deux jours suivants, les membres des Enquêtes discutèrent entre eux et le samedi 10 ils vinrent prendre séance à la Grand'Chambre. Mais le Premier Président, n'ayant reçu aucun avis du roi, refusa d'ouvrir la délibération et on passa ainsi l'audience à se regarder.[79]

By preventing the Parlement from discussing the King's actions, he hindered it from militating against the sovereign; in other words, he presided over its emasculation. Indeed, he had been appointed to this end as 'Richelieu named only experienced royal servants as *premiers présidents* in order to maintain a loyal representative in the highest position and also as an attempt to manipulate the actions of the Parlement in its relations with the monarchy'.[80] That Le Jay's tenure in office should affect Jacques Favereau, rather than any of the other contenders for authorship, is evident for two principal

---

[77] *Mémoires d'Omer Talon*, in *Nouvelle Collection des Mémoires pour servir à l'histoire de France depuis le XIIIe siècle jusqu'à la fin du XVIIIe*, ed. by Joseph-François Michaud and John-Joseph-François Poujoulat, 10 vols (Paris: Didot, 1836–39), VI (1839), 14.

[78] Ennemond Fayard, *Aperçu historique sur le Parlement de Paris*, 3 vols (Paris: Picard, 1876–78), II (1877), 77–113.

[79] Ernest Glasson, *Le Parlement de Paris: son rôle politique depuis le règne de Charles VII jusqu'à la Révolution*, 2 vols (Paris: Hachette, 1901), I, 155.

[80] Mark L. Cummings, 'The Long Robe and the Scepter: A Quantitive Study of the Parlement of Paris and the French Monarchy in the Early Seventeenth Century' (unpublished doctoral thesis, University of Colorado, 1969), p. 182.

reasons. Firstly, as a member of the Cour des Aides he belonged to a constituent institution of the Cour du Roi, together with the Parlement and the Chambre des Comptes.[81] The Cour des Aides was a sovereign body responsible for appeals involving taxation and finances and a series of confrontations between the government and the Cour des Aides arose as a result of increasing fiscal demands from the state; in 1631, the situation deteriorated to such a point that Louis XIII temporarily abolished the Cour des Aides.[82] Favereau participated in this action and is the only one of the writers suspected of the *Miliade*'s authorship to be party to the workings of the Cour at such close quarters, and accordingly had the most personal stake in the ramifications to Le Jay's complicity. Secondly, Étienne Pasquier, who had been his mentor and friend and into whose family he married, was a passionate defender of Parliamentary privilege and the institution played a significant role in his life from his entry in 1549. That he resigned his post as *avocat général* of the Chambre des Comptes in 1604, which he had held from 1585, shortly after Henri IV came into conflict with the Chambre and criticized their non-compliance with his orders to install a new *président* with haste and bypassing some of the usual forms.[83] Pasquier's resignation in favour of his son's succession ended over half a century of involvement with the sovereign courts and it is difficult not to interpret the timing of this step as a muted and personal reaction to the monarch's dismissive attitude to the authority of the Chambre. He was certainly a life-long supporter of the monarchy, but it is also telling that he was not reticent in deploring miscarriages of justice or the misuse of patronage, even if these occur at the highest level.[84] Pasquier considered that the sovereign court always reserved a right to remonstrance as a check and balance 'au Roy, pour luy faire

---

[81] For the workings of this body, see Martine Bennini, *Les Conseillers à la Cour des Aides (1604–1697): étude sociale*, Histoire et Archives, 9 (Paris: Champion, 2010). On documentation dealing with Favereau, see pp. 402–03.

[82] Philip Leo Sheehy, 'The *Cour des Aides de Paris*: Perspectives on the Seventeenth-Century French Magistrature' (unpublished doctoral thesis, University of California, Los Angeles, 1977), p. 357.

[83] Paul Bouteiller, 'Étienne Pasquier (1529–1615): sa vie et sa carrière' (unpublished doctoral thesis, Université de Lille III, 2001), pp. 218–21.

[84] L. Clark Keating, *Étienne Pasquier*, Twayne World Authors Series, 24 (New York: Twayne, 1972), pp. 79–80.

entendre que ses mouvemens doivent s'accorder à raison'.[85] Given that Pasquier showed such probity, it is little wonder that Favereau was so appalled at Le Jay's fervent role in the erosion of the Parlement's prerogatives.[86] In the absence of the Estates General, the Parlement was the only body powerful enough to assert the customary rights of remonstrance, a fact that was not lost on either the government or the Parlement itself.[87] It effectively became the only institutional vehicle through which public opinion could be expressed and the *Miliade* vigorously defends this privilege against Richelieu's attempts to emasculate it.

Bussy Pasquier

One further name that merits a mention in connection with the *Miliade* occurs in only one place, a manuscript of the poem that intriguingly contains an annotation after the poem's last line 'par Bussy Pasquier' in writing that appears to be seventeenth century, in slightly smaller script, apparently written in darker ink, and in an unmistakably different hand.[88] This refers to the Pasquier family of the Cognac region who held the title of *seigneurs de Bussy*.[89] At the time of the diffusion of the *Miliade*, Guy Pasquier was sieur de

---

[85] Étienne Pasquier, *Pourparlers*, ed. by Béatrice Sayhi-Périgot, Textes de la Renaissance, 7 (Paris: Champion, 1995), p. 102.

[86] J. H. Shennan views Le Jay's role during the skirmishes of January 1636 over the establishment of more offices as crucial to the imposition of an arbitrary decision on the part of the administration and sees the issue as 'whether the king had the authority to poach, in the name of state necessity, upon areas which traditionally he was expected to preserve from trespass', *The Parlement of Paris*, 2nd edn (Stroud: Sutton, 1988), pp. 244–53. Lauriane Kadlec underscores the difficulty of the clash of loyalties that Le Jay experienced, though concludes that '[l]e premier président se conduisit donc de façon ambivalente', *Quand le Parlement de Paris s'oppose à l'autorité royale: l'affaire de la chambre de l'Arsenal (14 juin 1631–mars 1632)*, Histoire et Archives, 7 (Paris: Champion, 2007), p. 102.

[87] 'Entre 1614 et 1789 il ne fut, en revanche, plus question des états généraux', François Bluche, *L'Ancien Régime: institutions et société* (Paris: Fallois, 1993), p. 37.

[88] Paris, Bibliothèque nationale, MS fonds français 22579, fols 46–62^v (62^v).

[89] Jean-Baptiste de Courcelles, *Histoire généalogique et héraldique des pairs de France, des grands dignitaires de la couronne, des principales familles nobles du royaume, et des maisons princières de l'Europe*, 12 vols (Paris: Bertrand, 1822–33), VIII (1827), 108.

Bussy. He came from a solidly intellectual family, for his uncle, Nicolas, was a writer of some distinction and his grandfather was Étienne Pasquier, the eminent laywer and historian.[90] Notwithstanding this literary genealogy, Guy Pasquier is an unlikely contender for the authorship of the poem for he was not a writer and in 1636 was still a minor who had not yet been legally emancipated. However, his sister, Marguerite, was married to Jacques Favereau, who was also legal guardian to the young Guy and his siblings, which is a curious link to a serious contender for the authorship of the *Miliade*.[91] Moreover, Favereau came to Paris from his native Cognac in order to study with Étienne Pasquier who was a close friend of his father's.[92] Since the origin of the annotation is unknown, it is possible that someone had muddled the gossip he or she had heard and, as a result of speculative cross-wires, assigned the work to Favereau's brother-in-law, François, who held the post of *auditeur en la chambre de comptes de Paris*, rather than to Favereau, or had quite simply confused the Favereau clan with the Pasquier family.[93] This would certainly be an easy mistake to make and it is also a logical one, given the strong familial and legal ties that bound the two families.[94] The 'Bussy Pasquier' annotation points us, once again, in the direction of Jacques Favereau.

Other Contenders

An unlikely name that has been advocated by a small number of critics is Pierre Corneille. The dramatist was first proposed by Pierre Louÿs in 1920 and his candidacy has recently resurfaced by proponents of Louÿs's thesis that Corneille was responsible for

---

[90] Nicolas was noted for his letters, several collections of which were published. See Denise Carabin, 'Les Lettres de Nicolas Pasquier: la lettre de consolation', *Revue d'Histoire Littéraire de France*, 102 (2002), 15–31.

[91] Louis Audiat, *Un Fils d'Estienne Pasquier: Nicolas Pasquier, lieutenant général et maître des requêtes. Étude sur sa vie et sur ses écrits* (Paris: Didier, 1876), p. 257.

[92] Michel de Marolles, *Tableaux du Temple des Muses Representant les Vertus, et les vices, sur les plus illustres fables de l'Antiquité* (Paris: Antoine de Sommaville, 1655), 'Éloge de M^r. Favereau', sig. [ĕ4]^v.

[93] Courcelles, *Histoire généalogique*, VIII, 108.

[94] Favereau had blood ties to the Pasquier family through his paternal grandfather, Audiat, *Un Fils d'Estienne Pasquier*, pp. 111–12.

comedies traditionally ascribed to Molière.[95] This possibility appears implausible for a number of reasons, not least of which is a complete absence of any contemporary insinuation of Corneille's involvement. Even if he had engaged in such a risky project while he was enjoying the Cardinal's patronage, the poem bears few of the playwright's stylistic hallmarks. Corneille's would bide his time and express his antipathy towards Richelieu's manipulation of the arts in the 'studied insolence' of the ambivalent eulogy contained in the dedication of *Horace* (1641).[96]

One further possibility that must be considered is that of collaborative authorship. However, the copious presence of anaphora and initial alliteration throughout the whole *Miliade* – there is no page that lacks this technique in the work – signals a consistency of style that points to sole authorship. Writing a couple of decades after the *Miliade*, Claude Le Petit and his circle of 'poëtes crottés' each contributed ten-line decasyllabic stanzas to compile two thousand-line poems entitled the *Milliade oratoire* and the *Milliade poétique*.[97] Le Petit, an author of libertine verse, holds the inauspicious distinction of being the only seventeenth-century writer to be burnt at the stake as a result of his writings, in 1662. The use of *Milliade* in the title of these poems seems to be a verbal nod towards the work's subversive content rather than emulating the manner in which the poetic namesake was written. In any case, the fact that the *Miliade* is not comprised of exactly 1000 lines undermines any hypothesis of collective authorship, since each poet would logically have been responsible for an assigned section of 100 lines or so. Georges Mongrédien proposes that Beys worked with Ételan on the poem; the idea of these two writers working together is an attractive one but

---

[95] See Henry Poulaille, *Corneille sous le masque de Molière* (Paris: Grasset, 1957), p. 165. The critics who most recently have defended Louÿs's hypothesis have followed his attribution of the *Miliade* to Corneille: see Philippe Vidal, *Molière-Corneille: les mensonges d'une légende* (Paris: Lafon, 2003), p. 171 and Denis Boissier, *L'Affaire Molière: la grande supercherie littéraire* (Paris: Godefroy, 2004), p. 300.

[96] Christopher Braider, *Indiscernible Counterparts: The Invention of the Text in French Classical Drama*, North Carolina Studies in the Romance Languages and Literatures, 275 (Chapel Hill: University of North Carolina Press, 2002), p. 114.

[97] Jean Rou, *Mémoires inédits et opuscules de Jean Rou (1638–1711)*, ed. by Francis Waddington, 2 vols (Paris: Agence Centrale de la Société, 1857), II, 317.

is more speculative than either of their particular claims taken on their individual merits.[98]

I believe that, taken together, the evidence such as it is, countenances the seriousness of Favereau's candidacy, and this effectively resolves the open question that even Richelieu was never able to answer and about which Tallemant resignedly admits 'Voyla mes conjectures; je ne voudrois pourtant rien asseurer'.[99] It is entirely reasonable to maintain that Favereau wrote the *Miliade* on the basis of a number of pieces of evidence taken collectively. One area that surprisingly failed to be relevant in evaluating the potential authorship was versification. Comparing the extremely small category of words whose syllabic count could vary in the seventeenth century yielded no pertinent results; this vocabulary was either not used in the poem or by the potential authors, or they were used in a consistent manner by all the authors.[100] The most common word that is variable, the adverb *hier*, is not present at all in the satire; this word proved to be an indispensible tool in allowing a recent editor to establish which specific act had been composed by which of the Cinq Auteurs in two collaborative plays.[101] The one variant that I found was in the use of 'fuir' which, while most commonly pronounced as a monosyllabic word, could occur disyllabically in some respected authors, particularly in the first half of the seventeenth century.[102] The verb occurs once in the *Miliade* and is used monosyllabically whereas Ételan favours a disyllabic

---

[98] Georges Mongrédien, *La Vie littéraire au XVIIe siècle* (Paris: Tallandier, 1947), p. 48.

[99] Tall, fol. 37^r. This line ends the final annotation to his copy of the poem; the note has been reproduced in full in this introduction.

[100] I consulted Antoine Phérotée de La Croix, *L'Art de la poësie françoise. Ou la methode de connoitre et de faire toute sorte de Vers* (Lyon: Thomas Amaulry, 1675), pp. 18–21 (Chapter 4; 'Doute sur le nombre de syllabes de certains mots') and Michel Mourgues, *Traité de la poësie françoise*, rev. edn (Paris: Jacques Vincent, 1724), pp. 126–58 (Chapter 2; 'Eclaircissemens de quelques doutes sur le nombre des syllabes de certains mots').

[101] Cinq Auteurs, *La Comédie des Tuileries; et, L'Aveugle de Smyrne*, ed. by François Lasserre, Sources Classiques, 87 (Paris: Champion, 2008). Lasserre's closely argued attribution of the acts of both plays is as magisterial as it is convincing.

[102] See Mourgues, *Traité de la poësie françoise*, pp. 145–46.

usage, contributing another corroborating factor against his authorship.[103] While I was completing the edition, it was reported in the media that Sir Brian Vickers had used anti-plagiarism software to assist him in comparing writing patterns in an unattributed play, *The Reign of Edward III*, and in other late sixteenth-century writers, leading him to conclude that the play is almost certainly a collaborative effort between Thomas Kyd and William Shakespeare.[104] I consequently ran the text of the *Miliade* through three major anti-plagiarism programmes which did not bring up any matches; this result was not entirely unexpected owing to the relatively negligible output of the suspected authors, together with the fact that a significant proportion remains inaccessible to the scope of this type of software because it is either not available online or only exists in manuscript form.

One thing is more certain in evaluating the poem's purported authors: by and large, almost without exception, all of these compelling and colourful characters have been unduly neglected by modern scholarship and closer critical interest into both their lives as well as their works is long overdue.

PUBLICATION HISTORY

The history of the printed versions of the *Miliade* has given rise to a certain amount of confusion, occasioned by the fact that it was reprinted with some additions at the beginning of the Fronde, thirteen years after it first appeared in 1636, while several reworked editions subsequently appeared from 1649 to 1652. Its final incarnation was its inclusion in a collection of anti-Richelieu and anti-Mazarin pamphlets that was printed in the Low Countries in 1693 and 1694.

---

[103] It occurs in line 288 of the *Miliade*. For its disyllabic use by Ételan, see 'Le Passage de Somme', fol. 551.

[104] Gaëlle Faure, 'How Plagiarism Software Finds a New Shakespeare Play', *Time*, 20 October 2009, <http://www.time.com/time/arts/article/ 0,8599,1930971,00.html> [accessed 2 April 2010].

The Octavo Edition

The earliest edition is identifiable by the fact it is in an octavo format whereas the versions appearing during the civil war were in quarto. Not only was the quarto format most associated with the pamphlets appearing in the capital during the Fronde,[105] but it is also possible to compare the corrections that have taken place between the two formats, with the inescapable conclusion that errors in pagination, orthography, and grammar have been improved in a successive timeline stemming from the octavo edition. This octavo format is compact, which has led some bibliographers to count it erroneously as a duodecimo.[106] In addition, there is some degree of amendments that have been introduced between versions of the octavo which strongly indicates two separate imprints, most likely produced within a matter of weeks of each other. Another proof that the octavo edition predates the quarto ones is the fact that it contains the locative information 'Envers' at the end; it was assumed the work emanated from the Low Countries and Tallemant, for one, believed this.[107] There was no need to posit a false place of publication during the Fronde and so this ending, anchoring the work to its appearance in print during the *année de Corbie*, is no longer present. Seven copies of the octavo edition are extant, which testifies to the thoroughness with which Richelieu tried to eradicate it, but, as with his investigations into the authorship, he did not entirely succeed. The seven copies are held in the following libraries: the Beinecke Rare Book and Manuscript Library, Yale University; Rare Book, Manuscripts, and Special Collections Library, Duke University; the Koninklijke Bibliotheek, The Hague; Patrimoine Fonds ancien, Bibliothèque Municipale Méjanes, Aix-en-Provence; three copies are held at the Bibliothèque nationale de France, one in the Département des manuscrits, Richelieu, and the other two at the Tolbiac site, with one being held in the Réserve and the other in the library's standard collections. Since there are so few remaining copies and given the almost complete absence of contemporary

---

[105] This was also Fournier's conclusion, *Variétés historiques*, p. 5n.

[106] Émile Bourgeois and Louis André, *Les Sources de l'histoire de France, XVIIe siècle (1620–1715)*, 8 vols (Paris: Picard, 1913–35), IV (1924), 264 and *Dictionnaire des lettres françaises: le XVIIe siècle*, ed. by Patrick Dandrey (Paris: Fayard, 1996), p. 856.

[107] *Hist*, I, 248.

sources to allow the order in which the work appeared to be pieced together satisfactorily, I have attempted to deduce a logical chronology for the satire on the basis of the meagre evidence as it stands.

Assuming that the original printed version or versions of the libel figures among the seven surviving octavo copies, I believe that the three copies held at the Bibliothèque nationale de France were undoubtedly published first of all, and the other four were printed at a later date. My reasoning for this is primarily textual. These three texts are almost identical to one another and even possess the same typographic errors in line 101, on page 9, where the letter 'a' is a couple of millimetres lower than the rest of the letters in the word 'grands' and indeed than the rest of the line, and in line 554 at the bottom of page 44 where 'qetit' is present instead of 'petit'. A further typographic error occurs with the word 'vice' in line 539, on page 44, which is unreadable save for the letters v and c; the missing vowels only occur in the three Paris copies. These two mistakes are not present in the other four copies. There are some minor differences between these three copies which indicate a small number of adjustments made by typesetters or, as is more likely, raising the possibility of another issue, but these remain cosmetic changes which are minor in nature. All of the three copies thus have same fault concerning the pagination: page 32 is followed by page 43 (which begins with line 519) and the work continues with this erroneous pagination all the way through from this point, an oversight that does not affect the poem's text. However, the third copy's pagination is different: in the copy held at the Réserve of the Bibliothèque nationale, page 30 is followed by 41, after which are pages 32 then 43. It would be logical to deduce that a fix has evidently been attempted to remedy the faulty pagination but has instead produced another mispagination. This leads us to conclude that the Réserve text at the Bibliothèque nationale is probably the first imprint of the surviving copies and could well be the first edition of the poem. The fact that efforts were made to rectify the confused sequence of page numbers yet which still produced an unsuccessful result indicates that the typesetter was inexperienced, numerically challenged, or simply slipshod. More plausibly, the persistence of errors might be accounted for by adrenalin as our typesetter was working under tremendous pressure and had more to lose than merely his livelihood for the Paris police's *règlement general* of 30 January 1635 invoked the death penalty for non-authorized works: 'Le pouvoir tient alors en main, sinon monopolise et confisque la parole publique: la production des libelles chutent, les publications clandestines sont de plus en plus risquées'.[108] The fact that the confused sequence of pagination is followed by the other four, presumably later, editions (which follow the second issue's series of page 32 followed by page 43 but without page 31 being affected) is a strong indicator that the same typesetter was responsible for the work coming off the same press in the case of all of the seven copies. Two of the three BN copies are affected by an identical defect concerning an uneven distribution of ink on the bottom of page 20: the last two letters of last word of line 304, 'canonades' are not visible and only the upper half of the 'd' may be made out, with the Richelieu copy being the exception. The minor differences between each of these three BN copies indicates that each of the three either represents distinct issues, presumably within a very short space of time, or else that the typesetter tried to correct some issues during the initial print run.

While these three texts are essentially identical, there are a substantial number of wide-ranging orthographical and grammatical infelicities present in these three BN copies which have been unequivocally corrected in the remaining four copies. This is not simply a question of a series of minor corrections and indicates a comprehensive programme to ameliorate the overall text. I do not propose detailing every such instance here since I record a number of such variants when they occur in the text, but will provide some representative examples to illustrate the extent of this phenomenon.

In the first place, there has been an attempt to rectify orthographical errors that obscure meaning. This includes changes in personal pronouns, so line 15 has 'nos debiles paupieres' in the Bibliothèque nationale copies, which has been corrected to 'vos' in the later versions; this provides clarification and conforms to the context since the surrounding passage directly addresses the reader, beginning with the first word, 'Peuple'. This is a frequent misreading of 'nos' in early modern manuscripts. In the preceeding line, the word 'nompareil' found in the Bibliothèque nationale copies has been replaced with 'non pareil'. The two variants existed, but it does seem to point to the work having being proofed and undergoing a certain degree of *nettoyage de texte*. In line 290, 'ces mains' makes more sense as 'ses mains', and a similar alteration revises 'Ce sage ce rit de ses fols' to 'Ce sage se rit de ces fols' (l. 317). The

---

[108] Françoise Hildesheimer, *Richelieu* (Paris: Flammarion, 2004), p. 324.

corrections also extend to spacing: thus the beginning of line 306 becomes 'Il terrasse' after having been 'Ilterrasse'. Similarly, many glaring mistakes have been put right so 'Qui gronde dessusnos ceste' is transformed to 'Qui gronde dessus nos testes' (l. 268). The wrongly conjugated verb in line 65, 'Il agit', is metamorphosed into 'Il agite'.[109] This type of correction compellingly implies that the cleaner version is posterior to a cruder text, namely the three Paris copies of the poem. Moreover, these copies lack two sets of couplets that are found in the other four editions on page 59 (ll. 809–10) and on page 60 (ll. 831–32).

The editorial intervention extends to the versification, which has been subject to correction: the rogue additional syllable in the original 'Et que l'on blesse la verité' is eliminated to produce the octosyllabic 'Et qu'on blesse la verité' (l. 73). Line 127 is recast from 'Ce molces à pour ses prestres' to 'Ce moloce a pour ses Prestres'. The seven syllables of 'Que ces cruels Commissaires' (l. 96) are rectified to 'Que ces deux cruels Commissaires'. There are other examples involving the addition of a syllable such as 'Son ame n'est jamais nüe' which becomes 'Et son ame n'est jamais nüe' (l. 148), and 'Et s'il traicte avec des sourds' benefits from the cosmetic supplement of 'que' in 'avecque' to produce 'Et s'il traitte avecque des sourds' (l. 166).[110] The following line, 'Les deçoit par son visage', has an extra 'Il' to give 'Il les deçoit par son visage', whereas 'bien' is inserted to the line 'Il faict chasque personnage', giving 'Il faict bien chasque personnage' (l. 195). A verb is replaced in line 246 to modify the line from 'Est plus clair que le Soleil' to 'Paroist plus clair que le Soleil'. An expletive 'le' is inserted before 'on' in order to inject another syllable into 'Traitter comme on fit Louvain' (l. 349) which remedies the missing syllable. While some

---

[109] At some point, an unknown owner of one of these copies (the one held in Tolbiac's standard collections) has not been able to resist the temptation to add the missing 'e' and, in fact, corrects most errors in this edition in the same fashion. While this edition is the only copy that has so far been digitised and made available on Gallica, these alterations in ink are sometimes impossible to spot, particularly since they have been made in a careful hand to blend in with the typeface.

[110] Claude Vaugelas admits the use of *avec* and *avecque* as 'tous deux bons', though goes on to assert that the two forms should be used in a systematic manner than just being reserved for poets availing themselves of a supplementary vowel, as is the case here. See *Remarques sur la langue françoise utiles a ceux qui veulent bien parler et bien escrire* (Paris: Jean Camusat and Pierre Le Petit, 1647), p. 311. This is the only appearance of 'avecque' in the entire poem.

care has been taken to implement a series of improvements, not everything has been caught. The six syllables of line 443, 'Les ordres Seraphines', remains in its initial state only to be modified in the first quarto version of the work where it becomes 'Les Ordonances Seraphines' (p. 8). This is probably owing to an incorrect reading of a contraction of the word 'ordonnances' in an early manuscript.

There is plentiful evidence of a programme of not only grammatical correction but also of stylistic improvements being implemented between the two editions. There are accordingly examples of different spellings; 'parjures' is preferred to 'perjeures' (it is, in fact, 'parieures', but I have resolved the i/j as an editorial practice) (l. 30); 'Le monstre des peuples François' to 'Le meurtre des peuples francois' (l. 254). Line 63 evokes Richelieu's 'haine pire et cruelle' which becomes 'haine fiere et cruelle', replacing the former with a more lucid adjective and undoubtedly rectifying a mistake resulting from an unclear hand in the manuscript at the time of typesetting.

The combination of these different alterations and improvements is ample proof of editorial involvement aiming to produce a less defective edition, a supposition that is more credible than a widescale degeneration in the opposite direction. Moreover, an identical fault with pagination that involves not only the three Paris copies but also one of the other copies, namely Duke's (the other three display page 55 correctly), does imply that the two versions of the work originate from the same press.[111] Among the four remaining copies, I would suggest that we have evidence of two separate issues. Thus on page 29 the name La Fabry is rendered as the abbreviated 'La F.' in line 463 in the Beinecke, Hague, and Aix copies, but is spelt in full in the three BN copies as well as the Duke copy, which signals that it was abbreviated at a later issue, namely the second issue of the corrected octavo edition. Another attribute shared only between the three Paris copies and Duke's and not

---

[111] This occurs with what should be page 55, which is inbetween 54 and 56; this page is erroneously numbered as another page 54 without loss of text. It may be concluded that the enhanced version of the *Miliade* which had been subject to corrections was undertaken by the same press, and that either a printer spotted and corrected the incorrect pagination resulting in two pages headed by 54 (an easier fix to enact than the substantial changes that would be involved in tweaking the sequence of a total of 33 pages from page 43, which should, in fact, be number 33), or that the correction was made during another subsequent issue.

present in the other three copies is a missing 2 from the number 29 at the heading of that page. The Duke copy is consequently the sole remnant of this first issue. Why this particular name was shortened in later satires, and this name alone, is inexplicable since the context indicates that this refers unambiguously to Séguier's wife, although it does add a forced element of scandal through apparently being necessitated to disguise identities. The four copies are identical save for one instance of mispagination.

As I have argued earlier, the work first appeared in print during the summer of 1636. Estimating when the reworked form was published is much less certain. Assuming that the author is Favereau, it would have to have been completed before the autumn of 1638, when he died. Nevertheless, the work would have lost something of its topicality in 1637 or 1638, since Richelieu had survived the events that seemed likely to bring him down, the Spanish had been routed, and the Queen was pregnant and gave birth to an heir in 1638, which neutralized the outrage occasioned by the treatment of the heir presumptive, Gaston d'Orléans, in the satire as well as weakening the powerbase of Marie de Médicis. In short, the position of the minister and, indeed, of Louis XIII, had been consolidated and there had been a shift in alliances, since Anne of Austria, as mother of an heir, now enjoyed a level of status that she never had as a childless queen. This leads to the conclusion that the amended version of the *Miliade* most likely appeared close to its predecessor, that is to say during the months July or August 1636. Some critics have referred to a revised version of the *Miliade* appearing in 1643 in Paris.[112] That year did see a number of anti-Richelieu pamphlets in the wake of his death in December 1642, so this remains a possibility but there is no corroborating evidence from contemporary sources or from any version of the poem itself to conclude that this is the case. It is also possible that a misunderstanding has arisen from the fact that one of the editions has had 'A Paris. / 1643.' added in pen at some point on the title page (BN Ye 4086), an unsubstantiated

---

[112] Barbier speaks of an octavo Paris edition of 1643, adding that 'Cette satire, publiée vers 1633, existe aussi sans indication de ville, sans nom d'impression et sans date (*Anvers*), in 8, 66p', *Dictionnaire des ouvrages anonymes*, II, col. 551. This seemingly alludes to a Parisian edition that does not display 'Envers' at the end, which is common to all seven surviving octavo copies. Barbier is therefore referring either to a version of the satire that is no longer extant or has confused it with other 1643 anti-Richelieu libels. Brunet also mentions the same 1643 Paris edition, *Manuel du libraire*, II, col. 1684,

and anonymous annotation that has been taken at face value by at least one critic.[113]

Moreover, there is nothing to indicate that the writer himself was directly involved with the publication of the poem. A more likely thesis is that he passed the work in manuscript form to carefully selected recipients, and that, at some point, a reader made the decision to commit it to a wider audience, perhaps without the author's approval, as was the case with Roger de Bussy-Rabutin's *Histoire amoureuse des Gaules* (1665) which caused the author's imprisonment in the Bastille, public disgrace, and exile from Louis XIV's court. The many errors to be found in the earlier copies reveal that the decision to publish the poem could well have been a rushed one, perhaps owing to the sharp downturn in Richelieu's popularity during the summer of 1636, but they just as well might be part of a purposeful strategy to throw Richelieu's agents off a trail that might have led to an accomplished poet, akin to a performer playing a musical instrument badly for comic effect yet who is perfectly capable of using the instrument correctly. Jean-Michel-Constant Leber maintains that the typography, inferior paper, and faults in French to be found in the work are part of a deliberate strategy to disguise the fact that this libel was printed domestically, most likely in a Parisian *cave*.[114] Given that the both versions of the octavo *Miliade* seem to emanate from the same press, on balance they almost certainly appeared within months, or even weeks, of each other. Despite there essentially being two editions of the octavo form of the poem, they all share the same printer's signatures, which also occur in the same place, another sign of a common origin.[115]

The Quarto Edition

The quarto version of the *Miliade* made its first appearance in 1649 as a fifteen-page pamphlet containing two columns on each page. It

---

[113] *Les Illustres Fous of Charles de Beys*, ed. by Merle I. Protzman (Baltimore: Johns Hopkins Press, 1942), p. 38.

[114] Jean-Michel-Constant Leber, *De l'état réel de la presse et des pamphlets depuis François Ier jusqu'à Louis XIV* (Paris: Techener, 1834), p. 100.

[115] The signatures are: B (p. 9); C (p. 17); D (p. 25); E (p. 43); F (p. 51); G (p. 59). The sig. B is, however, missing in the BnF Réserve copy and some signatures are only partially present in other copies owing to tightly-cut pages. There is no signature for A in any of the seven copies.

follows the text of the corrected octavo version and contains an additional two lines towards the end that are not present in any of the surviving octavo copies. Precise information is provided: Paris is given as the place of publication, the date is specified (17 March 1649), and the work is presented as a 'Nouuelle edition reueuë, & exactement corrigée'. To this end, the title has been adjusted to *LE TABLEAU DU GOUVERNEMENT PRESENT, OU ELOGE DE SON EMINENCE SATYRE DE MILLE VERS* as if to distinguish it from the earlier incarnation of the *Miliade*. Many Mazarinades of that year carried a date on their title page, and it may signify the actual date it was sent to the printers or was chosen since it was the day on which formal talks reopened at Saint-Germain between the court-in-exile and the rebellious members of the Paris Parlement. It also happened to be the date on which the English monarchy was abolished and the Commonwealth set up. This pamphlet has consequently been treated as a Mazarinade by some critics and is listed as such by Moreau, but is better to categorize it as a pseudo-Mazarinade, since it remained virtually unchanged and thus firmly anchored to Richelieu and his creatures as well as to events that had occurred up to two decades earlier.[116] That it could be printed without the need of a major textual overhaul persuasively implies that the work enjoyed an almost canonical status among the disenchanted. The existence of several manuscript copies of the work also attest to it having been widely disseminated before the 1649 reprint since a large proportion of the print runs had been seized. The readership was left to make the obvious and implicit connection between the *Miliade* and the Fronde: the wholescale corruption within the government was a result of the delegation of power to a self-serving minister, and Mazarin as the chosen heir to Richelieu, was perpetuating this self-same system.[117] Moreover,

---

[116] 'Ici, le texte de la première *Miliade* a été conservé. On sait que l'édition originale de ce pamphlet est de 1635. Elle est en caractères italiques. La critique ne s'est pas encore prononcée entre les auteurs présumés de cette terrible satire. Elle laisse le choix entre Favereau, conseiller à la cour des Aides, d'Estelan, fils du maréchal de Saint-Luc, et Beys, bon poëte du temps', Moreau, *Bibliographie des Mazarinades*, II, 11–12. Moreau lists this as Mazarinade number 1503.

[117] 'Un bon indicateur de la continuité mécanique établie entre la dénonciation de Richelieu et celle de Mazarin réside d'ailleurs dans une pratique largement répandue: la réutilisation pure et simple de pièces littéraires, parfois même sans adaptation', Laurent Avezou, 'La Légende de Richelieu: fortune posthume d'un rôle historique du XVIIe au XXe siècle' (unpublished doctoral thesis, Université Paris I, 2002), p. 69.

some of Richelieu's protégés, such as Chavigny and Séguier, were still in office.

While the text remains almost identical, some minor differences point to at least three separate subsequent printings of the text during the Fronde, all published under the original title and in quarto and without indication of place of publication and without any provision of a date. All of the quarto editions substitute 'FIN.' for 'Imprimé à Envers. Fin.' On page 6, some copies have a missing 'U' in the word 'Tour' of the line 'Et la d'Herbelay et de la Tour' (l. 685). Given that all of the extant copies of the pseudo-Mazarinade nonetheless share other quirks in addition to possessing the same text, it would seem logical to conclude that they originated from the same press. Most copies have three of the page numbers, located in the centre of the top of each page, directly above the column break, in italics (namely pages 8, 9, and 12). Other copies have only two page numbers italicized (pages 8 and 9). None of the page numbers are in italics in the edition of 1649.

Another edition must be mentioned, published in 1652, since it provides the date as well as the location of Paris on the title page, and appears under the modified title of *LE GOUVERNEMENT DE L'ESTAT PRESENT, Où l'on void les fourbes et tromperies de Mazarin*. Unlike the other four issues of the work during the Fronde, the name of Richelieu has systematically been replaced with that of Mazarin. Thus, the couplet 'D'avoir mesprisé Richelieu, / Dont le nom rime a demy Dieu' (ll. 321–22) is reconstructed as 'D'avoir mesprisé Mazarin, / Dont le renom ne vaut plus rien' (p. 7). In places this is somewhat forced, such as 'Il est valet de Richelieu, / Et l'adorateur de ce Dieu' (ll. 405–06) which appears as 'Il est valet de Mazarin, / Et l'adorateur de ce dain' (p. 8), though the fact that both cardinals had names containing exactly three syllables worked in this editor's favour. While the references to Mazarin do make the satire more topical, the specific allusions to the earlier political landcape have not been altered, which renders the editor's best intentions inescapably flawed; Richelieu's name might have been replaced but the references to his entourage remain untouched, notwithstanding the fact that some of them were no longer in office or alive. There are only four surviving copies of this work, at the Arsenal, the BN, Grenoble, and Auxerre. The last three are the only copies to have survived in their entirety, for the Arsenal's copy ends on page 12 at line 888. The other copies have a thirteenth page (with is given as an erroneously paginated second page 12) and has an additional couplet ending the poem and unique to this 1652 edition.

Finally, a quarto edition entitled *LA MILIADE OU L'ELOGE BURLESQUE DE MAZARIN, POUR SERVIR DE PIECE DE CARNAVAL*, with a date of publication given as 1651 on the title page and containing 30 pages of text set out in one column (unlike the quarto *Miliade* which is otherwise two columns per page), merits a mention in passing. This work possesses nothing in common with the *Miliade* other than having borrowed its name. It is in octosyllabic verse and it suffices to quote its introductory lines to demonstrate that, while it is not appreciably distant from the satirical register of its namesake, its reliance on bawdiness in its reference to Mazarin's family and the marital arrangements that were provided for his nieces sets it apart:

> GRAND Baladin Maistre Apolon
> *Alias*, jouĕur de Violon
> Ou Frere de ces neuf Pucelles
> Qui n'ayans dans leurs escarcelles
> Dequoy s'acheter un espoux
> Qui leur fretille les genoux
> Auront toujours leurs pucelages,
> Dautant qu'elles sont par trop sages. (p. 3)

This work was republished in 1663 following the death of Mazarin in 1661, and has been attributed to Paul Scarron, which raises the tantalising possibility of an indirect association between the *Miliade* and Louis XIV through his morganatic marriage to Scarron's widow.[118] The existence of this work signals that the very name of the satire had become synonymously resonant with subversive pamphlets by this point, almost acting to identify a subgenre of political lampoon in verse.

Anthology

The *Miliade* was included in an anthology published in 1693 and 1694 under the fictitious imprint of Pierre Marteau of Cologne and in duodecimo format. This volume, entitled *Le Tableau de la vie et du gouvernement de Messieurs les Cardinaux Richelieu et Mazarin, et de Monsieur Colbert* is a 'Recueil de vers satiriques – sonnets, épigrammes, épitaphes, rondeaux, etc. – contre Richelieu, Mazarin et Colbert. Les pièces concernant Fouquet lui sont souvent favorables,

---

[118] See *La Pure vérité cachée et autres Mazarinades rares et curieuses*, ed. by Pierre-Gustave Brunet (Amsterdam: [n.pub.], 1867), p. xxv.

ce qui est une façon de critiquer Colbert, et même Louis XIV'.[119] The *Miliade* is given pride of place with its positioning as the first satire in the 432-page compilation, an acknowledgement of its pioneering role in pamphlet history. Almost six decades after it first appeared to Richelieu's great irritation, the *Miliade* was still being called into service and had lost little of its polemical edge. In the 1690s the target was not a minister but rather the monarch whose authority had been consolidated by the collection's three subjects.[120] As with the Thirty Years War during the first half of the seventeenth century, France was at war and was also suffering from the ruinous effects of a devastating famine during 1693 and 1694 during which the lives of as many as 1.3 million lives out of a total population of around 22 million people would be claimed.[121] The compiler of the volume, possibly a disenfranchized French Huguenot writing from exile, does not offer any commentary other than a two-page 'Avertissement au Lecteur' in which he stresses the value of satire. The function of satirical literature is to present a balanced picture of great men: 'elles représentent les Vices aussi bien que les Vertüs d'une personne qui a fait dans le monde'. In the case of the two cardinals and Colbert, this is possible because 'chacun d'eux a été remply de tâches noires'.[122] Despite this discussion of the nature of this polemic genre, it is not difficult to draw the conclusion that it is, in truth, the construct of absolutism that is subtly attacked through some of its principal seventeenth-century architects. The *Tableau* had another edition with the following year's date, with identical contents and pagination from which we may surmise that it had gained a ready readership.

---

[119] Anne Sauvy, *Livres saisis à Paris entre 1678 et 1701*, Archives Internationales d'Histoire des Idées, 50 (The Hague: Nijhoff, 1972), p. 265.

[120] On the use of historical material to criticize the sovereign during this period, see Phyllis K. Leffler, 'French Historians and the Challenge to Louis XIV's Absolutism', *French Historical Studies*, 14 (1985), 1–22.

[121] Cormac Ó Gráda and Jean-Michel Chevet, 'Famine and Market in Ancien Régime France', *Journal of Economic History*, 62 (2002), 706–33 (pp. 709–10).

[122] Both citations are from the 'Avertissement au Lecteur' which is paginated with the following cipher, which is repeated on both pages:)°(2.

Manuscripts

There are seven copies of the satire in manuscript form, one at the Bibliothèque Sainte-Geneviève, two at the Bibliothèque de l'Arsenal, and four at the Richelieu site of the Bibliothèque nationale. With the exception of two of the four BN copies, these have passed entirely unnoticed by critics. However, I believe that none of these manuscripts predates the octavo text or could constitute either the source manuscript or a circulated version contemporary to the first edition. Close examination reveals that in all cases the text is almost identical to that of the quarto versions. Moreover, in the case of two of these manuscripts, the same handwriting is found in other texts collated in the same volumes which refer to Richelieu's death in 1642; a further one is in the same characters as a legal document dated 13 May 1642. One of the Arsenal's copies contains many words that have been partly or fully struck out and replaced; this systematic correction suggests that the manuscript was being copied from another document and corrections were being made to human errors that had crept into this transcribing. Six of the seven bear titles commencing with 'Le Tableau', which appeared only in the quarto editions from 1649, with the other one bearing the heading 'Les mil vers'. The manuscript located at the Bibliothèque Sainte-Geneviève is incomplete and ends abruptly with a full stop just above the middle of the page on line 842. Three of the manuscripts possess some marginal annotations. One of these is of especial interest (BN, MS f. fr. 19145) since it contains a series of annotations by Tallemant des Réaux.[123] With the exception of the concluding remarks made after the text of the poem and transcribed in part by Antoine Adam (quoted in its entirety earlier), these notes, written in Tallemant's 'main très rapide et difficilement déchiffrable', have never before been published and I include them in the endnotes to the *Miliade* text

---

[123] Adam's transcription is to be found in *Hist*, I. 922n, though contains some minor infelicities: for example Retz's title is rendered 'card.' whereas it is 'Coad' in the original, an abbreviation for *coadjuteur*. On the conclusive attribution of these annotations to Tallemant, see Hubert Carrier, *Les Muses guerrières: les Mazarinades et la vie littéraire au milieu du XVIIe siècle* (Paris: Klincksieck, 1996), p. 413n. This manuscript is known as the *Recueil de grand papier*, one of the designations provided by Émile Magne and used by critics to identify Tallemant's manuscript material: *Bourgeois et financiers du XVIIe siècle: la Fin troublée de Tallemant des Réaux d'après des documents inédits* (Paris: Émile-Paul, 1922), p. 391. The Bibliothèque nationale catalogue does not use Magne's categorizations.

because of their literary interest as well as the fact that they provide some useful elucidations to decipher the work's more impenetrable contemporary allusions.[124] Only a small number of these reflections are repeated in the *Historiettes*, so they provide an unexplored contemporary source. While the script appears different from the text it glosses, this is not unusual with the chronicler, as noted earlier, for not only did his handwriting vary, particularly when adding notes within limited space, but he also used scribes.[125]

The existence of so many manuscripts is curious but might be explained within the context of the scarcity of the octavo edition following the concentrated campaign to destroy it. La Porte alludes to a manuscript copy of the *Miliade* being in his possession and hidden in his affairs rather than the relatively slight dimensions of the small octavo whose compact size would have presumably made it easier to conceal. Indeed some bibliographers have mistaken it for a duocecimo format.[126] The most likely explanation is that, following Richelieu's death, the satire was modified and copied, after which this reworked copy was distributed among some like-minded and trusted individuals, finally being printed at the outbreak of the troubles in 1649. Once pamphlets began to be printed and read by the populace with the vogue for the Mazarinade, it would have been natural for someone to take the decision to make the most famous political libel of the first half of the seventeenth available to a wider audience.

THE *MILIADE* AS POLITICAL SATIRE

The *Miliade* incontestably struck a chord with certain readers of 1636, anxious about the current state of affairs in France and facing the real prospect of Paris itself being invaded, and the French nation

---

[124] Emma Gilby, 'Les textes qui nous restent de Tallemant de Réaux: mise au point bibliographique', *DSS*, 232 (2006), 513–21 (p. 515).

[125] Gédeon Tallemant des Réaux, *Le Manuscrit 673*, ed. by Vincenette Maigne (Paris: Klincksieck, 1994), p. 33.

[126] The Bibliothèque de l'Arsenal possesses a quarto edition of the satire catalogued as a duodecimo (shelf mark GD 44812), which seems to be a case of mistaken identity with the 1636 edition.

becoming the vassal of Spain. In this respect, the poem was a rallying-call crystallizing the generation of the *année de Corbie*. If we gauge its achievement in terms of longevity, then it was efficacious for it was a tenacious libel that knew three waves of success, during the 1630s, during successive incarnations as a pseudo-Mazarinade from 1649 to 1652, and finally in 1693 and 1694.

The work heralded a new phase in propaganda against the Cardinal since, while it drew on the archetypes of political satire, it differed from the tactics of previous tracts in several respects. Richelieu became the object of the most concerted and unrelenting campaign of criticism to be seen since the final years of the reign of Henri III. Donald Bailey discerns four categories of opposition to Richelieu: members of the royal family and their followers; a reaction against the centralizing tendencies of the monarchy which were implemented and consolidated by Richelieu and Louis XIII, evoking the particularist interests in the kingdom from social orders, economic corporations, provincial and municipal bodies as well as political and ecclesiastical interests; theological polemics from factions within the Church, some of which had political overtones or became of political significance, as would be the case with Richelieu's dealings with the cases of Urbain Grandier and Abbé de Saint-Cyran; finally, there was the political movement known by the names of *dévot*, *zélé*, or *bon catholique* and 'firmly based on a religious allegiance with political implications'.[127] Just as the assassination of the Guise brothers in 1588 had been the last straw for certain Catholics in France, the point from which Henri was unambiguously a tyrant and to be removed by any means, Richelieu's implication in the dubious legal process that resulted in the Marillac brothers' deaths in 1632 was similarly the catalyst for militating against the Cardinal.[128] Michel de Marillac in particular had a widespread reputation for sanctity and was held in great esteem by the *dévots*; his niece, Louise de Marillac, to whom he

---

[127] Donald Atholl Bailey, 'Writers Against the Cardinal: A Study of the Pamphlets which Attacked the Person and Policies of Cardinal Richelieu during the Decade 1630–1640' (unpublished doctoral thesis, University of Minnesota, 1973), pp. 1–3 (the quotation is from p. 3).

[128] One of the most prominent anti-Henrician works of the period is Jean Boucher, *De Justa Henrici Tertii abdicatione e Francorum regno, libri quatuor* (Paris: Nicolas Nivelle, 1589).

acted as tutor, worked closely with Vincent de Paul in the 1630s and would be canonized in 1934. Donald Bailey draws a parallel between Thomas More and Marillac, both of whom held the role of chancellor and were extremely pious laymen who had considered a vocation, with Marillac playing a signficant role as 'the renowned contributor to the Catholic renaissance in France'.[129]

There was a sizeable number of adversaries of Richelieu's policies, which leads us to the question of which group, if any, did the author of the poem identify with the most. It would seem that he did not belong to one of the principal factions, which would certainly ring true with Favereau, for the *Miliade* successfully combines grievances from all of these four currents. This reflects the diversity of some of his enemies: France's entry into the Thirty Years War in 1635, the excesses of which are poignantly captured by Jacques Callot's *Misères de la guerre*, and the alliances that were forged with Protestant nations against Catholic ones, made for some unlikely bedfellows united against the pursuit of this conflict.[130] War was also a costly venture necessitating much expenditure, borrowing, and taxation, which in turn contributed to the outbreak of popular revolts known as the *croquants* during 1635 and particularly during the summer of 1636. The war is patently not the *Miliade*'s only concern, however, for Richelieu's character undergoes a systematic polemical assassination from a political, religious, and personal perspective, though at the same time, it is evident that the poem owes its origins to the first two groups, namely political malcontents, since religious considerations are given relatively short shrift in the work. Marillac's death is mentioned, but only in a fleeting fashion. Similarly, the sin of ecclesiastics such as Richelieu and Père Joseph is primarily that of hypocrisy and war-mongering rather than bringing harm to the institution of the Church. The order of these priorities is certainly not that of a *dévot*, but rather reveals an author

---

[129] Nicolas Lefèvre, *La Vie de Michel de Marillac (1560–1632): garde des sceaux de France sous Louis XIII*, ed. and trans. by Donald A. Bailey (Laval: Presses Universitaires de Laval, 2007), p. xlviii.

[130] It is possible that Callot's etchings were part of the anti-war rhetoric that focused on Richelieu since he was held in high regard by Gaston d'Orléans and had known and worked for him since 1629. He was also resident in his native Lorraine at the same time as Gaston's refuge there, which is exactly the same period during which the *Misères* were executed. On the association between the prince and the artist, see Pierre Gatulle, 'La grande cabale de Gaston d'Orléans aux Pays-Bas espagnols et en Lorraine', *DSS*, 231 (2006), 301–26 (pp 303–05).

who uses these charges as further verbal artillery to be used against his target.

The substantial propaganda campaign against Richelieu testifies not only to his unpopularity, as well as his tenacious and successful hold on to the reins of power, but also represented a reaction against Richelieu's attempts to control and curtail anti-government literature. From an early stage he formulated a strategy: 'c'est avant tout contrôler l'expression écrite, avec ses deux aspects complémentaires: la censure et la propagande'.[131] He was particularly sensitive to the attacks of pamphleteers, and he went to great lengths to be kept informed of what was being disseminated. Indeed, he read and collected these pamphlets and recruited a group of writers which included Jean Chapelain, Abbé Boisrobert, and Paul Hay du Chastelet, who were commissioned to produce counter-pamphlets directly addressing the charges detailed in the most recent libels. So successful was this counter-offensive that the apologetic pamphlets were always produced in greater numbers than opposition works.[132] For Richelieu, this was an area of concern that preceded France's entry into the European arena of war:

> Long before he was fully in power in 1635, Richelieu worked from various positions in the king's council to shape the flow of public discourse. He was eventually able to curtail the pamphlet campaigns against his own administration and its policies and also to establish mechanisms for encouraging and sponsoring the publication of progovernment writings of all kinds. With his typical flair for administration and the skillful use of patronage, Richelieu made the existing organs of censorship and patronage more effective while putting new ones in place. By the mid-1630s antiadministration propaganda had been largely eliminated from France. In order to continue publishing, opposition pamphleteers such as Mathieu de Morgues had to flee the country.[133]

It is little wonder that Retz called him 'le ministre du monde le mieux averti'.[134] However, the fact that the prelate paid such an intricate and involved attention to these matters, – one might say it

---

[131] Georges Minois, *Censure et culture sous l'Ancien Régime* (Paris: Fayard, 1995), p. 77.

[132] Minois, *Censure et culture*, p. 94.

[133] Jeffrey K. Sawyer, *Printed Poison: Pamphlet Propaganda, Faction Politics, and the Public Sphere in Early Seventeenth-Century France* (Berkeley: University of California Press, 1990), p. 136.

[134] Retz, *Œuvres*, p. 146.

was a hands-on approach – does also seem to betray a sense that Richelieu was highly sensitive to any personal criticism.[135] His policy of involvement with censorship matters means that he did not rely on reports about the *Miliade* but rather that he read it himself and the work made him absolutely beside himself with fury. Tallemant relates:

> Les pieces qu'on imprimoit à Bruxelles contre luy le chagrinoient aussi terriblement. Il en eut un tel despit, que cela ne contribua pas peu à faire desclarer la guerre à l'Espagne: mais ce fut principalement pour se rendre nécessaire. L'escrit qui l'a le plus fait enrager depuis cela a esté cette satire de mille vers, où il y a du feu, mais c'est tout. Il fit emprisonner bien des gens pour cela; mais il n'en put rien descouvrir. Je me souviens qu'on fermoit la porte sur soy pour la lire: ce tyran-là estoit furieusement redouté.[136]

The son of one of Richelieu's *sécretaires d'État* (Henri-Auguste de Loménie, mentioned in line 498 of the satire) narrates the scene of the minister's first reading of the poem. After quoting the first eight lines of the satire, Brienne continues:

> Ces huit premiers vers du poème le plus mordant et le plus satyrique qui se soit jamais fait contre un ministre vindicatif, plurent infiniment au Cardinal quand il les lut, mais la suite lui fit bien connoître qu'il s'étoit trompé dans le jugement trop précipité que son orgueil avoit fait de cet ouvrage, et il se mit en une telle colère que Boisrobert, son lecteur ordinaire, s'enfuit de devant sa face irritée, tant sa peur fut grande que le ressentiment de son patron, qui ne se possédoit plus, ne retombât sur lui en qualité de poète. Il quitta donc la lecture fort brusquement et fit bien.[137]

This episode is particularly detailed and there is good reason to assume that Brienne heard it from a first-hand witness: his father. We know that these chroniclers' accounts are not prone to a significant degree of amplification, since the Cardinal was unwavering in his quest to find out who had written it. The determination with which he undertook this endeavour is seen in the unnerving testimony of La Porte about his arrival at the Bastille cited earlier. La Porte relates how he was beside himself with terror at the

---

[135] Anthony Levi holds that Richelieu's micromanaging tendencies were a result of his 'nervous energy', *Cardinal Richelieu and the Making of France* (London: Robinson, 2000), p. 144.

[136] *Hist*, I, 248.

[137] *Mémoires de Louis-Henri de Loménie, comte de Brienne, dit le jeune Brienne*, ed. by Paul Bonnefon, 3 vols (Paris: Laurens, 1916–19), I, 221–22.

prospect of his manuscript copy being uncovered; this narrative is as compelling as it is chilling almost four centuries later. We also have the image of Tallemant perusing his copy behind a locked door, making the enjoyment of the *Miliade* into a solitary vice that could be indulged only in private.

It is worth mentioning the other works which, according to Tallemant, were originating from the Low Countries, since these are the immediate forerunners to the *Miliade*. One figure stands out among the handful of writers agitating against the Cardinal: Mathieu de Morgues, abbé de Saint-Germain (1582–1670). This writer had been in Richelieu's pay until 1630, when apparent disgruntlement at having been passed over for the episcopate coupled with dissatisfaction with the political changes occasioned by the Day of Dupes motivated him to join Marie de Médicis's camp in exile, his venom fuelled by the heady fusion that only frustrated ambition and ideological conviction can generate.[138] His production of works against his former patron was unrelenting: 'Condamné à mort dans son pays, fugitif ruiné, maudit et insulté par les plumes officielles, il représenta presque seul contre tous l'opposition irréductible à la toute puissance de Richelieu'.[139] For Morgues, opposition to the Cardinal surpassed the level of personal resentment, as it is clear that the cleric was, to all means and purposes, driven to the point of obsession with undermining his former patron and he duly devoted vast resources of time, energy, and acrimony to this end. As with the writers suspected of the *Miliade*, a study devoted to Morgues is long overdue.[140] Morgues's ideological objections to Richelieu are summed up in a pamphlet he published after his nemesis's death when, having failed in seeing him fall from office during his lifetime, he derived some satisfaction from continuing to sully his posthumous reputation:

---

[138] Joseph Bergin, 'Richelieu and His Bishops: Ministerial Power and Episcopal Patronage under Louis XIII', in *Richelieu and His Age*, ed. by Joseph Bergin and Laurence Brockliss (Oxford: Oxford University Press, 1992), pp. 175–202 (p. 182).

[139] Yves-Marie Bercé, 'Richelieu: la maîtrise de l'histoire et le conformisme historique', in *Idéologie et propagande en France*, ed. by Myriam Yardeni (Paris: Picard, 1987), pp. 99–106 (p. 104).

[140] For an excellent assessment of Morgue's career and a bibliography of his output, see Donald Bailey, 'Les pamphlets de Mathieu de Morgues (1582–1670): bibliographie des ouvrages disponibles dans les bibliothèques parisiennes et certaines bibliothèques des États-Unis', *Revue Française d'Histoire du Livre*, 18 (1978), 3–48.

> Il a violé le respect qu'il devoit au Frere unique du Roy, et a voulu perdre sa personne. Non seulement il a mis la mauvaise intelligence entre l'Enfant et la Mere, et entre les Freres; mais il a voulu faire le mesme entre le Mary et la Femme. Il a faict decapiter le Mareschal de Marillac contre droict et Justice. Le Duc de Montmorency par un droict souverain, et absolu. Le Marquis de Cinqmars avec droict et injure, et le Conseiller d'Estat de Thou, avec plus d'injure que de droict. Il a écarté, et obligé à la fuite quelques Princes: a emprisonné beaucoup de Grands, en a chassé de la Cour un bon nombre, et a proscrit toutes les personnes qui se pouvoient opposer à ses desseins, sans avoir espargné les plus vertueuses Princesses et Dames.[141]

According to the cleric, Richelieu's tyranny consists of perpetuating a cleavage in the heart of the royal family and of lacking respect for the social hierarchy and the due process of the law.[142] These charges are mirrored in the *Miliade*: the King's brother is treated with blatant disrespect (l. 37); Monsieur's contracted marriage is dissolved (l. 845); Marillac and other *maréchaux* have been unjustly executed (ll. 88–89); princesses have been exiled (l. 39); individuals of high rank have been incarcerated (ll. 43–46).

There is no doubt that the creator of the *Miliade* and Morgues are united in their objectives. Where they diverge is in their format. Morgues's narrative provides comprehensive accounts of Richelieu's abuses and failings. Together with this analytical approach, he also dissects the Cardinal's official propaganda through glossing the contact of prominent tracts. The *Miliade* does not belong within this tradition of scholarly commentary, though it must be added that Morgues's style is a blend of closely argued assessments of the actions of Richelieu's government peppered with *ad hominem* judgements against the prelate. This latter tendency became more predominant with the passage of time. Morgues's denigration of Richelieu is certainly more measured than the *Miliade* but is every bit as vehement:

> L'ingratitude, l'avarice, l'ambition, et la cruauté sont les quatre vices qui deshonnerent sa vie, et les bourreaux qui tourmentent son ame. Tous les maux qu'il a fait aux hommes, ne sont que les effects de sa peur. Il ne croit pas estre meschant et infame, en faisant les violences

---

[141] [Mathieu de Morgues]. *Abrege de la vie du cardinal de Richelieu pour luy server d'epitaphe* ([Antwerp]: [n.pub.], 1643), p. 5

[142] As Seung-Hwi Lim maintains, however, Morgues was not an unconditional supporter of royal authority, for he supported the traditional rights of the Paris Parlement several years before the Fronde, 'Mathieu de Morgues, Bon Français ou Bon Catholique?', *DSS*, 213 (2001), 655–72 (pp. 672).

qui servent à sa conservation; parce que la presomption luy fait croire qu'elle est necessaire à la France.[143]

This portrait of the Cardinal, published a matter of months before the poem, purports to be psychologically incisive, reminding the reader that is made by someone who had occasion to observe him at close quarters for a number of years. The *Miliade* concentrates on these same traits, yet they are cast in a radically different manner than in Morgues. While the poem marks a departure from the cleric's particular brand of closely argued pamphlet, at the same it also owes a debt to Morgues's corpus, a lineage that is, perhaps, acknowledged by the mention 'Envers' at the close of the poem, which evokes the province from which Morgues operated. In the 'Passage de Somme', Ételan pens a more explicit homage to Morgues, depicting Isaac de Laffemas burning his proscribed works.[144]

The originality of the *Miliade* is that it takes aim at Richelieu with a similar authorial agenda as that of Morgues and other pamphleteers but uses a different vehicle, one that draws in and combines elements from literary parodies, polemic political tracts, and popular songs. The blend of these features marks a new stage in the alliance of politics and literature which characterized the anti-ministerial discourse.[145] The octosyllabic verse, together with the rhyming couplets, make the poem ideal for singing and the more salacious and memorable sections, which are plentiful, could well have lent themselves to this purpose.[146] At the same time, the

---

[143] [Mathieu Morgues], *La verité defendue: ensemble quelques observations sur la conduite du Cardinal de Richelieu* (1635), in *Diverses pieces pour la defense de la Royne Mere du roy tres-chrestien Louis XIII* ([Antwerp]: [n.pub.], [1637]), pp. 435–511 (p. 494).

[144] 'Et St Germain est mis au rôlle des proscrits, / Le Bourreau, tout joyeux, jettant au feu ses écrits', Ételan, 'Passage de Somme', fol. 553.

[145] 'Il semble bien que la réalité politique et la fiction littéraire se rejoignent et se nourrissent l'une de l'autre, pour forger des sensiblilités nouvelles, sans cesse ressourcées par les réalités politiques, les événements et la politique de Richelieu', Jean-Marie Constant, 'Le discours sur la guerre de l'opposition nobiliaire à Richelieu: amorce d'une autre vision politique et philosophique du monde', in *Armées, guerre et société dans la France du XVIIe siècle: actes du VIIIe Colloque du Centre international de rencontres sur le XVIIe siècle, Nantes, 18–20 mars 2004*, ed. by Jean Garapon, Biblio 17, 167 (Tübingen: Narr, 2006), pp. 25–35 (p. 34).

[146] The presence of couplets, particularly end-stopped ones, not only allow for parts of the *Miliade* to be sung but also form part of a larger authorial strategy as they

apparently *faux naïf* style is underpinned by a rich vein of complex tropes and stylistic devices which are all employed to deride the entire cast of untrustworthy characters who are deemed to be leading France to its destruction. The work's popularity is owing to several factors, not least of which its timing, but it also benefits from its quotability since it seems to be composed of a whole series of sound bites and this is perhaps what so incensed Richelieu: here was a tract that was equally at home in the salon or in the saloon. The *Miliade* committed to print a panoply of urban legends, the stuff of tavern jokes and street ditties, ensuring it appealed to market-traders as well as marquis.

The work's title of 'La Miliade' is both appealing and memorable. In fact, while this might have been the most common appellation, it was one of two alternative subheadings: 'LE GOUVERNEMENT PRESENT OU ELOGE DE SON EMINENCE. *SATYRE OU LA Miliade*. The first part does not betray any satirical intent, but 'Éloge de son Éminence' introduces an ironic note since the tract is anything but encomiastic, as revealed by the final 'satyre'.[147] It is only in the third part of the title that 'Miliade' is offered. Contemporary sources largely refer to the concluding portion of the title as set out on the title page. It may well be the case that the poem was originally entitled 'Les mil vers' when it was circulated in manuscript prior to printing, assuming that it did pass around, for it is referred to by this name by several sources, including Tallemant and Patin, though La Porte does use *Miliade*. The 1649 edition eschews *Miliade* in favour of 'satyre de mille vers' and Montplaisir entitles his sonnet of self-vindication 'Contre la satyre Qu'on appelle vulgairement la piece de mille vers'. It is also used as the title of one of the manuscript versions of the poem. It is possible that 'mille vers' was used prior to publication during which time *Miliade* was devised, perhaps by one of Favereau's circle or even himself, then used in the first edition. At any rate, this was a shrewd choice since it provided the work with a distinctive descriptor. This name inscribes the work into a vogue for

---

'permit a satirist to resist closure, because the tension of the individual couplet sends us back to its internal parallels and contrasts, and because the march of successive couplets keeps us moving forward', Dustin Griffin, *Satire: A Critical Reintroduction* (Lexington: University Press of Kentucky, 1994), p. 114.

[147] This part of the title situates the work within the tradition of *éloges paradoxaux*; see Patrick Dandrey, *L'Éloge paradoxal de Georgias à Molière* (Paris: PUF, 1997), in particular pp. 175–209.

mock-epic poems ending in -ade during the second half of the sixteenth and first half of the seventeenth century.[148] The creation was not a neologism, however, since its first recorded use in early modern French is by Nostradamus in his 'Épître à Henri II' (1558), presumably already existing as a Latin derivative used in is native Provence.[149] I have found only one other example of it being used during the sixteenth century and a single occurrence from the seventeenth century before the publication of the poem which implies it was far from being in common usage.[150] Given the name, it is somewhat disappointing to discover that the satire is only composed of 952 lines in its first octavo version and 956 lines in the subsequent one. Whether this was always the case is a matter of speculation, although it might be noted that the manuscript versions average around 30 lines per page (32 lines in the case of the copy at the Bibliothèque Sainte-Geneviève and BN, MS f. fr. 19145), so it is always possible that a leaf went astray in the original manuscript prior to it being printed.

SATIRICAL TARGETS

The *Miliade* addresses itself firstly to the people of France. In inviting the reader to see the state of affairs of the nation, 'le

---

[148] Klára Csűrös explains that this 'vogue des titres pseudo-épiques explique sans doute ceux d'un grand nombre de tragédies, parmi lesquelles certaines font honneur à la *Franciade* de Ronsard', *Variétés et vicissitudes du genre épique de Ronsard à Voltaire*, Littérature Générale et Comparée, 21 (Paris: Champion, 1999), p. 38.

[149] 'À *L'Invictissime*, Très-Puissant et Très-Chrétien *Henri*, Roi de *France* Second: Michel Nostradamus, très-humble et très obeissant serviteur et sujet, Victoire et Félicité', in Edgar Leoni, *Nostradamus: Life and Literature* (New York: Exposition, 1961), pp. 324–47 (p. 324). The astrologer is speaking of having made a thousand prophecies. I have been unable to locate the word in any Franco-Provençal dictionary.

[150] It occurs as an emphatic way of denoting a thousand in Pierre Boaistuau, *Histoires prodigieuses extraictes de plusieurs fameux autheurs grecs et latins, sacrez et prophanes, mises en notre langage* (Paris: Jacques Macé, 1567), p. 282. François de Sales similarly uses the term when speaking of 'cette miliade de Martyrs, Confesseurs et Docteurs qui nous ont precedés', Discours XLVI, in *Œuvres completes de saint François de Sales, évêque et prince de Genève*, ed. by Henry-Joseph Crelier and Adolphe-Charles Peltier, 12 vols (Paris: Vivès, 1866), VIII, 436.

gouvernement présent' of the title, it ends with begging the monarch to address the political catastrophe it depicts. The work strikes at the core of Richelieu's administration, his reliance on a system of creatures, through providing a series of portraits of the principal actors. It is not surprising that the quarto editions modified the title to 'Tableau du gouvernement présent'. Orest Ranum has detailed Richelieu's careful cultivation of his creatures at the heart of government, a network of allegiances that centred around and depended on him.[151] No key player is left out of this cast with Machaud and Laffemas being mentioned first as Richelieu's henchmen who carry out his bloodthirsty orders (ll. 95–118). His reliance on the friendship of his confidants, Père Joseph and Abbé Boisrobert, is suitably mocked (ll. 233–34). The 'grands Oracles' of Des Noyers, Séguier, and the elder and younger Bouthillier are not spared (l. 353–54), neither is Bullion (ll. 580–82) or La Tour d'Auvergne (l. 685). The entire network is subject to satirical scrutiny from *maiîtres de requêtes* and *surintendants* to the four *secrétaires d'État* and finally the first minister himself. During Louis XIII's reign, Richelieu and his creatures were careful to ensure that they remained in the monarch's good graces: '[t]hey controlled his correspondence, surrounded him, and sheltered him from other would-be favourites and courtiers opposed to Richelieu and his policies'.[152] While, as Claude Abraham points out, we do not read satire for its plot, the sequence of *tableaux* does contribute a cohension to the *Miliade*.[153] The quirks and failings of Richelieu and his supporters are laid bare: we encounter Le Jay's penchant for alcohol and ladies of easy virtue; we read the titbit of Père Joseph's lackeys being renowned, in a subclass noted for its coarse language, for being the most foul-mouthed in the capita; and we a provided with a jovial description of Séguier's pedantry and lack of social graces. The reliance on anecdotal revelations of these characters tends to reinforce the sense of veracity rather than detract from it since this was an integral marker of historical narrative and 'anecdotes not only played a privileged role in understanding

---

[151] Orest A. Ranum, *Richelieu and the Councillors of Louis XIII: A Study of the Secretaries of State and Superintendants of Finance in the Ministry of Richelieu 1635–1642* (Oxford: Clarendon Press, 1963).

[152] Ranum, *Richelieu and the Councillors*, p. 22.

[153] Claude Abraham, *Norman Satirists in the Age of Louis XIII*, Biblio 17, 8 (Tübingen: Narr, 1983), p. 49.

history, but were also crucial for its successful transmission'.[154] All in all, there is an overwhelming impression of widespread disorder at the heart of government, since every representative of the regime is shown to be personally and morally corrupt.[155] They are adulterers, fornicators, vainglorious, thieves, liars, and all of this relates to their service of Richelieu, the kingpin who presides over this band of degenerates. Favouritism and the abuse of patronage is a significant preoccupation of the poem: Richelieu enjoys the King's favour, and the potential for such royal reliance to infect the equilibrium of the state is illustrated by the mention of Richelieu being 'ce neuveau conchine' (l. 950). In the *Miliade*, favouritism passes down from the monarch in a kind of apostolic succession of cronyism: Louis delegates affairs of state to Richelieu who in turn relies on his own creatures and these figures also cultivate their own systems of allegiance.

The portraits sketched in the poem attain a universal quality because they are not dependent on inside knowledge to be appreciated, while at the same time the reader is drawn in through the conspiratorial tone of the sharing of such information. Richelieu's unprecedented reprisals aimed at the author of this satire have much to do with its novel format combining political commentary with tavern humour but I believe that the Cardinal was also attempting to deflect potential damage away from his sovereign. The final salvo of the poem contains a markedly disrespectful register in its address to Louis XIII, one which breaches the convention of the monarch led astray by an iniquitous minister which had been frequently employed by previous pamphleteers, thus absolving him of personal responsibility. During the wave of pamphlets that appeared during the summer of 1636, writers were adept in distinguishing between Richelieu and the King: 'ce fut là une tactique d'une grande habileté, indispensable au fond, au succès de l'entreprise'.[156] The ruler is directly addressed in the final twenty

---

[154] Malina Stefanovska, 'Exemplary or Singular? The Anecdote in Historical Narrative', *Substance*, 118 (2009), 16–30 (p. 21).

[155] It is not only by the presentation of unflattering portraits that this sense of unbalance is achieved, for 'the basic technique of satire is distortion, usually in the form of exaggeration, understatement, and pretense; and distortion implies disorder', Leonard Feinberg, *Introduction to Satire* (Ames: Iowa State University Press, 1967), p. 4.

[156] Hugues de Montbas, *Richelieu et l'opposition pendant la Guerre de Trente Ans (1635–1638)* (Paris: H. Champion, 1913), p. 18.

lines (ll. 937–57). The fact that the poem unexpectedly veers away from its purported target, the Cardinal, and addresses the King, captures the reader's attention as does the unanticipated change in register, for from a series of meandering comic caricactures, we suddenly encounter a grave monition.[157] It is not so much a plea at all, but rather an indictment in which the informal second person is used, creating a tone of casual informality which is consolidated by the use of regal attributes which would generally be accompanied with a second-personal plural form or at least an impersonal form ('ta puissance' (l. 937); 'ton estat' (l. 940); 'Ton triomphe' (l. 941); and 'ton bras' (l. 943). This vein of insolence reinforces the sense of irony of the ostensibly loyal and sincere request: 'Grand Roy banny par ta puissance, / La servitude de la France' (ll. 937–38). This conforms, almost to the letter, to the tradition of appeals routinely formulated by Morgues: 'Arretez son ambition, son avarice, et sa violence, GRAND ROY'.[158] The crucial difference is that Morgues employs the markers of respect in order to moderate any sense of admonishing the King. When the *Miliade* implores Louis to act in this concluding passage, his track record of failure to act is put under the spotlight. The audaciously strong imperative contained in line 943, 'Ouvre les yeux, arme ton bras', is a circuitous manner to underscore Louis's blindness to the perilous state of France and his impotency to deal with the situation. This would have been a grave accusation to make at any time, but within the context of a nation at war and the enemy within a couple of days' march of the capital, it assumes an even more solemn register. The stakes are high as Louis is urged to abandon the minister to save himself: 'Et fuys en sauvant la Couronne' (l. 953).

In fact, the escalating tone of recrimination reminds the reader not so much of Richelieu, but rather of the person in whose name he has acted and by whose authority he has been able to oppress the people: 'Faicts punir l'autheur de nos maux, / L'autheur de mille et mille impots' (ll. 947–48). The reader is invited, by the plural noun in the prophecy of the poem's terminal line, to reflect on the master as well as the minister: 'Les tyrans n'ont point de tombeau' (l. 956),

---

[157] There is a fleeting preview of the final sequence in lines 631–2 when talking of Bullion: 'Que Louys d'un coup de tonnerre, / Doit exterminer de la terre', which is markedly more respectful in its use of the third-person singular.

[158] Mathieu de Morgues, *Diverses pieces pour la defense de la Royne Mere du roy tres-chrestien Louis XIII*, p. 97.

particularly since the poet has already prophesized, not without a sense of resignation, 'Ton triomphe sera funeste' (l. 941). Moreover, Louis evades living up to his sobriquet as Louis le Juste, as he patently does not punish and, which is more, resists divine justice being enacted (l. 949).[159] The reference to Concini's death in line 950 ('Accable ce neuveau conchine') serves a twofold function of providing a precedent to the dangers of dependency on a favourite, albeit that of Marie de Médicis, as well as pitting this decisive action on Louis's part to his current inertia, compounding the sense of his lethargic incapability to accomplish his duty.

Throughout the *Miliade*, there are two principal charges with which Richelieu is damned and as a result of which he is portrayed as a double tyrant: the minister has abused his power in order to oppress the people while at the same time usurping the royal prerogative.[160] As I have mentioned, the author of the *Miliade* resists a formulaic depiction of a misled but basically decent king and, in its stead, presents an entirely enfeebled king who is presiding over the ruin of the state, and is therefore largely responsible: the father of the nation is effectively impotent.[161] If Richelieu has taken it upon himself 'D'estre plustost Roy que subject' (l. 834), then Louis has conversely been debased, and there is the ultimate insult of the monarch being talked to as a *vigneron* by the first president of the Paris Parlement, Nicolas Le Jay, a scenario in which the client of Richelieu treats his monarch as his servant (l. 717). Such criticism of the monarch must be understood within the context of the lack of an heir for 'durant la plus grande partie du règne de Louis XIII (du moins jusqu'à l'arrivée heureuse de Louis "Dieudonné", le futur Louis XIV) comme au début du règne de Louis XVI, l'attente d'un

---

[159] On the cultivation and propagation of this sobriquet, see A. Lloyd Moote, *Louis XIII, the Just* (Berkeley: University of California Press, 1989), pp. 72–73.

[160] These two elements loom large in Morgues's accusations against the Cardinal, particularly the humiliation of the monarchy by his minister's power base; see Laurent Avezou, 'Richelieu vu par Mathieu de Morgues et Paul Hay du Chastelet: le double miroir de Janus', *Travaux de Littérature*, 18 (2005), 167–78 (pp. 174–75).

[161] I have argued that Corneille draws on the relationship between the King and his minister in *Le Cid*, which was composed during this period, to build up the portrait of an apparently weak sovereign, who does, however, assert his authority at the end of the play. See Paul Scott, '"Ma force est trop petite": Authority and Kingship in *Le Cid*', *Forum for Modern Language Studies*, 45 (2009), 292–304 (particularly pp. 303–4).

héritier mâle pour le trône de France alimente des discours'.[162] This specific historical moment echoes the reign of Henri III and explains the tone of anxiety that underpins the *Miliade* on this subject for it seemed to be very unlikely that Louis would now produce any children in 1636, given the age of his wife (Anne of Austria was in her mid-thirties) coupled with his notorious predilection for handsome young male favourites.[163] On top of this, Louis's health was precarious and he had before come very close to death on at least one occasion. While the issue of the succession is never explicitly set out – indicating the extent of the taboo surrounding it – it is nonetheless clearly manifested in the outrage expressed in the satire in respect to Richelieu's treatment of the heir presumptive and other members of the royal family. There is an unspoken implication that might easily be drawn: namely that the fruitless marriage constitutes a divine punishment for the warped state of affairs at the heart of government. Here, a direct parallel may be drawn with the last few months of Henri III's reign.

I would like to suggest that Richelieu sensed that the seditious insolence of the *Miliade* was not aimed solely in his direction but also set its sights on Louis XIII, which might go some way to explain his extraordinary and unique display of fury and the subsequent punitive steps, as well as significantly, the lack of a specially commissioned printed rebuttal. The antagonistic register of the concluding passage would not have gone unnoticed by Richelieu who set great store by these things: 'Courtesy was the very lifeblood of this society, as Richelieu knew all too well when he repeatedly exhorted Louis XIII not to suffer any indignity or disobedience from his subjects.'[164] For, in acting in this way, Richelieu spectacularly gave the impression that this scurrilous work was a personal affront and forged this association in the public consciousness. The public heard about this anti-Richelieu lampoon even if they did not manage

---

[162] Annie Duprat, *Les Rois de papier: la caricacture de Henri III à Louis XVI* (Paris: Belin, 2002), p. 52.

[163] On Louis's same-sex attachments, see Maurice Lever, *Les Bûchers de Sodome: histoire des "infames"* (Paris: Fayard, 1985), pp. 128–36. Tallemant circumspect when probing the King's affections, but lists his male favourites beginning with the coachman Saint-Amour. When considering his female dalliances, Tallemant adds, somewhat intriguingly, that '[s]es amours estoient d'estranges amours; il n'avoit rien d'un amoureux que la jalousie' (*Hist*, I, 334 and 338).

[164] Orest Ranum, 'Courtesy, Absolutism, and the Rise of the French State, 1630–1660', *Journal of Modern History*, 52 (1980), 426–51 (p. 427).

to consult a copy. In redirecting blame away from the King, Richelieu successfully neutralized the tract's most subversive and most potentially damaging critique directed towards the person of the monarch. In this, the *Miliade* had much in common with Cornelius Jansen's *Mars Gallicus* (1635), a philippic in Latin which attacked both Richelieu and the monarch who sustained him in office and which earned the author a bishopric and pension from Philip IV, King of Spain, in the following year.[165] Like the *Miliade*, the *Mars Gallicus* was widely distributed in France despite tightened censorship controls.[166] Roger Chartier establishes that the period of 1629 to 1648 marks a trough in the production of anti-governement pamphlets, largely because of the draconian controls enforced by Richelieu: 'la verve pamphlétaire se tarit et le libellistes, tenu en bride, se mettent au seul service de la propagande royale'.[167] Jansen and the *Miliade* spectacularly breached this polemic lull; since the *Mars Gallicus* was not translated into French until 1637 its popular draw was somewhat limited.[168] Nonetheless, there is no doubt that the work influenced the *Miliade*'s author during the events of the summer of 1636 and it owes a greater debt to the spirit of this work than to the pamphlets of Morgues.[169]

---

[165] It has been claimed that the reprisals taken by Richelieu against Jansen's tract 'set the pattern for royal policy towards Jansenism for the rest of the century', Geoffrey Treasure, *Mazarin: The Crisis of Absolutism in France* (London: Routledge, 1995), p. 96.

[166] Hélène Duccini, *Faire voir, faire croire: l'opinion publique sous Louis XIII* (Seyssel: Champ Vallon, 2003), p. 451.

[167] Roger Chartier, 'Pamphlets et gazettes', in *Histoire de l'édition française*, ed. by Henri-Jean Martin and Roger Chartier, 4 vols (Paris: PROMODIS, 1982–86), I, 405–25 (p. 407).

[168] Cornelius Jansen, *La Mars françois ou la guerre de France, En laquelle sont examinées les raisons de la Justice pretendu des Armes, et des Alliances du Roi de France* ([Paris?]: [n.pub.], 1637).

[169] For an incisive study of the anti-monarchical ideology of this work, see Gérard Ferreyolles, 'Jansénius politique: le *Mars Gallicus*', in *Justice et force: Politiques au temps de Pascal. Actes du colloque "Droit et pensee politique autour de Pascal", Clermont-Ferrand, 20–23 septembre 1990*, ed. by Gérard Ferreyolles (Paris: Klincksieck, 1996), pp. 95–108.

TECHNIQUES OF DISCONTENT

It is instructive to examine the opening section, the first twelve lines, of the *Miliade* to discern the representative authorial strategies in place from the beginning. Colette Arnould has noticed that many of the satires against Richelieu begin in a similarly anodine fashion before they descend into piquancy and the *Miliade* is no exception.[170] The poem is addressed to the people, and the opening two verses contain puns on Richelieu's ecclesiastical status ('autels and 'éminent'). The three cardinal-statesmen mentioned in lines 6 and 7 had been employed as historical examples of ecclesiastics' involvement in affairs of state by Richelieu's propagandists, such as a 1631 life of Cardinal d'Amboise by one of Richelieu's most tireless apologists, Jean Sirmond.[171] Robert Knecht maintains that 'such comparisons served to justify Richelieu's administration and justify its superiority'.[172] We see immediately that the satirist is meticulously invoking the precise substance and style of cardinalatial plaudits, but entirely suborns them with irony. Similarly, the hyperbolic inflation of the number of the Cinq Auteurs in line 12 reminds the reader that, despite the prelate's solicitude to have artists in his purse, the very existence of the *Miliade* and the fact these remarks have been committed to print roundly proves that attempts to channel propaganda and enforce censorship have not been entirely successful. This is the first mention in a series of direct allusions to Richelieu's own propaganda machine for from line 5, a solar metaphor is used in respect of the cardinal. Not only is he 'ce soleil des Cardinaux' (l. 5) but also 'Ses rayons percent les tenebres' (l. 11), and spectators are blinded before this celestial creature. Richelieu had frequently been represented as the sun in both iconography and verse, typified by an engraving completed by Abraham Bosse in 1627.[173] The satirist is, then, appropriating the

---

[170] Colette Arnould, *La Satire, une histoire dans l'histoire* (Paris: PUF, 1996), p. 98.

[171] The title of the work reveals its polemic intent: Jean Sirmond, *La Vie du cardinal d'Amboise, en suite de laquelle sont traités quelques points sur les affaires présentes* (Paris: Étienne Richer, 1631).

[172] Robert Knecht, *Richelieu* (London: Longman, 1991), p. 177.

[173] As a poetic example of solar imagery brought into service to extol the minister, Hilaire Soulas rearranges the prelate's name to give 'Sol radians, spes es una Mundi', an anagram of 'Armandus Ioannes du Plessis', *Anagrammes sur les noms*

cardinal's own arms to use against him. However, the use of this trope is further mined in the poem for it is adroitly used to depict the network of Richelieu's associates revolving around him like satellites in order to do his bidding.[174] At the same time it stands as a commentary on Richelieu's unseemly appropriation of the central position that a monarch should occupy within the state, for Richelieu had assumed a royal trope. While particularly associated with Louis XIV, it was a long-standing one that had been used in respect of his father and grandfather.[175] This is far from coincidental since 'Bosse s'est probablement inspiré d'un modèle antérieur représentant Louis XIII au centre d'un soleil dont les rayons composent l'acrostiche de son nom'.[176] Richelieu's appropriation of regal allegory extended to painting, for Philippe de Champaigne's portraits of the minister would borrow from Van Dyck's commissions of King Charles I of England.[177] At the same time as parodying Richelieu's self-promotion, the solar trope also serves as a critique of his displacement of the King, a multifaceted use of metaphor which, once again, stresses that the *Miliade* is the product of an urbane mind.

This complexity that runs counter to the satire's apparent simplicity as a lampoon is best detected in the robust presence of several tropes which function on several levels of meaning. The *Miliade* is, above all, a deceptive work; while it might appear to be loaded with innuendo and bawdiness it is far from simplistic. One of the great appeals of the poem, apart from its enjoyable and deft

---

du Roy, de la Reyne, de M^r le Cardinal de Richelieu, de M^r le Cardinal de Lyon, et de Monsieur l'Evesque de Poictiers (Poitiers: Veuve d'Antoine Mesnier, 1633), p. 5. On Bosse's inventory, see Roger-Armand Weigert and Maxime Préaud, *Inventaire du Fonds français: graveurs du XVIIe siècle*, 17 vols (Paris: Bibliothèque Nationale, 1939–2008), I (1939), 473.

[174] The term is used in line 112 where Machaud and Laffemas are selected to be 'ses fideles satellites'.

[175] It had also been used in the sixteenth century; see, for example, Ewa Kociszewska, 'The Sun King in the Realm of Eternal Winter: The Unknown Medal of Henri de Valois, King of Poland (1573)', *French Studies Bulletin*, 113 (2009), 78–82.

[176] Guiliano Ferretti, 'Richelieu, le "Ministre-soleil" de la France, d'après une gravure d'Abraham Bosse', *Genèses*, 48 (2002), 136–53 (p. 138).

[177] José Gonçalves, *Philippe de Champaigne: le patriarche de la peinture, 1602–1674* (Paris: ACR, 1995), pp. 36–37.

character assassinations, is the sophistication of the multi-layered wealth of historical, contemporary, classical, and scriptural references. It works on a basic level as an appealing invective, but also invites us to delve into its many allusions. There are four dominant tropes present in the satire, and I would like to discuss each one, particularly from the perspective of polyphonic layers. These tropes are nautical, theatrical, bestial, and sexual. These are by no means exhaustive; there are many others present in the satire. However, these four stand out since they are exploited the most frequently and at the greatest length.

The nautical trope occurs at several points, namely lines 265–288, 460, 607–17, and 779–782, totalling forty lines. In the first occurrence, a hyperbolic description of Richelieu alone braving the elements is provided: 'Luy seul commande aux elemens, / Luy seul est le maistre des vents' (ll. 269–70). The amplified praise contained in this feigned eulogy is all the more humorous since it echoes the standard formulae of praise to be found in the many dedications and apologies made in Richelieu's honour while at the same time embodying a Canute-like reminder of the limitations of terrestrial power. It is not only the spirit of obsequiousness which is emulated, as nautical imagery was also employed as a commonplace in dedicatory works to the prelate. In a work published in the year before the *Miliade*, a poet proclaimed of the minister: 'C'est à vous à mener la Barque / Ou de sainct Pierre, ou de LOUYS'.[178] In the light of such government-sponsored propaganda which, without missing a beat, manages to elevate Richelieu's status above that of the papacy and the monarchy, the *Miliade* is simply borrowing from rather than expanding on such verse. In the same collection, which constituted a *festschrift* of some of the finest encomiastic verse that had been written in the Cardinal's honour since his accession to power in 1624, Richelieu's name is paired no fewer than seventeen times with 'Dieu' in the singular or plural, reinforcing the *Miliade*'s observation about Richelieu, 'Dont le nom rime a demy Dieu' (l. 322). This rhyme is used more modestly in the *Miliade*, coming into service on five occasions (ll. 322–23; 405–6; 729–30; 793–94; 809–10). It has been argued that Ételan and Saint-Évremond's *Comédie des Académistes* consciously parallels sections of this work, *Le Sacrifice*

---

[178] Claude de l'Estoile, 'Ode à Monseigneur le cardinal de Richelieu, in *Le Sacrifice des Muses, au grand cardinal de Richelieu* (Paris: Sebastien Cramoisy, 1635), pp. 82–83 (p. 82).

des Muses, since it was '*de rigueur* reading in court circles' and this deformation would be recognized without much effort; the *Miliade* is employing an identical strategy a couple of years earlier.[179]

As well as nautical imagery being a standard tactic among writers currying the minister's favour, it also alludes to the allegory of the ship of state. However, this metaphor had been modified from the monarch alone at the helm to Louis XIII standing beside, or even behind, Richelieu, a scene which was used both positively in pro-government pamphlets but also negatively as in the case of the *Miliade*. While this libel depicts the nation as being misled by Richelieu's navigation ('Laisse Armand mener le vaisseau / Nul autre pilote nouveau' (ll. 265–66)), other tracts of the 1630s are kinder: thus La Vicane comments: 'Sa Divine bonté vous a fait naistre un Judicieux Pilotte, lequel sous l'honneur de vos Commandemens, conduit et gouverne si bien vostre Estat.'[180] It was also put into service in iconographical as well as written endorsements of the chief minister.[181] So effective was this trope that almost six decades later, Furetière cited the Cardinal to illustrate his definition of *pilote*.[182]

The nautical trope also taps into the Cardinal's association with maritime matters. In 1626, the King authorized Richelieu to take up the *grande maîtrise de la navigation et du commerce* and the *généralat des galères*. It was a groundbreaking decision to allocate the office to such a high-ranking official as Richelieu, already encumbered with the burden of running the government, but it does make sense when Richelieu's passion for naval issues is taken into account, demonstrated by the fact that he immediately concentrated on centralizing the service. With his characteristic rancour, Tallemant recounts that the minister only gained the post after

---

[179] Eugène Joliat, 'Saint-Évremond's *Les Académistes*, succès de scandale', *Studi Francesi*, 28 (1984), 286–89 (p. 287).

[180] Sieur de La Vicane, *Lettre au Roy, Sur les Vertus Eminentes de Monseigneur le Cardinal Duc de Richelieu, Dans les heureuses Conduittes et Succez des Affaires de sa Majesté* (Paris: Pierre Mettayer, 1633), p. 6.

[181] For example, Eris van Pasce executed an engraving of Louis XIII and Richelieu in 1628, with both figures aboard a boat with the devise 'Va navire ne crains point ton pilote est un Dieu / Jamais ancre ne fut en un plus Riche Lieu', *Le roi et le cardinal dans une nef sur la Seine*, BN, B12052/ Qb1 1628.

[182] 'Le Cardinal de Richelieu étoit un bon *Pilote*, il avoit en main le timon des affaires', *DU*, III, sig. N3^{r-v}.

falsely notifying Louis XIII that a fleet of Spanish ships were headed to Bayonne.[183] His attention went beyond the administrative for '[s]a décision d'avoir et d'entretenir une flotte de trente vaisseaux pour lutter contre les Espagnols à partir de 1635 constitue les origines de la marine moderne et un symbole des ambitions maritimes françaises'.[184] Gone were the days when the the rank of admiral was an honorific title denoting an administrator of ports and shipping held by unreconstructed landlubbers such as Gaspard de Coligny (1519–1572); Richelieu abolished the rank altogether and transferred their powers to the *grand maîtrise*. Strengthening the French navy was a central preoccupation with Richelieu, and the *Miliade*'s nautical trope takes this fixation and suborns it.[185] Indeed, the Cardinal's personal intervention in the navy was part of his wider concern with promoting a certain aspect of his image, one which Orest Ranum has fittingly termed 'la psychologie morale de guerrier'.[186] The *Miliade* goes further than portraying the Cardinal, however ironically, as single-handedly steering the ship of state, for it also turns this representation on its head with the statement that he is 'plus cruel qu'un corsaire' (l. 456), and his subordinates, Cornuel and Bullion, are 'deux horribles corsaires' (l. 612). This inversion of the nautical trope consolidates the sense of usurpation of the heart of the state which runs throughout the poem. It may, at the same time, remind the reader that, for all the Cardinal's efforts to revitalize maritime trade, piracy remained an endemic problem which he had failed to eradicate during his tenure.[187] As a final example of the manifold layers to be drawn out of this trope, there is a personal maritime connection in Richelieu's family: the minister's paternal grandfather, François, had been governor of Le Havre-de-Grâce, an

---

[183] *Hist*, I, 246.

[184] Alan James, 'L'évolution de la stratégie navale française du XVIe au XVIIe siècle: la guerre de trente ans en Méditerranée', *Cahiers de la Méditerranée*, 71.2 (2005), 1–25 (p. 1).

[185] Evidence of Richelieu's naval interest is to be found in his *testament* in which he states: 'la puissance des armes requiert non seulement que le Roi soit plutôt fort sur la terre, mais elle veut en outre qu'il soit puissant sur la mer', *Testament politique*, ed. by Louis André (Paris: Laffont, 1947), p. 440.

[186] Orest Ranum, 'Richelieu, guerrier héroïque?', in *Armées, guerre et société*, ed. Garapon, pp. 269–81 (p. 270).

[187] Pierre Castagnos, *Richelieu face à la mer* (Rennes: Ouest-France, 1989), p. 278.

office which was granted to the Cardinal in 1626.[188] On assuming control of the admiralty, the Cardinal added a supporting anchor to the shield of his family coat of arms, a heraldic adjunct that had hitherto been reserved exclusively for admirals, the naval post he had abolished and subsumed into his own functions.[189] The Cardinal's governance of the *marine* was a substantial source of his personal fortune, as Joseph Bergin has underscored. Moreover, it was emblematic of his wide-ranging and unprecedented powers as 'Louis XIII practically handed over French maritime affairs to the Cardinal in October 1626, retaining no formal control of them thereafter'.[190] Richelieu manifestly felt the sea was in his blood and his involvement in seafaring matters was a source of revenue and prestige, as well as being an indication of the increasing trust invested in him by the King; unconcealed mockery of this must have succeeded, and by all accounts did succeed, in getting his blood boiling.

Another recurrent trope is the dramatic: the theatre and matters theatrical are mentioned on a number of occasions. This tunes into Richelieu's love for the stage, which is denounced as both unseemly and excessive. When his mind should be on serious matters, Richelieu is depicted as giving himself to frivolity: 'Il trace une piece nouvelle, / Quand on emporte la capelle' (ll. 231–32). During times of crisis, Richelieu resorts to Boisrobert's acting skills for his consolation (l. 233).[191] Tallemant confirms that the minister did indeed depend on Boisrobert to raise him out of his not infrequent depressive states.[192] This image of his associate playing the clown casts Richelieu as a mercurial tyrant in need of a jester to amuse him,

---

[188] On Richelieu's heraldic arms, see Yvan Loskoutoff, *L'Armorial de Calliope: l'œuvre du Père Le Moyne S.J. (1602–1671). Littérature, héraldique, spiritualité*, Biblio 17, 125 (Tübingen: Narr, 2000), p. 145.

[189] Louvan Géliot, *Indice armorial ou Sommaire Explication des mots usitez au Blason des Armoiries* (Paris: Pierre Billaine, 1635), p. 13.

[190] Joseph Bergin, *Cardinal Richelieu: Power and the Pursuit of Wealth* (New Haven and London: Yale University Press, 1985), p. 53. On the lucrative fiscal rights related to his control of the *marine*, see pp. 96–99.

[191] In reality, his theatrical-related activity was at its lowest point during 1636 and 1637; see *Europe, comédie héroïque. Attribuée à Armand du Plessis, Cardinal de Richelieu et Jean Desmarets Sieur de Saint-Sorlin*, ed. by Sylvie Taussig (Turnhout: Brepols, 2006), intro. p. 32.

[192] *Hist*, I. 268.

another reinforcement of the leitmotiv of tyranny.[193] Public shows were forbidden to ecclesiastics and professional actors would be under interdict until the edict of 1641 removed them from a status of infamy, a piece of legislation that was largely the work of Richelieu.[194] The fact that Richelieu enjoys this pastime in private, albeit legitimately, makes it a surreptitious pleasure. The Cardinal's passion for the stage has been unflatteringly termed *théâtromanie*, not without reason.[195] As well as being a pastime to enjoy, the prelate is seen to mix business with pleasure in his promotion of writers willing to laud him while at the same time controlling the patronage of the arts typified in the establishment of the Cinq Auteurs (l. 12).[196] The motif is taken further in lines 188–234, where Richelieu figures as a consummate actor, 'Sans masque il est tousjours masqué' (l. 189) as well as a 'charlatan sur son theatre' (l. 199), and a skilled hypocrite pretending to work for the good of France and the Church, the two institutions he represents, a service symbolized by his scarlet dress as well as the blue ribbon, the highest honour to be bestowed by France's king (l. 746). Richelieu is said to be 'ce Matamore orgueilleux' (l. 758), a topical reference to Pierre Corneille's *Illusion comique* which was being performed in the Théâtre du Marais in 1636. It is also a two-edged allusion, for just as Richelieu has been penetrated by Hispanic theatrical influences so too have the Spanish penetrated the very heart of the state because of his bellicose policies.

---

[193] Explicit mentions of the term occur in lines 69, 83, 131, 197, 559, 732, 837, 954, and 956. The concept is in fact reinforced in the final line. Ételan develops this more explicitly: 'Qu'il voulût triompher des miseres publiques; / Tel qu'on voyoit jadis un Empereur Romain', 'Le Passage de Somme', fol. 553. Once again, the manner in which this same point is explored serves to underscore different authorial approaches.

[194] See Henry Phillips, 'Richelieu and the Edict of 1641', *Seventeenth-Century French Studies*, 15 (1993), 71–84. Elsewhere, Phillips proposes that this distrust was not only based on the texts themselves and the lascivious stimulation offered by actresses to an overwhelmingly male audience, but also because 'of the whole nature of the experience' in offering a rival arena to churches; *Church and Culture in Seventeenth-Century France* (Cambridge: Cambridge University Press, 1997), p. 61.

[195] Léopold Lacour, *Richelieu dramaturge et ses collaborateurs: les imbroglios romanesques, les pièces politiques* (Paris: Ollendorff, 1926), p. 16.

[196] Georges Couton comments that 'le Cardinal s'est decidé à avoir une politique culturelle et spécialement une politique théâtrale', *Richelieu et le théâtre* (Lyon: Presses Universitaires de Lyon, 1989), p. 7.

According to the *Miliade*, it is through the double dissimulation of his emotions and actions that Richelieu manages to maintain his hold on power, which pairs his art of deception with his political ideology: 'Les destours de sa politique, / Les secrets de son art comique' (ll. 339–40). He carefully prepares his role and plays it well: 'Il deguise ses actions, / Dissimule ses passions, / Compoze son geste et sa mine' (ll. 149–50).[197] There is an almost imperceptible element of grudging admiration in this picture of Richelieu's ability to use his own body language so advantageously. Among his arsenal of deception, he uses the ability to cry to his advantage: 'Si les Roynes l'ont en horreur, / Il pleure pour gaigner leur cœur' (ll. 173–74), yet these are crocodile tears (l. 179). This is not mere poetic licence, for, according to Tallemant, Marie de Médicis, on hearing of the prelate's distress at her refusal to see him during the strained period in their relations before she went into exile, remarked 'Je ne m'estonne pas, répondit-elle, il pleure quand il veut'.[198] She had been a first-hand witness at how effective his lachrymosity could be, on the Day of Dupes. His minions in their turn are depicted in terms of being stage fools because of their acquiescence to Richelieu; thus Le Jay is 'ce buffle supresme' (l. 652). If Richelieu proficiently stage-manages affairs of state, this does leave the question of the sovereign's place within this schema. As Timothy Murray concludes, 'it was Richelieu, who, with the aid of theatrical ruses, produced and directed Louis's histrionic appearances as king'.[199]

The government is populated with figures who are comic caricatures of incompetence and self-interest, a situation that would be humorous were it not leading to an inevitable tragic dénouement: the ruin of France (ll. 205–07). The *Miliade* forges a connection between Richelieu's love of performance and his personality, which, at the same time, draws on the trope of *theatrum mundi*. This is not merely an assault on the Cardinal's duplicitous personality for at the

---

[197] Françoise Hildesheimer sees Richelieu as 'un acteur virtuose du contrôle du monde intellectuel', *Relectures de Richelieu* (Paris: Publisud, 2000), p. 208.

[198] *Hist*, I, 242. Anthony Levi is less harsh than Marie in this respect: 'If Richelieu was readily moved to tears, it was not on account of any unusual sensitivity of feeling, but the simple result of nervous stress, a consequence of the intensity wth which he committed himself even to minutiae in the management of affairs', *Cardinal Richelieu*, p. 146.

[199] Timothy C. Murray, 'Richelieu's Theater: The Mirror of a Prince', *Renaissance Drama*, 8 (1977), 257–98 (p. 297).

same time it undermines a central tool of his political tenets: 'Under the ministry of Richelieu, spectacular display and the theatrical performance of power and sovereign political authority were essential to the emerging absolutist culture'.[200] At the same time, it is posited as an ineffectual policy and Peter Shoemaker considers that, in the satire, 'the language of theatricality and illusion expresses not the mystery of power, but rather the affinity between self-deception and political impotence'.[201] With its repeated focus on the theatrical trope and its use as a parody of the minister's unseemly predilection for the stage, as well as denoting his cultivation of an artistic propaganda machine, in addition to the insinuated evocation of *theatrum mundi*, the poem manages to spread its nets wider than the minister. It this, it forms a critique of absolutism itself, another instance of the promiscuous use of a metaphor that typifies the work. Behind this depiction of the risible excesses of an administration plummeting further into degradation, I would like to think that we catch a glimpse of a world-weary, disillusioned Favereau, weaned on the potency of the humanistic *theatrum mundi* allegory from his mentor, Étienne Pasquier, and having to endure this hapless comedy of errors as a privileged but helpless spectator.[202]

The driving force with which Richelieu conceals his true nature and projects an image that is chimeric suggests that there is something monstrous lurking beneath the surface. This is an apposite moment to turn to animalistic tropes, another well-used theme in the work and situating it within a long strand of satirical tradition which often employs bestial characteristics, symbols, and characters.[203] On several occasions Richelieu is cast as being postitively reptilian: he is a serpent who gnaws at the country's

---

[200] Erec R. Koch, *The Aesthetic Body: Passion, Sensibility, and Corporeality in Seventeenth-Century France* (Newark: University of Delaware Press, 2008), p. 96.

[201] Peter W. Shoemaker, *Powerful Connections: The Poetics of Patronage in the Age of Louis XIII* (Newark: University of Delaware Press, 2007), p. 189.

[202] For a solid discussion of early modern uses of the theatrical trope in politics, see Derek A. Watts, 'Le sens des métaphores théâtrales chez le cardinal de Retz et quelques écrivains contemporains', *Travaux de Linguistique et de Littérature*, 13 (1975), 385–400.

[203] 'See George A. Test, *Satire: Spirit and Art* (Tampa: University of South Florida Press, 1991), pp. 198–99. Duprat devotes a chapter to the use of animal metaphors against monarchs, particularly Henri III and Louis XVI; see *Les Rois de papier*, pp. 203–46.

interior (l. 930) and he possesses a basilisk's stare with his words being impregnated with asp's venom (ll. 137–38). The basilisk is fitting to represent someone who held episcopal orders since its head was reputedly endowed with a mitre-shaped crest.[204] Moreover, both the names for both these snakes denoted artillery weapons, so with one deft stroke the metaphor connotes that the prelate is vicious, pugnacious, and inhuman.[205] As well as these deadly serpentine attributes, he sheds crocodile tears for his victims (l. 179). His subordinates share similar brutish attributes, with Machaud and Laffemas presented as 'deux monstres nouveaux' (l. 78) and also 'Tygres audacieux' (l. 122). The wife of Chancellor Séguier is a 'dragon qui rapine tout' (l. 465). Bullion is a 'gros taureau' (l. 625) and 'un serpent enflé de venin' (l. 630).

The persistent insistence on beast-like features augments the sense of the Cardinal's barbarity which in turn is emphasized through the recurrent use of the adjective *cruel* or noun *cruauté* which come into service no fewer than fourteen times. The insistence on Richelieu's animalistic qualities goes further than dehumanizing him, however, since it also evokes a diabolic nature. He is labelled 'le demon de l'univers' (l. 34) and 'le demon de ton etat' (l. 940; this is addressed to the monarch). His life is patterned on 'vertus infernalles' (l. 28). The fact that his aggressive nature is leonine (ll. 923–26) recalls St Peter's injunction to beware of the marauding figure of Satan (1 Peter, 5.7). This sinister side is manifested in his host of deceitful acts and the web of malice he weaves, as well as in his sadism: he bathes in the tears of his victims and their blood, prison, and suffering represent 'ses plus aimables delices' (l. 60).[206] This prince of the Church even manages to outwit and surpass Satan with the extent of his infernal malice: 'Le demon à peine devine, / Le mal qu'il cache dans son sein' (ll. 152–53). In short, the nation is being dragged to Hell by the minister's machinations. Demonic and infernal allegories have a long history of

---

[204] Ulysse Aldrovandi, *Serpentum et draconum historiæ* (Bologna: Clement Ferroruium, 1640), p. 364.

[205] See Furetière, who states that the asp denotes 'une ancienne piece d'artillerie', *DU*, I, sig. R2ʳ.

[206] 'The etymology of the word 'diable' – devil, calumniator, divider, deceiver – was well known to early modern writers on slander', Emily Butterworth, *Poisoned Words: Slander and Satire in Early Modern France*, Research Monographs in French Studies, 21 (Oxford: Legenda, 2007), p. 28.

alignment with satire with perhaps the most obvious example being Dante. W. H. Auden argues that the two most common satirical devices are either to present to object of the satire as a lunatic, therefore not fully responsible for their actions, or demonic, in which case they hold complete liability for what they do, since they have freely embraced evil.[207] Seventeenth-century satirists frequently resorted to this theme and it is particularly present in Scarron's work.[208] During the second decade of the century, 'authors channelled the Ravaillac and Concini affairs into a larger narrative about demonic threats to the French body politic'; this polemical strategy constitutes a recent and obvious heritage for the *Miliade*.[209] This politico-religious rhetoric constructs an image of Richelieu being whole-heartedly aligned with the forces of darkness with the inescapable conclusion being that Richelieu is evil and serving another master: Satan.[210] Thus the animalistic characteristics of Richelieu are aligned to scriptural references and, in a psalm that patristic authorities interpret as addressing the messiah, all of the sub-human properties assigned to Richelieu are employed by the psalmist: 'Thou shalt walk upon the asp and the basilisk: and thou shalt trample under foot the lion and dragon' (Psalm 90.13; Douay Rheims). The Cardinal is not only anti-Christian, he is also anti-Christ.

The fourth trope that occupies a large part of the *Miliade* is sexual. The erotic foibles of Richelieu's entourage are set out in unambiguous terms. The Chancellor is being cuckolded by a priest, a doubly humiliating infidelity for someone representing justice within the state. Bullion is depicted as having a sexual appetite to match his gastronomic one (l. 624). A minor government official, Jacques Coquet, provides Cornuel with mistresses in return for access to this administrator's wife. This theme of procuring is sustained in the following section of the poem, a term which fits in well with the pun available with the office of *procureur*.[211] Le Jay has 'une garce

---

[207] W. H. Auden, 'Notes on the Comic', *Thought*, 27 (1952), 57–71 (p. 67).

[208] L. S. Koritz, *Scarron satirique* (Paris: Klincksieck, 1977), pp. 74–83.

[209] Anne E. Duggan, 'Criminal Profiles, Diabolical Schemes, and Infernal Punishments: The Cases of Ravaillac and the Concinis', *Modern Language Review*, 105 (2010), 366–84 (pp. 367–68).

[210] Laurent Testu is termed 'Digne Prevost de lucifer' in line 82.

[211] For example, Mme Herbelay is said to be 'grosse de procureurs' in line 702.

infame' installed in his country home as his mistress (l. 664), who is reported to have died in his arms while they were engaged in carnal congress: 'Qui dans cette extase brutalle / Approcha de l'onde infernalle' (ll. 667–68). This is an archetype of political smear if its frequency is anything to go by – similar stories regularly feature in twenty-first century headlines – and is all the more indecent because Le Jay has become the efficient cause of eternal damnation for this woman, resulting in a vigorous and disquieting mix of fornication and necrophilia that transgresses natural and divine law. His home is described as facilitating other pleasures of libidinous excess, for he not only sleeps with the wife, but also the daughter not of one, but no fewer than three, officials (l. 679). One of these women, Herbelay's wife, cuckolds her husband at his instigation as long as those who enjoy her company pay him 'une offrande' (l. 700). This prostitute is legendary among tailors for her lasciviousness (l. 701). The sartorial trade aims to provide a pleasing exterior for its clients, so there is a touch of the whited sepulchre brand of hypocrisy implied in this defamatory observation. Furthermore, with a network reaching across the capital, there is a particular type of shame about this unsavoury reputation being trumpeted all over the capital. Richelieu's family is not exempt, for the rumours about his niece's same-sex liaisons are repeated (ll. 860–61). It is interesting that the titillating tales of erotic misdemeanours do not extend to Père Joseph, whose respect of his vow of chastity was never the object of serious discussion by contemporaries; that he is not similarly libelled indicates that the *Miliade* is repeating and expanding on scurrilous gossip rather than creating it. This is an important distinction since it adds weight to the conclusion that the *Miliade* is a synthesis of both facts and rumours concerning the government, a compendium of political and moral failure.

Richelieu himself largely escapes the taint of sexual impropriety, despite contemporary hearsay linking him to three different women: the duchesse d'Aiguillon, his niece; the wife of the maréchal de Chaulnes; with the most forceful reports naming a young lower-class woman from the capital called Marion de Lorme.[212] However, while an erotic trope is not used explicitly in respect of the minister, there is an example of a subdued intimation of a past indiscretion when speaking of his relationship with Léon Bouthillier, comte de Chavigny.

---

[212] *Hist*, I, 264–65.

> L'amour qu'Armand luy porte est telle,
> Qu'[e]lle esgale la paternelle,
> Et si son pere n'estoit doux,
> Il en pourroit estre jaloux. (ll. 547–50)

On one level, this serves to create the sense that Richelieu has appropriated a paternal role within this family which, as I will discuss later, corresponds to a similar assumption of responsibility that is not rightly his within the state and particularly in respect to the sovereign. At the same time, this is also an indirect allusion to popular claims that Richelieu had fathered Chavigny while he was bishop of Luçon.[213] They were certainly close collaborators and it would account for Chavigny's meteoric rise to power, although this assertion is somewhat tempered by the fact that his father and grandfather had been devoted servants of the Crown. As with the other tropes employed in the poem, the paternity of the minister's favourite is not the only question that is entertained here, for another suggestion comes into play. The poet states that Chavigny's position is unassailable and 'Qu'il est le premier favory / De ce ministre au cul poury' (ll. 533–34). This alludes to Richelieu's long-suffering health problems as the result of haemorrhoids; this couplet exemplifies Laurent Avezou's judgement that 'les hémorroïdes de Richelieu jouissent alors d'une notoriété internationale et déterminent toute une poétique de la trivialité'.[214] At the same time, however, the couplet pairs the ambiguous term 'favory' with Richelieu's putrified rectum creating an intimation of sodomy and sexually transmitted infection. This is further reinforced by the following lines which relate Chavigny's lascivious immoderation culminating in the observation 'Et par les femmes il est dompté' (l. 538), such excessive devotion to women constituting an early modern marker of effeminacy.[215] Sodomy is not raised here as an actuality; we know that Richelieu

---

[213] Tallemant relates that Gaston d'Orléans, on hearing a joke made at the Cardinal's expense by Chavigny, replied '*Et tu quoque, fili?* car on disoit qu'il estoit filz du Cardinal, qui estant jeune, avoit couché avec Mme Bouthillier', *Hist*, I, 355. François Bluche, while admitting the possibility of an actual relationship between the prelate and Lorme, considers the question of his paternity of Chavigny 'possible, peu probable, mais de toute façon invérifiable', *Richelieu: essai* (Paris: Perrin, 2003), p. 107.

[214] Laurent Avezou 'Le tombeau littéraire de Richelieu: genèse d'une héroïsation', *Hypothèses*, 1 (2001), 181–90 (p. 183).

[215] David M. Halperin, 'How to Do the History of Male Homosexuality', *GLQ: A Journal of Lesbian and Gay Studies*, 6 (2000), 87–123 (p. 94).

was resolutely disposed towards women, but rather as a subtle suggestion of a scatological and sodomitical slur that points not to acts but rather to a wider implication that this disruptive relationship embodies Richelieu's whole government which creates and cultivates disorder in the body politic.[216] The nature of this concept to be gleaned in the *Miliade* is one that invokes 'the widespread early modern understanding of sodomy as a sympton of cosmic or cultural disorder'.[217] It is France which is passively enduring the sustained rape of Richelieu's ministry, a theme that is also raised in the verdict that 'Armand possede Louys' (l. 915).[218] The depiction of Richelieu's sick and frail body with its rectal ailments is analogous to the suffering and divided body politic, as if Richelieu were an incurable and lethal virus that has contaminated France. One tract published after the execution of Louis de Marillac pulls no punches in asserting that the recurrent 'maladies du corps' experienced by Richelieu are divine retribution for the minister's part in his downfall.[219] In this aspect, the *Miliade* heralds writers militating against Mazarin during the Fronde, particularly Scarron, for whom sodomy went beyond insinuations of perversion to encompass tyranny itself.[220]

---

[216] Richelieu's heterosexuality is encapsulated in Tallemant's knowing comment: 'Le Cardinal aimoit les femmes', *Hist*, I, 265. While the Mazarinades would take up similar bestial and erotic tropes, sodomitical references went beyond the political, since rumours about his same-sex relationships were widely assumed to possess more than a grain of truth. For a probing assessment of this aspect of the pamphlets, see See Jeffrey Merrick, 'The Cardinal and the Queen: Sexual and Political Disorders in the Mazarinades', *French Historical Studies*, 18 (1994), 667–99.

[217] Lewis Seifert, *Manning the Margins: Masculinity and Writing in Seventeenth-Century France* (Ann Arbor: University of Michigan Press, 2009), p. 158.

[218] Gregory W. Bredbeck proposes that 'sodomy does not create disorder; rather disorder demands sodomy', *Sodomy and Interpretation: Marlowe to Milton* (Ithaca: Cornell University Press, 1991), p. 77.

[219] *L'Esprit bien-heureux du Mareschal de Marillac, à l'esprit mal-heureux du Cardinal de Richelieu* ([n.p.]: [n.pub.], 1632?), p. 42.

[220] Lewis C. Seifert, 'Masculinity and Satires of "Sodomites" in France 1660–1715', in *Homosexuality in French History and Culture*, ed. by Jeffrey Merrick and Michael Sibalis (London: Routledge, 2002), pp. 37–52 (p. 44). One Mazarinade used a courtier's constipation as a metaphor for the moribund state of France under Mazarin: *Le Constipé de la cour. Avec une prophétie burlesque* ([n.p.]: [n.pub.], 1649?).

While supposedly working for the benefit of France and for the Crown, Richelieu is depicted as abusing his relationship to the nation, the eldest daughter of the Church and to the King, the father of the nation, and to Rome, Holy Mother Church.[221] The dominant themes of the satire essentially serve this wider familial topos, what might be termed a master trope: Richelieu does not respect social or familial hierarchy and his original sin is disloyalty to Marie de Médicis, who had graced him with her patronage. The *Miliade* echoes Morgues's analysis of '[t]he ungrateful client Richelieu subvert[ing] the Christian character of the monarchy in favor of an authoritarian tyranny that did not respect the family as the moral touchstone of society'.[222] The uninhibited scheming of the Cardinal stands at the root of the disasters afflicting the nation and its king, reflecting the belief that 'ambition clashed with the early modern view of a rigidly hierarchical society in which everyone knew and kept his place. It also clashed with the claim of the Bourbon Monarchy to absolute power because ambitious men were politically disobedient'.[223]

As well as his infidelity towards the synedochical family of the Church and in his filial relationship to the monarch, Richelieu has maintained his grasp on power through creating a cleavage at the heart of the royal family between mother and son and between siblings. His victory on the Day of Dupes in 1630 was the turning-point of his ministry and unequivocally confirmed his supremacy. This was done at the expense of the residual influence of, and Louis XIII's relationship with, his mother. There was a great irony in this turn of events, since Richelieu had won the trust of the King 'as the one man who offered some hope of healing their differences [between Louis and his mother] and ending the rift in the royal family'.[224] Jean-François Dubost has argued that the Queen Mother's life was radically transformed as a result of and following this event,

---

[221] 'Le nom de pere appartient au chef de la maison, le nom de pere de la patrie appartient au Prince', François de Colomby, *De l'Autorité des roys, premier discours* (Paris: Toussainct Du Bray, 1631), p. 14.

[222] Katherine Crawford, *Perilous Performances: Gender and Regency in Early Modern Europe* (Cambridge, MA: Harvard University Press, 2004), p. 91.

[223] Sharon Kettering, 'Patronage and Kinship in Early Modern France', *French Historical Studies*. 16 (1989), 408–35 (p. 412).

[224] J. H. Elliott, *Richelieu and Olivares* (Cambridge: Cambridge University Press, 1991), p. 37.

which constituted an absolute failure on her part since she did not present a credible alternative to Richelieu's ministry. Dubost proposes that her quest for legitimacy was founded on the realm of the visual, an illusion of power from which she was excluded whereas 'un Richelieu, virtuose de la parole et maître de la clarté discursive, n'a guère besoin du secours des images pour convaincre'.[225] How galling then, must he have found the *Miliade*, which became a byword for opposition to himself and his policies.

THE *MILIADE*'S LEGACY

In a sense the *Miliade* defined a generation in the same way as Corbie did and there is no doubt that the memory of the poem remained as much a part of the collective public imagination from 1636 as the Spanish advance towards the capital. An example of how far this work penetrated the public consciousness may be seen in one of its most accomplished jokes, that Richelieu 'Introduit par toute la France / Le crime de leze Eminence' (ll. 739–40). I have found no instance of this type of pun before the *Miliade* and it appears to be an original one-liner. However, within a matter of months, this particular wordplay finds its way into an author involved in the *querelle du Cid*: 'Je ne croy pas estre criminel de leze amitié, pour en avoir receu quelques copies, comme les autres, et leur avoir donné la loüange qu'ils méritent'.[226] The fact that witticisms from the poem soon found an echo in other writers indicates that it had permeated its audience. In a similar vein and almost three decades later, Molière's Monsieur Purgon would complain of Argan having committed 'un crime de lèse-Faculté'.[227] The playwright was no doubt influenced either by the format of the

---

[225] Jean-François Dubost, *Marie de Médicis: la reine dévoilée* (Paris: Payot, 2009), p. 875.

[226] Jean Clavaret, 'Lettre du Sr Clavaret au Sr Corneille, soy disant autheur du Cid', in *La Querelle du Cid (1637–1638)*, ed. by Jean-Marc Civardi, Sources Classiques, 52 (Paris: Champion, 2004), pp. 537–43 (p. 538).

[227] Jean-Baptiste Poquelin de Molière, *Le Malade imaginaire*, in *Œuvres complètes*, ed. by Georges Forestier and Claude Bourqui, 2 vols (Paris: Gallimard, 2010), II, 699 (II. 6).

joke having passed into regular use, in which case a new variation of a familiar joke is invariably humorous, or he took his inspiration from the quarto versions of the satire which appeared during the Fronde. Clearly the *Miliade* had a ready readership and was a publishing sensation. It is not, however, the formulation of such sound bites which signal the work's enduring success. This is perhaps best illustrated in a judgement made by Mathieu Marais during the reign of Louis XV. Marais, a lawyer at the Parlement de Paris, reflects on the ministry of Cardinal Dubois to conclude: 'C'est un rare prélat qui aura bien quelque jour la *Milliade*, comme le cardinal de Richelieu. Cette *Milliade* a de certains vers excellents'.[228] Almost a century after it first appeared, under the reign of the great-great-grandson of Louis XIII, the *Miliade* is spoken of as an eminent exemplar of political satire and as a benchmark of the genre.[229] There is no doubt that the work inspired the subsequent course of polemics. Théophraste Renaudot, who was recruited by Richelieu to found the *Gazette* as a popular organ propagating his policies, acknowledged that the *Miliade*'s sentiments were favourably echoed by Protestant writers, and even among sections of the higher nobility.[230]

The *Miliade* represented an important milestone in evading official censorship while at the same time it pioneered a new wave of political comment that would culminate in the Mazarinade, and it is

---

[228] *Journal et mémoires de Mathieu Marais, avocat au Parlement de Paris, sur la régence et le règne de Louis XV (1715–1737): publiés pour la première fois d'après le manuscrit de la Bibliothèque impériale*, ed. by Adolphe Mathurin de Lescure, 4 vols (Paris: Firmin-Didot, 1863–68), II (1864), 401. While Dubois may have not provoked an adversarial work such as the poem, he did fulfil the prophecy at the end of the *Miliade* that tyrants do not have tombs; Jean-Pierre Thomas wants to redress this omission and underlines that there is 'aucune rue de Paris et aucun monument public ne commémore le nom alors que tant d'inutiles traîneurs de sabre imposent leur souvenir éphémère dans chaque recoin de la capitale', *Le Régent et le cardinal Dubois: l'art de l'ambiguïté* (Paris: Payot, 2004), p. 238. The comparison between Dubois and Richelieu is an apposite one according to Guy Chaussinand-Nogaret who believes that Dubois 'voulait être un autre Richelieu et n'entendait pas qu'une parcelle d'autorité échappât à la monarchie', *Le Cardinal Dubois, 1656–1723* (Paris: Perrin, 2000), p. 83.

[229] Célestin Moreau opines that, while the Mazarinades represent a crucial development in political satire, 'elle [la Fronde] n'a rien de plus hardi, de meilleur, de plus fameux que la *Miliade*', *Choix de Mazarinades*, 2 vols (Paris: Renouard, 1853), I, v.

[230] *Mémoires de Théophraste Renaudot*, ed. by Christian Bailly (Paris: Albatros, 1981), p. 84.

in these pamphlets that the most immediate and significant impact of the 1636 satire may be seen. This influence goes further than being emboldened by the *Miliade*'s success: Jacques Prévot convincingly goes so far as to suggest that the 'formes fixes, le pamphlet en vers dans la tradition de la *Miliade*' of the Mazarinade stem from the original satire.[231] The Mazarinade might therefore owe its genesis directly to the *Miliade*. I contend that an indicator of this linguistic lineage might be discerned in the very name of the pamphlet. The term Mazarinade was coined at beginning of Fronde, with its first recorded usage being in July 1648, and it caught on rapidly. Hubert Carrier proposes that the inspiration of this word stems from satirical tradition: 'Le sens est clair: *mazarinade* a été formé comme *trivelinade, turlupinade* ou *tabarinade*, c'est un tour de farceur, une singerie de bouffon.'[232] As I have discussed earlier, I believe that this observation holds true of the origins of the title of the *Miliade*. Nevertheless, it is credible to believe that Mazarinade was not referencing this earlier strand of satire but rather belies its immediate heritage thus paying homage to the *Miliade*, to which it owed so much.

In a recent study concentrating on the eighteenth century, Robert Darnton lists anecdotes, portraits, and news as the three essential constituents of libels of this period. Moreover, the intimate association that Darnton observes between sex and politcs and decadence and despotism could well apply to the *Miliade*, as could his description of the full assault of the libel on eighteenth-century institutions: 'As pictured in the literature of libel, *les grands* inhabited a kind of satanic fairyland where they could give full rein to the pursuit of lust and power'.[233] In deeply infusing the public consciousness, whether directly during its three separate waves of printings or indirectly through the genre it inspired during the Fronde, the *Miliade* could well have influenced the course of anti-

---

[231] Jacques Prévot, *Cyrano de Bergerac, poète et dramaturge* (Paris: Belin, 1978), p. 255.

[232] Hubert Carrier, *La Presse de la Fronde (1648–1653): les Mazarinades, la conquête de l'opinion* (Geneva: Droz, 1989), p. 60.

[233] Robert Darnton, *The Devil in the Holy Water or the Art of Slander from Louis XIV to Napoleon* (Philadelphia: University of Pennsylvania Press, 2010), p. 6. On the basic ingredients of libel, see pp. 257–339. 'Sex and Politics' is treated in Chapter 26 (pp. 360–74) and 'Decadence and Despotism' in Chapter 27 (pp. 375–96).

governmental discourse in the following century and might be seen as a forerunner of eighteenth-century libels which shared its features but went further in their criticism of the sovereign and would culminate in revolution.

The *Miliade* may not have reached its aim of contributing to the removal of Cardinal Richelieu, yet this apparent failure is unimportant; it almost did. It immensely rattled its target. The fact that its author was never unmasked and punished represents a triumph against the egregious excesses of Richelieu's ministry and his tightly controlled system of restricting works appearing in print overseen by censors, inspectors, and spies. This might appear, at first glance, to be a minor victory, yet it is an unquantifiable one in terms of the psychological boost it brought to its clandestine readership during the 1630s, then during its subsequent incarnations during the Fronde, and finally during the 1690s. It embodied the spirit of resistance and its very existence stands as a compelling demonstration that, even when ruthlessly stifled, free speech can and does always find a vehicle of expression.[234] Reading it in the twenty-first century, we might not understand every contemporary reference, pun, or joke, but that is entirely beside the point. As Ronald Knox observes, 'Humour is of an age, satire is of all ages; humour is of one particular civilization, satire of all countries. [...] Satire has a wider scope, too. It is born to scourge the persistent and ever-recurrent follies of the human creature as such'.[235] The *Miliade* is endowed with a certain timelessness irrespective of its seventeenth-century topicality. As I hope to have shown, the work is significant in its historical and political import, and it is a pleasure to be able to present it to a new audience.

---

[234] 'To some extent, of course, the political joke *is* a safety valve or, as some observers would say, a way in which an oppressed people preserves its sanity. Jokes may not be able to topple a dictatorial regime; but there is one important point which adds to the effectiveness of political humour: the oppressors have no defence against it. If they try to fight back they appear only more ridiculous', Egon Larsen, *Wit as Weapon: The Political Joke in History* (London: Muller, 1980), p. 3.

[235] Ronald A. Knox, 'On Humour and Satire', in *Satire: Modern Essays in Criticism*, ed. by Ronald Paulson (Englewood Cliffs: Prentice-Hall, 1971), pp. 52–65 (p. 61).

ESTABLISHMENT OF THE TEXT AND EDITORIAL PRACTICE

The text I have chosen as the basis of this critical edition is the corrected, later octavo edition, and I have used the copy held at The Hague as the source text, the bibliographical information for which is provided below. First and foremost, this was an early version of the *Miliade* which almost certainly appeared within a few weeks or months of the first edition. The text is freer of the not inconsiderable quantity of errata that plagued the first edition, notwithstanding the question of whether they were purposeful or not. Since it almost certainly originated from the same press, there is every likelihood that the author or at least someone closely associated with the production of the original version had a hand in the production of the enhanced volume. Since the quarto edition appeared some time after the original political situation, printing, and authorial intervention of the octavo version, there is no imperative reason to select it over its predecessor.

I have listed variants between the seven octavo editions in the form of footnotes, with the exception of differences occurring because of the orthographical and grammatical corrections that were carried out from the first to the second edition, as well as obvious typesetting errors such as the absence of a space between two words; these have been systematically and silently amended. I have operated a selective rather than exhaustive policy in the listing of variants occurring in the quarto editions and between the octavo and the quarto versions: only substantial disparities such as changes of words or in the word order rather than variants in spelling or typographical differences have been recorded Similarly, since the manuscript copies of the poem almost certainly postdate the octavo and possibly even the quarto editions, I have limited mention of variants to noteworthy occurrences in these copies which tend to confirm this posterior status.[236] I have resolved i/j and u/v to modern

---

[236] With regard to the common occurrences of variants, it is clear that Ars 1, Ars 2, and Gen bear many affinities and it is probable that Ars 2 and Gen are copies of the former. RMS bears many similarities to Tall (1649), including the inclusion of lines 809–10, and is most likely a copy of the printed edition.

usage and replaced the ampersand with 'et'. Other that this, the use of upper and lower-case has been retained exactly as it occurs in the original, save for a small number of lines beginning with a lower-case letter, which have been altered to an upper-case one in each occurrence. Spellings are transcribed as they occur in The Hague copy with the exception of the letter 'a', which has been silently corrected in instances when it carried or lacked an appropriate accent in accordance with modern usage. The page numbers of this copy (which are common to five out of the seven copies) are provided to the right-hand side of the text in italics.

In order to avoid weighing down the text with an ungainly amount of annotations, I have listed the variants in the form of footnotes, and have reserved endnotes for commenting on the poem itself. For the glossing of the text, I have not provided references to readily available biographical information about people and events. Rather than a glossary, which would add another layer of scholarly apparatus to the footnotes and endnotes, I have commented on unclear and rare terms in my notes to the text. Finally, I have provided the poems written by Beys, Ételan, and Montplaisir in their defence since two (Beys and Montplaisir) have not been published in a modern edition and Ételan has never been edited. I also include four other poems by Beys that have a direct bearing on the *Miliade*, one addressed to Laffemas and another to Richelieu, both written in the Bastille, as well as an epigram and sonnet written in honour of Condé during his imprisonment.

LE / GOVVERNEMENT / PRESENT OV ELOGE / DE SON EMINENCE, / *SATYRE OV LA* / *Miliade*.

Collation: 8°. [A]–G[4]. 66 p.

Signatures: only the first leaf of each gathering is signed. A is unsigned.

Pagination: the following errors occur: 29 is mislabelled 9; 43 = 33. This jump in pagination from 32 to 43 affects the rest of the text, so 44 = 34, etc.

Location: Koninklijke Bibliotheek, The Hague (KW 757 D26).

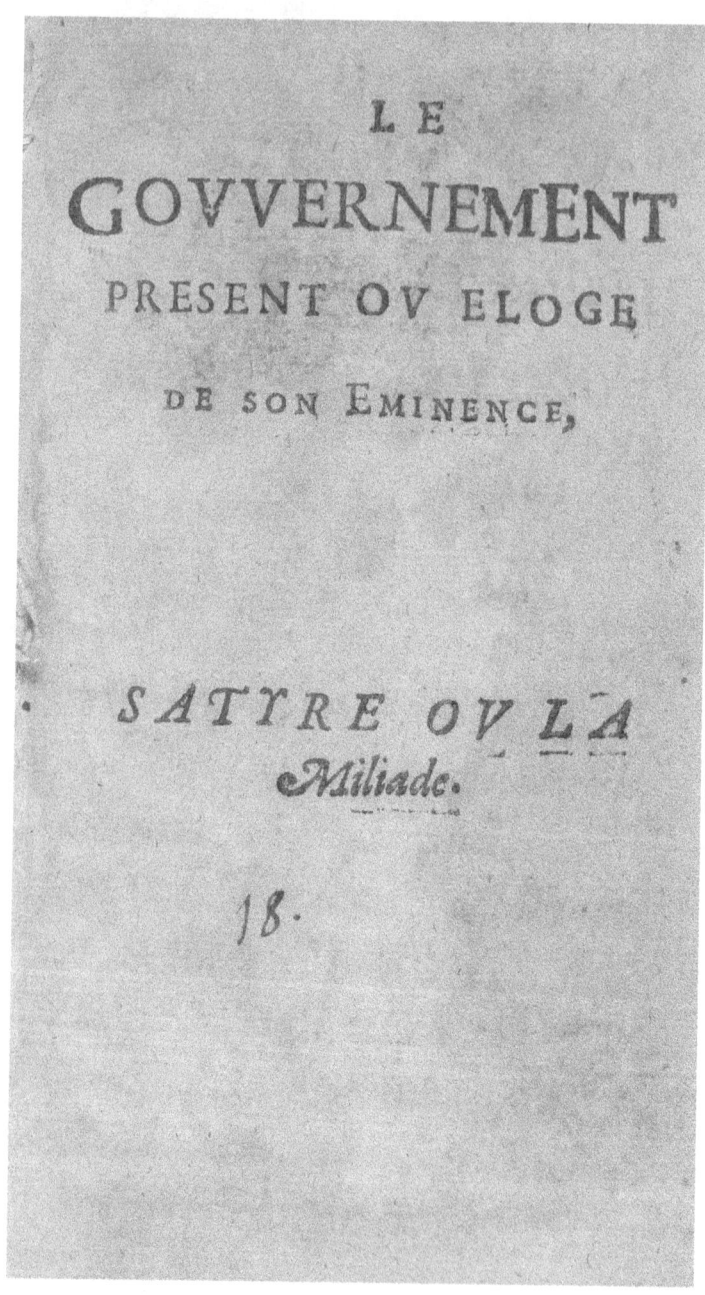

Figure 1. Title page from *Le Gouvernement present, Eloge de son Eminence, Satyre ou La Miliade* ([Paris?]: [n.pub.], 1636?). This title is common to the seven surviving octavo copies of the poem and would be modified when it was reprinted in 1649 to *Le Tableau du gouvernement present*. Reproduced by courtesy of the Beinecke Rare Book and Manuscript Library, Yale University.

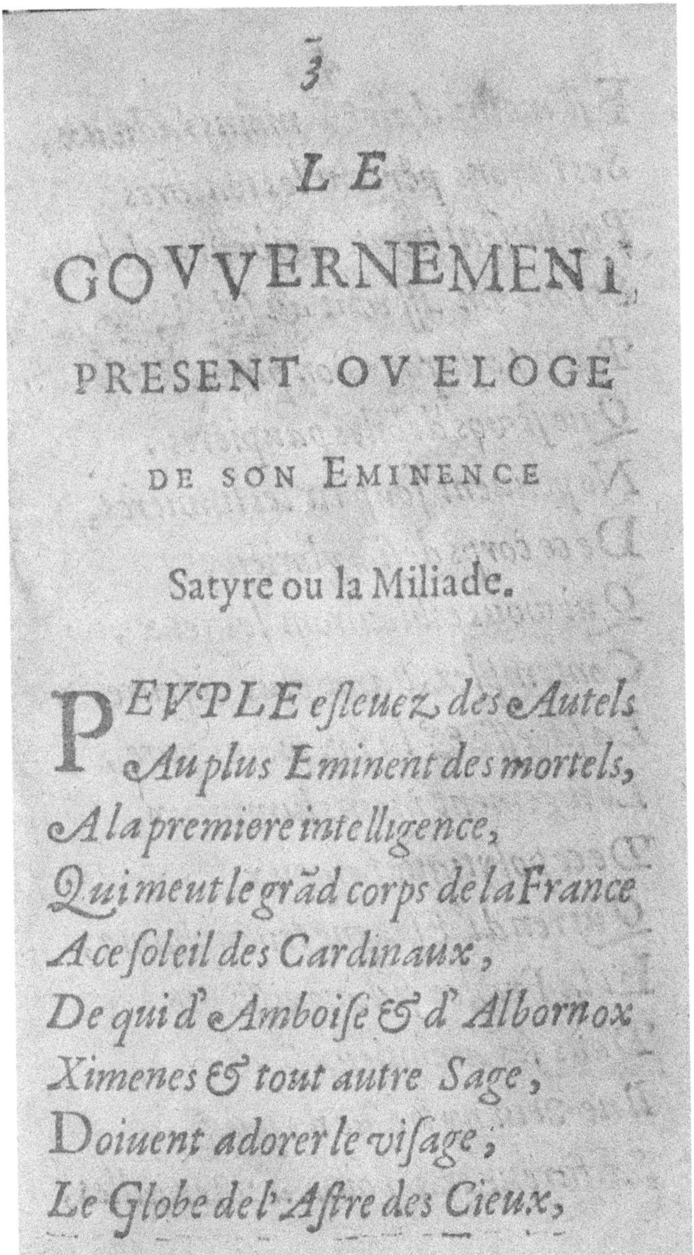

3

LE GOVVERNEMENT PRESENT OV ELOGE

DE SON EMINENCE

Satyre ou la Miliade.

PEVPLE esleuez des Autels
Au plus Eminent des mortels,
A la premiere intelligence,
Qui meut le grãd corps de la France
A ce soleil des Cardinaux,
De qui d'Amboise & d'Albornox
Ximenes & tout autre Sage,
Doiuent adorer le visage,
Le Globe de l'Astre des Cieux,

Figure 2. *Le Gouvernement present, Eloge de son Eminence ou Satyre en mil vers*, p. 3. This first page of the poem contains the error of the first word being in the singular which would be corrected in the 1649 quarto edition and in four of the manuscript versions. Reproduced by courtesy of the Beinecke Rare Book and Manuscript Library, Yale University.

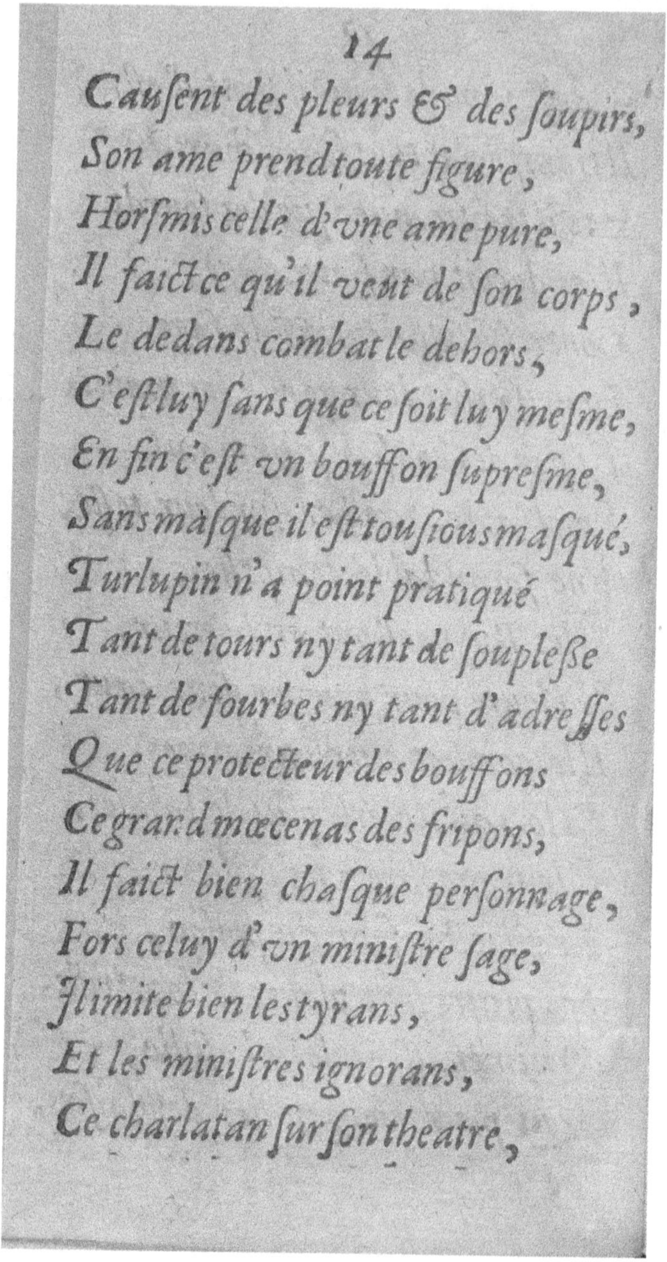

14

Causent des pleurs & des soupirs,
Son ame prend toute figure,
Horsmis celle d'vne ame pure,
Il faict ce qu'il veut de son corps,
Le dedans combat le dehors,
C'est luy sans que ce soit luy mesme,
En fin c'est vn bouffon supresme,
Sans masque il est tousious masqué,
Turlupin n'a point pratiqué
Tant de tours ny tant de souplesse
Tant de fourbes ny tant d'adresses
Que ce protecteur des bouffons
Ce grand mæcenas des fripons,
Il faict bien chasque personnage,
Fors celuy d'vn ministre sage,
Il imite bien les tyrans,
Et les ministres ignorans,
Ce charlatan sur son theatre,

Figure 3. *Le Gouvernement present, Eloge de son Eminence ou Satyre en mil vers*, pp. 14–15. These two pages display a striking use of anaphora which touches almost half of this section, one of the stylistic features that points to Jacques Favereau's authorship. Reproduced courtesy of the Beinecke Rare Book and Manuscript Library, Yale University.

Croit voir tout le monde idolastre,
De ses discours de ses leçons,
De ses pieces de ses chansons,
On souffriroit ses comedies,
Quoy que foibles & peu hardies,
Si des tragiques mouuemens
N'entroubloient les contentemens,
S'il n'auoit affoibly la France,
En destruisant son abondance,
En augmentant tous les impotz,
En multipliant tous les maux,
En tirant le sang des prouinces,
En persecutant les grands princes,
En ontrageant les potentats,
En leur vsurpant tous leurs estats,
En formant vne lonque guerre,
En l'attirant dans nostre terre,
En nous liurant aux estrangers,

LE
GOVVERNEMENT
PRESENT OV ELOGE
DE SON EMINENCE
Satyre ou la Miliade.

PEUPLE[1] eslevez des Autels
Au plus Eminent des mortels,
A la premiere intelligence,
Qui meut le grand corps de la France
5 A ce soleil des Cardinaux,
De qui d'Amboise et d'Albornox
Ximenes et tout autre Sage,
Doivent adorer le visage,
Le Globe de l'Astre des Cieux,
10 Est moins clair et moins radieux,
Ses rayons percent les tenebres
Produisent trente autheurs celebres,
Et font un affront au soleil,
Par cet ouvrage non pareil,[2]
15 Que si vos debiles paupieres,
Ne peuvent souffrir les lumieres,
De ce corps desja glorieux,
Qui vous esblouiront[3] les yeux,
Contemplez l'ame plus obscure,
20 La sagesse et la foy moins pure,
Le jugement moins lumineux,
De ce polytique fameux[4]
Qui rend l'Espagne triomphante,
Et la France si languissante,
25 Dans ses ambitieux souhaits:
Il ne veut ny trefve ny paix,
Sa fureur n'a point d'intervalles
Il suit les vertus infernalles,

---

[1] *PEUPLES*: Tab (1649), Ars 1, and Ars 2.

[2] *nompareil*: BnF.

[3] *éblouïroit*: Ars 1, Ars 2, and Gen.

[4] *furieux*: Gen. There is an additional line following this one in Gen: *Qui mesprise mesme les Dieux.*

LE GOUVERNEMENT PRESENT

        Les fourbes et les trahisons,
30   Les parjures et les poisons,
        Rendent sa probité celebre,
        Jusqu'en l'empire des tenebres,[1]
        C'est le ministre des enfers,
        C'est le demon de l'univers,
35   Le fer le feu la violence
        Signallent par tout sa clemence,
        Les freres du Roy mal traittez,
        Les Mareschaux decapitez,
        Quatre Princesses exilées,
40   Trente[2] Provinces desolées,
        Les magistrats emprisonnez,
        Les grands Seigneurs empoisonnez
        Les gardes des Sceaux dans les chaisnes.
        Les gentils-hommes dans les gesnes
45   Tant de genereux Innocents,
        Dans la Bastille gemissans,
        Cette foule de miserables,
        Où les criminels sont coulpables,
        D'avoir trop d'esprit ou de cœur,
50   Trop de franchise ou de valeur,
        Tant d'autres celebres victimes,
        Tant de personnes magnanimes,
        Qu'il tient soubs ses barbares loix,
        Dont il ne peut souffrir la voix
55   Dont il redoute le courage:
        Dont il craint mesme le visage,
        Ce grand nombre de mal-heureux
        Qui sentent son joug rigoureux:
        Leur sang, leurs poisons,[3] leurs supplices.[4]
60   Sont ses plus aimables delices,
        Il se nourrit de leurs mal-heurs,

---

[1] *Jusques dans l'Empire funèbre*: Ars 1.

[2] *Tant de*: Gen.

[3] *prisons*: BnF.

[4] *Leurs prisons, leur sang, leurs supplices*: Ars 1. *Leur prison leur sang leur supplice*: Ars 2. *Leur poison leur soing leur supplices*: Gen. *Leur sang, leurs prisons, leurs supplices*: RMS.

Il se baigne en l'eau de leurs pleurs,
Et sa haine fiere¹ et cruelle
Dans leur mort mesme est immortelle,
65 Il agite² encor leur repos
Il trouble leur cendre³ et leurs os,
Il deshonnore leur memoire,
Leur oste la vie et la gloire,
Ce tyran veut que ces martyrs
70 N'ayent que d'infames souspirs,
Dans leur plus injuste souffrance,
Qu'on approuve ses violences,⁴
Et qu'on blesse la verité,
Pour adorer sa cruauté,
75 Il ayme les fureurs brutales,⁵
Des trois suppots de sa caballe,
De ce pourvoyeur de bourreaux,
Et de ces deux monstres nouveaux,
Qui plus terribles qu'un cerbere,
80 Deschirent sans estre⁶ en colere
De Testu⁷ cette ame de fer,
Digne⁸ Prevost de lucifer,
Cet⁹ instrument de tyrannie,
Qui rend la liberté bannie,
85 Ce Geolier qui de sa maison,
Faict une cruelle prison,
Et qui traitte avec insolence
Les braves Mareschaux de France,
Lors qu'il les conduit à la mort,

---

¹ *pire*: BnF.

² *agit*: BnF.

³ *leurs cendres*: BnF.

⁴ *ses insolences*: Gen.

⁵ *la fureur brutale*: Tab (1649), Ars 1, Ars 2, Gen, and RMS.

⁶ *ordre*: Ars 2.

⁷ *destestant*: Gen.

⁸ *du pire*: Ars 2.

⁹ *Est*: Ars 2 and Gen.

90   Lors que l'estat pleure leur sort,
     Lors que leur destin miserable
     Rendroit un Tygre pitoyable:
     Mais quels insignes attentats
     N'ont faict MACHAUD et L'AFFEMAS,[1]
95   Quels Juges sont aussi severes,
     Que ces deux cruels Commissaires
     Ces bourreaux[2] de qui les souhaits,
     Sont de peupler tous les gibets,[3]
     De qui les mains sont tousjours prestes,
100 A couper des illustres testes,[4]
     A faire verser à grands flots,
     Le sang dessus les eschaffaux,
     La mort naturelle et commune,
     Leur desplait et les importune,
105 Et la sanglante à des appas,
     Ou leur cœur prennent[5] leur esbats,
     En decapitant ils se jouent,
     Ils sont encor plus guays[6] s'ils rouent,
     Mais leur plus agreable jeu,
110 Est de brûler à petit feu,
     ARMAND à choisi ces deux Scythes,
     Pour ses fideles satellites,
     Pour monstrer qu'il tient en ses mains
     La vie et la mort des humains
115 Et qu'il regne par sa puissance,
     Comme les Roys par leur naissance,
     Ses Juges menassent les grands,
     Et font trembler les innocens,
     Castrain, Marillac et de Jarre
120 Ont paty[7] devant ces barbares,

---

[1] This line is incomplete in Gen giving only *nous font* at the beginning.

[2] *Voleurs*: Gen.

[3] *gibaits*: BnF.

[4] This couplet is missing from 1694.

[5] *trouve*: Ars 1 and Ars 2. *treuve*: Gen.

[6] *guaye*: BnF.

[7] *pâly*: Ars 1 and Tall. *palli*: Gen.

>   Et veu leur mort dedans les yeux
>   De ces Tygres¹ audacieux,
>   ARMAND voulant des sacrifices,
>   De cruauté et d'injustice,
> 125   Pour paroistre ses serviteurs
>   Ils sont les sacrificateurs,
>   Ce molocle² a pour ses Prestres,³
>   Il arme de cousteaux ces traistres,
>   Pour immoler sur ses⁴ Autels,
> 130   Non des bestes mais des mortels,
>   Le vieux tyran des Arsacides
>   A moins commandé d'homicides,
>   Que ce moderne phalaris,
>   Ce monstre entre les favoris,
> 135   Son œil farouche et sanguinaire,
>   S'alume dedans sa colere,
>   Ses regards sont d'un bazilic,
>   Sa langue a le venein d'aspic,
>   Elle sert d'arme à sa malice,
> 140   Elle couvre son injustice,
>   Et mesle la douceur du miel
>   A l'amertume de son fiel,
>   Et sa parolle est infidelle,
>   Autant que sa main est cruelle,
> 145   Il ne perce⁵ qu'en caressant,
>   Et n'estouffe qu'en embrassant,
>   Il flatte lors mesme qu'il tue,
>   Et son ame n'est jamais nüe,
>   Il desguise ses actions,⁶
> 150   Dissimule ses passions,
>   Compoze son geste et sa mine
>   Le demon à peine devine,

---

¹ *Lyons*: Ars 1, Ars 2, and Gen.

² *molecles*: BnF. *Moloc*: Tall.

³ *sa prebstrise*: Ars 2.

⁴ *des*: BnF.

⁵ *parle*: BnF.

⁶ *ambitions*: Gen.

> Le mal qu'il cache dans son sein
> Il lit à peine en son dessein,[1]
155 Il ayme les lasches finesses,
> De perdre malgré ses promesses,
> De lancer soudain dans les airs
> La foudre sans bruict sans esclairs,
> De faire esclater un orage,
160 Lors que le ciel est sans nuage,
> Il est meschant il est trompeur,[2]
> Il est brutal il est menteur,
> Ses baizairs sont baizers de traistre
> Il n'est jamais ce qu'il feint d'estre,
165 Il trompe par tout ses discours,
> Et s'il traitte avecque[3] des sourds
> Il les deçoit[4] par son visage,
> Contrefaict le doux et le sage,
> Leur sousrit leur presse les mains,
170 Et par des conseils inhumains,
> Faict apres tomber[5] sur leur teste,
> Une formidable tempeste,
> Si les Roynes l'ont en horreur,
> Il pleure pour gaigner leur cœur,
175 Il les combat avec leurs armes,
> Et lors qu'il verse plus de larmes,
> Il leur prepare une prison,
> Et s'il est besoin du poison,
> Ses pleurs sont pleurs de cocodrille,[6]
180 Qui[7] menassent de la bastille,
> Qui pour venger des desplaisirs,
> Causent des pleurs et des soupirs,

---

[1] *A peine il lit dans son dessein*: Ars 1.

[2] The second *il est* in this line and the following one is replaced with *et* in Ars 1 and Ars 2.

[3] *aux*: BnF.

[4] *trompe*: Ars 1 and Ars 2. BnF lacks the initial *Il*.

[5] *tomber apres*: Ars 1, Ars 2, and Gen.

[6] Corrected to *crocodille* in Tab (1649).

[7] *Il*: Ars 2.

Son ame prend toute figure,
Hormis celle d'une ame pure,
185 Il faict ce qu'il veut de son corps,
Le dedans combat le dehors,
C'est luy sans que ce soit luy mesme,
En fin c'est un bouffon supresme,
Sans masque il est tousjours masqué,
190 Turlupin n'a point pratiqué
Tant de tours ny tant de souplesse
Tant de fourbes¹ ny tant d'adresses
Que ce protecteur des bouffons
Ce grand mœcenas des fripons,²
195 Il faict bien chasque personnage,
Fors celuy d'un ministre sage,
Il imite bien les tyrans,
Et les ministres ignorans,
Ce charlatan sur son theatre,
200 Croit³ voir tout le monde idolastre,
De ses discours de ses leçons,
De ses pieces de ses chansons,
On souffriroit ses comedies,
Quoy que foibles et peu hardies,
205 Si des tragiques mouvemens
N'en troubloient les contentemens,
S'il n'avoit affoibly la France,
En destruisant son abondance,
En augmentant tous les impotz,
210 En multipliant tous les maux,
En tirant le sang des provinces,
En persecutant les grands⁴ princes,
En outrageant les potentats,
En leur usurpant leurs⁵ estats,
215 En formant une longue guerre,
En l'attirant dans nostre terre,

---

¹ *tours*: BnF.

² *Ce Mecenas de ce fripons*: BnF, Ars 1, Ars 2, and Gen.

³ *Veult*: Gen.

⁴ *En destruisant les plus grands*: Gen.

⁵ This is preceded by *tous* in BnF, Duke, and Tab (1649).

En nous livrant aux estrangers,
En mesprisant les grands¹ dangers,
En desgarnissant les frontieres
220 En n'assurant point les rivieres,
Bref en abandonnant les Lys,
A la fureur des ennemis,
Au sort des armes si funestes,
A la faim la guerre la peste,
225 Lors qu'il doit penser aux combats,
Il prend ses comiques esbats,
Et pour ouvrage se propose,
Quelque² poesme pour belle rose,
Il descrit de fauces douleurs,
230 Quand l'estat sent de vrays malheurs,
Il trace³ une piece nouvelle,
Quand on emporte la capelle,
Et consulte encor Bois-robert,
Quand⁴ une Province se pert,
235 Les peuples sont touchez de crainte
Le parlement porte⁵ leur plainte,
Implore⁶ le Roy pour Paris,
Sans offenser les favoris.
ARMAND, toutesfois le querelle,
240 Enflamme sa face cruelle,
Et d'un regard de furieux,
Le traite de seditieux,
Certes illustre compagnie,
Tu doibs adoucir⁷ ce genie,
245 Dont le jugement nompareil,
Paroist⁸ plus clair que le Soleil,

---

¹ *en nous exposant aux*: Gen.

² *Un*: Ars 1, Ars 2, and Gen.

³ *traicte*: BnF.

⁴ *Lors que*: Ars 1, Ars 2, and Gen.

⁵ *portan*: Ars 2.

⁶ *Imploran*: Ars 2.

⁷ *adorer*: Ars 1 and Ars 2. *avouer*: Gen.

⁸ *Est*: BnF.

        Luy seul descouvre toute chose,
        Previent les effects dans leur cause
        Perse la nuict de l'advenir,
250   Sçait tout deffendre et tout munir,
        Il a pris l'attaque du Liege,
        Par une fraude[1] et par un piege[2]
        Il a preveu ce que tu vois,[3]
        Le meurtre[4] des peuples francois,
255   Dix mille bourgades pillées,
        Un grand nombre d'autres bruslées,
        L'horreur, la mort de toutes parts,
        Trente mille habitans esparts,
        Cachez[5] dans les lieux solitaires,
260   Dix mille deja tributaires,
        Et les fers encor preparez,
        Aux foibles et moins remparez,
        Demeure donc dans le silence
        Auguste oracle de la france,
265   Laisse Armand mener le vaisseau
        Nul autre pilote nouveau
        Ne peut conjurer[6] la tempeste,
        Qui gronde[7] dessus nos testes,[8]
        Luy seul commande aux elemens,
270   Luy seul est le maistre des vents,
        Luy seul bride le fier Neptune,
        Lors que son onde l'importune,
        Il luy faict des escueils nouveaux,
        Il se promene sur ses eaux,
275   Et d'une digue merveilleuse
        Dompte sa nature orgueilleuse,

---

[1] *ruse*: Tab (1649), though *fraude* in Tab.

[2] BnF, Ars 2, Gen, RMS, and Tall give *pour* in the place of *par*.

[3] *Crois*: Gen.

[4] *monstre*: BnF.

[5] *Chassez*: Gen.

[6] *calmer*: Ars 2.

[7] *grossit*: Ars 1, Gen, and Tall; *grossist*: Ars 2.

[8] *nostre teste*: Tab (1649), RMS, and Tall.

Le Gouvernement Present

         Sy le Dieu de toutes les mers,
         C'est veu[1] captif dessous ses fers,
         Ne domptera il pas l'espagne,
280   S'il la rencontre à la campagne,
         Les humains flechiront ils pas
         Voyants que les Dieux sont à bas,
         Il a vaincu les Nereides,
         Terrassé les troupes humides,
285   Fouldroyé cent mille Tritons,
         Et ne crains vingt mille fripons,
         Et c'est Espagnol[2] canaille,
         Qui fuira devant la bataille,   *20*
         ARMAND, le plus grand des humains,
290   Porte le tonnerre[3] en ses mains,
         Il gouverne la destinée,
         Tient[4] la fortune enchesnée,
         Son esprit faict mouvoir les cieux,
         Brave les Roys et les Dieux,[5]
295   Crains tu de n'avoir point de poudre
         Ce iupiter porte la foudre,
         Crains tu de manquer de canons,
         Il est trop au dessus des noms,
         Au dessus des tiltres vulgaires,
300   Au dessus des loix ordinaires,
         Pour employer dans les combatz,
         Autre tonnerre que son bras,
         Ses moins fortes rodomontades
         Sont bien plus que des canonades,
305   Dans ses plus foibles visions,   *21*
         Il terrasse dix legions,
         En parlant avec ses esclaves,
         Il faict desja peur aux plus braves,
         Avec ses seules vanitez,

---

[1] *Ses vœu*: BnF.

[2] *cette Espagnolle*: Ars 1, Ars 2, Tall, and Gen (followed by *racaille* in the latter).

[3] *La foudre*: Gen.

[4] *Il tient*: Tab (1649), Ars 1, Ars 2, Gen, RMS, and Tall.

[5] *et demi-dieux*: RMS.

310 Il reprend desja des citez,
     Et dans sa plus froide¹ arrogance,
     Conçoit une Riche esperance,
     Il plaint quasi ces estrangers,
     De s'estre mis dans les² dangers,
315 Ou se sont mis Valence et Dosle,
     Par leur temerité frivolle,
     Ce sage se rit de ces fols,
     Et les croit voir à deux genoux
     Excuser leur outrecuidance,
320 D'avoir irrité sa prudence,
     D'avoir mesprisé Richelieu,
     Dont le nom rime à demy Dieu,³
     D'avoir d'une atteinte mortelle,
     Esbranlé sa pauvre cervelle,
325 D'avoir resveillé ses humeurs,
     Qui l'ont agité de fureurs,
     D'avoir terny toute sa gloire,
     D'avoir esmeu sa bile noire,
     D'avoir rendu son poil plus blanc,
330 D'avoir trop eschauffé son sang,
     Et d'avoir reduict son derriere
     A sa disgrace coustumiere,
     Il croit se voyant à cheval,
     Voir Alexandre et Bucefal,⁴
335 Il croit que⁵ sa seule prudence,⁶
     Le renom de son insolence,
     Le son de ses trente mulets,⁷
     Le grand nombre de ses valets,

22

---

¹ *foible*: Ars 2.

² *en ce*: Gen.

³ *Que l'on ryme avec Demy-dieu*: Ars 1 and Tall.

⁴ *Bucœbal*: BnF.

⁵ *par*: BnF.

⁶ *présence*: Ars 1 and Tall.

⁷ This line is missing in Gen, though a marginal addition of *mulet* has been inserted next to the previous line in the same hand as the manuscript.

         Les destours de sa politique,
340   Les secrets de son art comique,
         Le vert esclat de ses lauriers,   23
         Le bruit de ses actes guerriers,
         Le feu¹ de son masle courage,
         Et les rayons de son visage,
345   Glaceront les timides cœurs
         De ses fiers et cruels vainqueurs,
         Il croit desja piller Bruxelle,
         Et par des vengeances cruelles,
         Traitter² comme l'on fit Louvain,
350   Apres la bataille d'Avain,
         Pour faire de si beaux miracles,
         Il consulte de grands Oracles,
         Le Moyne des Noyers, Seguier,
         Le jeune et le grand³ Bouthillier,
355   Voila les Conseillers⁴ supresmes,
         Qu'il consulte aux perils extremes.
         Le Moine imite S[aint]. François,
         Il protege⁵ les Suedois,
         Il a le Zele Seraphique,   24
360   Il travaille pour l'heretique,
         Il est percé du divin traict,
         Mais non⁶ encor tout à faict,
         Car il porte bien les stigmates,
         Mais non les marques d'escarlates,
365   Son Capuchon Piramidal,
         Ne luy plaist qu'estant à cheval,
         Sur la beste luxurieuse,
         Qui prend la posture amoureuse,
         Et par le branle et par le chocq
370   Faict dresser la pointe du frocq,

---

¹ *fruict*: Ars 2.

² *La traitter*: Tab (1649), Ars 1, Ars 2, Gen, and RMS.

³ *Le jeune et chaud*: Ars 1, Ars 2, and Gen; 'on appelle un *chaud* ami, un homme prompt à rendre service', *DU*, I, sig. Zz2ʳ.

⁴ *Sont les Politiques*: Ars 1.

⁵ *En protégeant*: Ars 1.

⁶ This is followed by *pas* in Gen.

>   Il n'a plus le simple equipage
>   Du fameux mulet de bagage,
>   Qui n'avoit comme un cordelier,
>   Pour train qu'un asne regulier,¹
> 375 Ceste vieille beste de somme,²
>   A pris le train d'un Gentil-homme,
>   Que bien³ quand le vin l'animoit,
>   Le brave cavallier se nommoit,
>   Il a suivant et secretaire
> 380 Il a carosse, il a cauterre,⁴
>   Il a des laquais insolens
>   Qui jurent mieux que ceux des grands,
>   Il est l'oracle des oracles,
>   Il est le faiseur de miracles,
> 385 L'esprit S[aint] forme ses d'iscours,
>   Un Ange les escrit tousjours,
>   Ils font par tout fleurir la guerre
>   Ils le canonizent en terre,
>   Il est des saincts reformateurs
> 390 De l'ordre des freres mineurs,
>   Il fait une regle nouvelle
>   Pour grimper au Ciel sans eschelle,
>   Pour y monter à six chevaux,
>   Et par des ambitieux travaux,
> 395 Gaigner Dieu⁵ par ou les ames
>   Gaignent les eternelles flammes
>   Pour estre capucin d'habit,
>   Pour estre esclave de credit,
>   Pour estre eminent dans l'Eglise,
> 400 Pour empourprer la couleur grise,
>   Pour estre martyr des enfers,
>   Pour estre un monstre en l'Univers,
>   Seguier Race d'Apothiquaire,¹

---

[1] *qu'un asne pour train regulier*: Gen.

[2] *difforme*: Gen.

[3] *Qu'Hebron*: Tab (1649) and RMS. *Qu'Ebron*: Ars 1 and Ars 2. *Que bran*: Gen.

[4] *litiere*: Tab (1649) and RMS; *littieres*: Gen.

[5] *Pour gagner Dieu*: Ars 1; *Pour gaigner Dieu*: Ars 2 and Gen.

　　　　　Est un esclave volontaire,
405　　Il est valet de Richelieu,
　　　　　Et l'adorateur² de ce Dieu,
　　　　　Il prend pour regle de Justice,
　　　　　Ce bon sainct sans fard ny malice,
　　　　　Il dict le voyant en Tableau,
410　　Le Ciel n'a rien faict de si beau,
　　　　　Ses volontez luy sont sacrée,
　　　　　Les Aigres injures succrée,
　　　　　Il tremble, il fleschit les genoux,
　　　　　Il est prest á souffrir les coups,
415　　L'appelle Monseigneur et Maistre
　　　　　Et pour luy violant et traistre,
　　　　　Pour luy ne cognoist plus de loix,
　　　　　Pour luy viole tous les droits,
　　　　　Sur son billet n'ose rien dire,
420　　Scelle trente blancs³ sans les lire,
　　　　　Trahit son sens et sa raison,
　　　　　Tant il redoute la prison,
　　　　　Il est morne et melancholique,
　　　　　Il est niais et lunatique,
425　　Une linotte est son jouet,
　　　　　Il est solitaire et muet,
　　　　　Tousjours pensif et tousjours morne
　　　　　Tumine⁴ comme beste à corne,
　　　　　Il auroit esté bon⁵ Chartreux
430　　Car il est sombre et tenebreux,
　　　　　Son humeur pedantesque et molle,
　　　　　Sent tres-bien⁶ son maistre d'escolle,⁷
　　　　　Il n'a point noblesse de cœur,
　　　　　Quoy qu'aye dit un lasche flateur,

---

[1] Every word in this line is capitalized in Duke.

[2] *Lorateur*: Gen.

[3] *Scelle, traicte, rand*: Gen.

[4] *Rumine*: Tab (1649), Ars 2, Gen, and RMS.

[5] This is followed by *pour* in Ars 2 and Gen.

[6] *si bien*: Ars 2 and Gen.

[7] *N'est propre qu'aux maîtres d'école*: Ars 1.

435 Sa perruque en couvrant sa teste,
　　 Couvre en mesme temps une beste,[1]
　　 Car[2] des bastons au temps jadis,
　　 Ont rendu[3] ses sens estourdis,
　　 Il va tous les jours à la Messe,
440 Sans que son injustice cesse,
　　 Les moynes Gouvernent son sceau,
　　 Quand ils veulent il faict du veau,
　　 Les ordres[4] Seraphines,
　　 Luy tiennent lieu de loix divines,
445 Et la plus saincte faculté,
　　 Par luy n'a plus[5] de liberté,
　　 Si Richelieu,[6] devient injuste　　　　　　　　 *[2]9*
　　 Contre le Parlement Auguste,
　　 Il a l'ardeur d'un[7] renegat,
450 Et soubs mains les choque et lesbat:
　　 Mais son avarice est extreme,
　　 Et dans sa dignité supreme,
　　 Il fait le geux et le faquin
　　 Comme s'il n'avoit pas du pain,
455 Son ame basse et mercenaire
　　 Le rend plus cruel qu'un corsaire
　　 S'il y va de son interest,
　　 Ou quand quelque maison luy plaist,
　　 Il ne croit pointt[8] d'illustre ouvrage,
460 Que de s'enrichir davantage,
　　 Et pleure de n'avoir encor,
　　 Peu gaigner un million d'or,
　　 La F[abry][1] cette serrurierre,

---

[1] *Marque cette tragique fête*: Ars 1.

[2] *Où*: Ars 1.

[3] *Rendirent*: Ars 1.

[4] *Ordonnances*: Tab (1649), Ars 1, Ars 2, Gen, RMS.

[5] *N'a plus par luy*: Ars 2.

[6] Richelieu is capitalized in Duke and none of the other octavo copies.

[7] *Il traicte comme un*: Ars 2.

[8] This mistake is also common to Bein and Aix.

           Cette laide, cette fripiere,
465   Ce dragon qui rapine tout,
           Qui court Paris de bout en bout,
           Pour avoir[2] aux ventes publiques,
           Les meubles les plus magnifiques,
           Et ne donnant qu'un peu d'argent,
470   Elle faict trembler[3] le sergent,
           C'est à Seguier une harpie,
           Un demon, qui sans cesse crie,
           Qu'il faut[4] voler à toutes mains,
           Que sans biens les honneurs sont vains,
475   Elle contrefaict la bigotte,
           Et se laisse lever la cotte,
           Assoisonnant ses voluptez,
           D'eau beniste et de charitez,
           Son mary carresse les moines
480   Elle carresse les chanoines,
           Et faict avec[5] chacun deux
           Ce qu'on peut faire estant deux,
           Des Noyers nouveau secretaire,
           Merite bien quelque salaire,
485   Car il est assez bon valet,
           Quoy que ce ne soit qu'un triboulet,
           Et ne cognoist point de prudence,
           Que la plus lasche complaisance,
           Et cherche son eslement,[6]
490   Par un infame abaissement,
           Sa vertu n'est point scrupuleuse,[7]
           Et d'une adresse merveilleuse,
           Quitte le bien et suit le mal,

---

[1] *La FABRY* in BnF and Duke, but *La F.* in the other octavos, Tab (1649), and Tab.

[2] *ravir*: Gen.

[3] *Et intimidan*: Ars 2. *Et faisan trembler*: Gen.

[4] *fault*: Duke.

[5] *avecque*: Ars 1 and Gen.

[6] *élevement*: Tab (1649), Ars 1, Ars 2, Gen, and RMS.

[7] *somptueuse*: Gen.

Le Gouvernement Present

      Selon qu'il plaist au Cardinal,
495 Une legere suffisance,
      Passe en luy pour grande science,
      Et le signalle entre ses veaux,
      De Lomenie et Phelipeaux,[1]
      Son ame est esgalle à sa mine,
500 Elle est petite foible et fine,
      Et n'a poinct du tout cet[2] esclat,   32
      D'un grand secretaire d'Estat,
      Sa splendeur n'estant que commune,
      Ne peut aux yeux estre importune,
505 Et son naturel bas et doux,
      Luy donne fort peu de jaloux,
      Servient[3] ton noble genie,
      Ta faict sortir[4] la tiranie,
      De ce regne ou les genereux,
510 Sont tous pauvres et malheureux,
      Ainsi lastre par la lumiere,
      Esclatte[5] une vapeur grossiere,
      Qui ternit tout[6] la clarté,
      Et qui nous cache[7] sa beauté,
515 Que si le soleil chasse l'ombre,
      Il[8] perce le nuage sombre
      Espere que les envieux;
      Te verront un jour glorieux:
      Mais le plus beau des[9] politiques   43
520 Est Chavigny, dont les pratiques
      Luy procurent avant le temps

---

[1] Lines 497–98 do not figure in Gen.

[2] *Elle n'a point le grand*: Ars 1.

[3] *Servien* in Tab (1649) and Gen, which makes it clear that this is a proper name.

[4] *sentir*: Ars 1, Ars 2, and Gen. *fuir*: RMS.

[5] *Excite*: Ars 2. *Exalle*: Gen.

[6] Corrected to *toute* in Tab (1649), Ars 1, Ars 2, and Gen.

[7] *Et nous dérobbe*: Ars 1, Ars 2, and Gen.

[8] *S'il*: BnF, Duke, Ars 1, Ars 2, and Gen.

[9] *Mais les plus braves*: Gen.

Le venin des plus vieux serpens,
Il est fourbe, il est temeraire,
Armand l'a pour son emissaire[1]
525 Et vers Monsieur et vers le Roy,
Et vers tous deux il est sans loy,[2]
Il tromperoit son propre pere,
Trahiroit[3] sa propre mere,
Si le cours de ses passions
530 Rapportoit[4] à ses actions,
Il a tant apris d'un tel maistre
Le mestier de fourbe et de traistre
Qu'il est le premier favory
De ce ministre au cul poury,
535 Ses prodigieuses richesses,
Le font brusler pour deux[5] metresses
Par la gloire il est emporté,
Et par les femmes il est dompté,
Son esprit embrasse les vices,
540 Son corps embrasse les delices,
Qui corrompent le jugement,
Par le brutal debordement,
Il se flatte de l'esperance,
De se voir Duc et Pair de france,
545 Et dans son desir violant,
Trouve que son remede[6] est lent,
L'amour qu'Armand luy porte est telle,
Qu'[e]lle[7] esgalle[8] la paternelle,
Et si son pere n'estoit doux,
550 Il en pourroit estre jaloux,
Sa femme apprend d'un[1] bon stoique[2]

---

[1] *commissaire*: Gen.

[2] *foy*: Ars 1, Ars 2, and Gen.

[3] *Il trahiroit*: Tab (1649), Tab, Ars 1, and Ars 2. *Et trahiroit*: Gen.

[4] *Le portoit*: Ars 1, Ars 2, and Gen.

[5] *des*: Gen.

[6] *bon-heur*: Ars 1 and Ars 2. *desir*: Gen.

[7] *Quelle*: BnF.

[8] *passe*: Gen.

La naturelle politique,
Est que tout vice estant esgal,
L'adultere est un petit mal,
555 Mais pour punir ceste coquette,
Il luy rend ce qu'elle luy preste,
Voilla les ieannins les sullys,
Les villeroys les sillerys,
Dont ce fier tyran de la france,
560 Consulte la rare prudence,
Si tu demande des herauts,
Qui nous deslivrent de nos maux
Les Brezay et les Meillerayes
Sont les medecins de nos playes,
565 Si tu veux des foudres de mars,
Qui servent de vivans rempars,
Coeslin dans la plaine campaigne
Sert plus qu'une haute montaigne
Courlay dans l'empire des flots,
570 Faict un grand rocher de son dos,
Ces deux bosses preservent[3] la france
De toute maligne influance,
Tous ses braves avanturiers,
Nous promettent mille lauriers
575 Ils outragent les capitaines,
Ils font des entreprises vaines,
Et quoy qu'ils craignent les hazars.
Ils veullent passer pour des Cezards,[4]
Mais qui regne sur les[5] finances,
580 Bullion dont les violences,
Sont le principal instrument,
De cet heureux gouvernement,
Le plus cruel monstre d'Affrique,
Est plus doux que ce frenetique,

---

[1] *du*: Ars 1, Ars 2, and RMS.

[2] *de cette intrigue*: Gen.

[3] *gardent*: Tab (1649) and RMS. *couvrent*: Gen.

[4] *pour soldarts*: Gen.

[5] *gouverne les*: Ars 2.

585 Qui triomphe de nos malheurs,
Qui s'engraisse de nos douleurs,
Qui par ces advis detestables
Rend tous les peuples miserables,
Qui par ses tiraniques loix,
590 Les faict pleurer d'estre François.
Qui surpasse[1] les bourreaux mesme,
Ce plaist dans leurs tourmens extremes
Qui d'un exil s'est trempé les[2] mains,
Dans le sang de cent mille humains;
595 Qui leur blessure rénouvelle,
Du fer[3] de sa plume cruelle,
Et rit en leur faisant souffrir,
Mille morts[4] avant que mourir,
Est il un merite si[5] rare,
600 Qui[6] puisse adoucir ce barbare,
Le grand Veimard et sa[7] valeur,
Peuvent-ils flechir ce voleur,
Il ne cognoist point de justice,
Que les fougues de son caprice,
605 Il outrage les officiers,
Il[8] gourmande les Chancelliers,
Armand soustient son insolence,
Volle avec luy toute la France,
Et pour confirmer les Edicts,
610 Rend les magistrats interdicts
Tous les François sont tributaires,
De ces deux horribles corsaires,
Jamais Pirates sur les mers,

---

[1] *surpassant*: Ars 1, Ars 2, and Gen.

[2] *Qui d'un exil trempe ses*: Tab (1649) and Ars 1. *Qui d'un œil sec trempe ses*: Gen.

[3] *fiel*: Gen.

[4] *maux*: Gen.

[5] *assez*: Ars 2.

[6] *Qu'il*: Ars 1.

[7] *Le grand renom ni la*: Gen.

[8] *Et*: Ars 1.

N'ont faict tant[1] de larcins divers
615 Ce nautonnier à ce pillotte,
Rapeinnt[2] avec une flotte,
Cornuel meut les avirons,
Et vaut luy seul trente larrons,[3]
Bullion par ses avarices,[4]
620 Entretient son luxe et son vice,
Ce gros Guillaume racourcy,
A tousjours le ventre farcy,
Et plain de potage et de graisses,
Baise ses imfames maistresses,[5]
625 Le gros coquet ce gros taureau,
Est son honneste macquereau,
Voila la fidelle peinture,
D'un avorton de la[6] nature,
D'un bacchus d'un pifre[7] d'un nain
630 D'un serpent enflé de venin,[8]
Que Louys d'un coup de tonnerre,
Doit exterminer de la terre,
PARIS pour illustre tombeau,
Luy prepare un sale Ruisseau,
635 Promet de longues funerailles,
A ses tripes et[9] ses entrailles,
Et s'oblige à graver son nom,
Sur les pilliers de montfaulcon
Il fera bien la mesme grace,
640 A un moreau qui le surpasse,
En blasphesmes et juremens,

49

---

[1] *N'ont tant fait*: Ars 1 and Ars 2.

[2] *Rapinant*: BnF, Duke, Tab (1649), and RMS. *Y rappine*: Gen.

[3] *Luy seul vaut trente larrons*: BnF and Duke.

[4] *son avarice*: Tab (1649) and Ars 2.

[5] *son infame maistresse*: Tab (1649), Ars 1, Ars 2, Gen, and RMS.

[6] *la* is missing in BnF and Duke.

[7] *pigmé*: Gen.

[8] *Vray successeur de Laretin*: Gen.

[9] *à*: BnF, Duke, and Ars 1.

        Et l'esgalle en debordemens,
        Ce magistrat est adultaire;
        Injuste fripon temeraire,
645   Et pour estre fils de Martin,
        N'est pas moins fils de putain,
        Dans Paris il vent[1] la justice:
        Il exerce encor la police,[2]
        Mais on y méprise sa voix,
650   Et l'on hait[3] ses injustes loix,
        Grand Senat tu hais tout de mesme
        Ce le Jay ce buffle supresme,
        Le chef honteux d'un noble corps,
        L'horreur des vivans[4] et des morts,
655   Cet infame qui sans naissance
        Sans probitè sans suffisance,
        Et sans avoir servy les Roys,
        Se voit sur le trosne des loix,
        Cet animal faict en Colosse,
660   Ce grand[5] ce vieux Rosse,
        Qui n'est bon que pour les harats,
        Et[6] pour ses amoureux combats,
        Qui dans maison rouge se pasme,
        En baisant une garce[7] infame
665   Qui parut mort entre ses bras,
        Qu'on trouva couché entre[8] ses dras,
        Qui dans cette extase brutalle
        Approcha de l'onde infernalle,

---

[1] *tient*: Gen.

[2] *qua bon droit on nomme injustice*: Gen.

[3] *fuit*: Ars 2.

[4] *vivant*: BnF.

[5] Followed by *puant, et*: Tab (1649) and RMS. This addition remedies the syllabic deficiency as does *ce gros, et* in Ars 1, *ce gros et* in Ars 2, and *et ce gros* in Gen, though BnF contains only two supplementary syllables with *ce gros*.

[6] *Que*: Ars 1.

[7] *grosse*: Gen.

[8] *en*: Tab (1649), which omits the superfluous syllable.

LE GOUVERNEMENT PRESENT

C'est pour¹ couronner son bon-heur
670   S'il mouroit en son lict² d'honneur,
Cet yvroigne n'a rien d'honneste³
Son ame est l'ame d'une beste,
Et n'a que de lasches desirs,
Et rien que sales plaisirs,⁴
675   Sa maison est une retraicte
Ou loge l'ardeur indiscrette,
Ou regnent venus et Bacchus
Des macquereaux et des cocus
Cursi⁵ d'Herbelay et de Courville,
680   Dont il voit la femme et⁶ fille,
Il se plaist d'estre yvre souvent,
C'est alors qu'il paroist sçavant,   *52*
Et que ceint d'un laurier bacchique
Il discours de la republique,
685   Et⁷ la d'Herbelay et de la Tour,
De leur beauté de son amour,
Il vieillit sans devenir sage,
Il fuit tousjours le mariage,
Il estoit gendre et tres-meschant,
690   Du grand capitaine marchand,
Il estoit civile⁸ à sa femme
Brusloit⁹ d'une impudique flamme,
Elle de sa part l'encernoit,
Prodigue vers qui luy donnoit¹⁰

---

¹ *Et creut*: Ars 1 and Ars 2.

² *en ce lit*: BnF and Duke. *dans ce lit*: Ars 2.

³ *honnesteté*: BnF and Duke.

⁴ The two lines of this couplet begin with *Il n'a que* in Ars 1 and only the first one in Ars 2.

⁵ *Cugy*: Tab (1649) and RMS. *Cuigy*: Ars 1, Ars 2, and Gen.

⁶ *ou la*: Ars 1; *et la*: Ars 2 and Gen.

⁷ *De*: Ars 1, Ars 2, Gen, and RMS.

⁸ *cruel*: Gen.

⁹ *Brûlant*: Ars 1, Ars 2, and Gen.

¹⁰ There are four additional lines in Ars 1 following this line, which are not present in the printed versions: 'Elle aymoit dessus sa

695	Ce Boucquin pour nourrir son vice,
	Vend publiquement la Justice,
	D'Herbelay la mise¹ à l'encamp,
	Tire huict mil escus par an,
	Fais ordonner ce qu'on demande
700	Pourveu qu'on luy porte une offrande
	Se vante parmy les tailleurs,²
	Qu'elle est grosse de procureurs,
	Qu'elle enfantera vingt officiers,³
	Le digne prix de ses services,⁴
705	Que s'il est sale en ses amours
	Il est plus sot en ses⁵ discours,
	Ses harangues sont pedantesques
	Et plaine⁶ d'infinie grotesques,
	Empruntant tousjours son Rollet,
710	D'un Esprit pedant et follet,
	Il ayme si fort la nature,
	Qu'il parle au Roy d'agriculture,
	De bien semer de bien planter,
	Desmonder clacquer hanter,
715	Il discours tout⁷ d'un art si rare,
	Que dans les jardins il s'esgare,
	Traitte Louis¹ de Vigneron,

53

---

poitraine / Une piece de forme humaine, / Et ne desiroit pour tombeau / Que celuy dont rit Isabeau'. Ars 2 and Gen include these lines though the second additional line reads 'Une forme de chair humaine'. Gen gives 'armoit' instead of 'aymoit' in the first additional line. Tall also contains these lines and adds as a marginal note: 'une epig. du Cabinet satirique – monter dessus et puis escrire / Icy dessous gist Isabeau', fol. 33ᵛ.

¹ *met*: Ars 1 and Gen.

² *railleurs*: Ars 1, Ars 2, and Gen.

³ *Offices*: Tab (1649), Ars 1, and Gen.

⁴ *Juste prix de ses bons services*: Ars 2. *Pour punir tous nos malefices*: Gen.

⁵ *Il est fat en ses grans*: Ars 1. *Il est fat en ses*: Ars 2. *Il lest deffaict en ses*: Gen.

⁶ *Si remplies*: Ars 2.

⁷ *tant*: Ars 1, Ars 2, and Gen.

Le Gouvernement Present

       Adjouste ce tiltre à son nom,
       Compare un grand arbre à la France
720 Et ce bel astre à sa prudence,
       Qu'il[2] sçait esbranler les estats,
       Qu'il sçait couper les potentasts,
       Qu'il sçait anter guerre sur guerre,
       Qu'il[3] sçait bien cultiver les terres,
725 Aisi ce sublime orateur,
       Ce sage et delicat flatteur,
       Ce Satyre à la gorge ouverte,
       Ce beau porteur de cire verte,
       Cet Athée ennemy de Dieu,
730 S'est fait amy de Richelieu,
       Il est traistre à sa compagnie,
       Les[4] soubmet à la tyrannie,
       Denonce les plus gueux,[5]
       Excite Richelieu contre eux,
735 Et fait qu'il ordonne un supplice,
       Pour le courage et la Justice,
       Il[6] bannit les bons magistrats,
       Comme perturbateurs d'estats,
       Introduit par toute la France
740 Le crime de leze Eminence,
       Vange avec moins de cruauté
       Celuy de leze Majesté,
       Il fait reverer sa personne,
       Plus que Louis[7] et sa couronne
745 Par ses services[8] dignes de feu

---

[1] *le Roy*: Gen.

[2] *Qui*: Ars 1 and Ars 2 (and for the following three lines).

[3] *Qui*: BnF and Duke.

[4] *La*: Ars 1 and Ars 2. *Le*: Gen.

[5] *genereux*: Tab (1649), Ars 1, Ars 2, Gen, and RMS. The original rendering is probably a misreading of a contraction in a manuscript.

[6] *Qu'il*: Ars 2.

[7] *loix*: Gen.

[8] *ces crimes*: Ars 1. *Pour les crimes*: Gen.

Il a gaigné le cordon bleu,
Cordon qui servira de corde,
Si on luy fait misericorde,
Car la rouë à peine[1] est le prix
750 Des attentats qu'il a commis,
Armand a ces ames si pures,
Dispanse les magistratures,
Et faict regner sur les subjets
Ceux qui sont dignes de gibets,
755 C'est[2] la conduite admirable,
De ce ministre incomparable,
De ce capitan sourcilleux,
De ce Matamore orgueilleux,
De ce jeune hercule des Gaulles,
760 Qui les porte sur ses espaules,
Qui soubs ce faix n'est jamais las,
Qui n'a point besoing d'un Athlas,
Et qui dessus sa maigre eschine
Veut porter la ronde machine,
765 Ce Courtisan subtil et vain,[3]
A fait le Politique en vain,
Les fautes sont toutes visibles
Et ne nous sont que trop sensibles,[4]
Les premieres prosperitez
770 L'ont signalé de tous costez,
Mais les avantures sinistres[5]
L'ont mis au rang des sots ministres,
Et est[6] que dans les grands mal-heurs
Que l'on reconnoist les grands cœurs
775 L'esclat des heureuses fortunes,
Rend rares les ames commune,[7]

---

[1] *peyne*: BnF and Duke.

[2] This is followed by an additional word, *là*, in Ars 1, Ars 2, and Gen.

[3] *fin*: Ars 2.

[4] *nuisibles*: Gen.

[5] *sinestres*: BnF and Duke.

[6] *Ce n'est*: Ars 2.

[7] *Rend rare les ames communes*: BnF and Duke.

> Et les ouvrages du hazard,
> Passent pour chef-d'œuvre de l'art,
> Tout pilote est bon sans orage
> 780 L'imprudent alors paroist sages:
> Mais il se monstre ingenieux
> Lors que les flots montent aux cieux,
> Quand Dieu punissant[1] l'infidelle,
> Quand il foudroioit les rebelles,
> 785 Quand il vangeroit le droict des Rois
> Quand il combatoit pour les loix,
> Quand il chatioit la Savoye,
> Quand il nous la donnoit en proye,
> Quand il se servoit de nos mains,
> 790 Pour delivrer les souverains:
> Armand estoit esgal aux Anges,
> Et les flateurs[2] dans les loüanges
> Donnoit au bras de Richelieu
> Les miracles du droict[3] de Dieu,
> 795 Non que par ses soins et ses veilles,
> Il n'ait eu part à ces merveilles,
> Et que Dieu n'ait des instrumens,
> Des plus fameux evenemens:
> Mais la divine providence,
> 800 Conduisoit sa foible prudence,
> La force des astres[4] divains,
> Mettoit la force en ces mains
> Dieu regloit les causes secondes
> Et calmoit la fureur des ondes,
> 805 Il leur faisoit baiser alors,
> Nostre digue ainsi que leurs bords,
> Et la providence eternelle,
> La destruict apres La Rochelle,
> Donnons-en la louange à Dieu,[5]

---

[1] *punissoit*: Ars 1, Ars 2, Gen, and RMS.

[2] *Autheurs*: Ars 2 and Gen.

[3] *doigt*: Tab (1649), Ars 1, Ars 2, and RMS. *ce que lon doit tenir*: Gen.

[4] *arrets*: Ars 1 and Ars 2.

[5] Lines 809–10 are missing from BnF, Ars 2, and Gen.

810 Non pas au nom¹ de Richelieu,
Dans Ré dans Cazal et Mantouë
Qui n'a point veu que Dieu se jouë
Des vains et des ambitieux,
Qui pensent escheller les Cieux,
815 Lors que le seigneur des batailles,
Attaque ou deffend des murailles,
Les foibles domptent les puissans,
Et les Nains vainquent les Geans,
Soubs luy les hommes obeissent,
820 Soubs luy les elemens flechissent,
Il retient le cours du soleil,
Il destourne un sage Conseil,
Il glace de peur les armées,
Il les rend d'ardeur enflammées,
825 Il meut leur corps,² pousse leur bras,
Dresse leurs mains regle leur pas,
Et par des detours invisibles,
Conduit les ouvrages sensibles,
Armant faisoit fleurir les lys,
830 Quand Dieu perdoit nos³ ennemis,
Armant ne trouve⁴ point d'obstacles,
Quand Dieu nous faisoit des⁵ miracles,
Mais quand il a pris pour object,
D'estre plustost Roy que subject,
835 De faire adorer sa prudence,
Plus que sa Royale puissance,
D'estre le tyran des François,
Et le⁶ fleau des plus grands Roys,
D'eterniser dedans la terre,
840 Le triste flambeau de la guerre,
De violer tous les traictez,

---

¹ *bras*: Ars 1.

² *cœurs*: Ars 1, Ars 2, and Gen.

³ *leurs*: Ars 1 and Ars 2.

⁴ *trouvoit*: Ars 2.

⁵ *Quand Dieu produisoit ces*: Gen.

⁶ *D'estre*: Ars 1 and Ars 2.

De voler toutes les Citez,[1]
D'usurper toute la Loraine,
D'emprisonner sa souveraine,
845 De separer ce que Dieu joinct,[2]
De mespriser ce qu'il enjoinct,
De rendre l'Eglise asservie,
De ne luy laisser que la vie,
De la faire esclave des Roys,
850 De ravir ses biens et ses droicts,
De dissoudre un sainct mariage,
Pour faire un ridicule ouvrage,
Pour joindre avec des jeunes lys,
Des grateculs et seps[3] viellis,
855 Pour mesler le sang de la france
Au vil sang de son Eminence,
Pour faire Reyne Gombalet
La veufve d'un pauvre Argoulet,
La posterité d'un notaire,
860 L'hermaphrodite voluntaire,
L'amante et l'amant de vigean,[4]
La princesse au teint de saffran,[5]
La Nayade, qui dans sa chambre
Tient une fontaine d'eau d'ambre,
865 Et le chaste Dieu des jardins,
Parmy ses lys et ses jasmins,
Quand renversant le cours des choses
Il a faict des metamorphoses,
A rendu vierge combalet,
870 La femme d'un maistre mulet,
Alors les celestes puissances,
N'ont pû souffrir ses insolences,

---

[1] Gen ends at this point with a full stop.

[2] The bottom of Hague is so tightly cut that this verse is almost entirely lacking save for a small portion of the top of the letters (but still with not displaying enough text to be able discern any of the words).

[3] *secs et*: Ars 1 and Ars 2.

[4] *La main de la main du vigent*: BnF.

[5] *s'affrant*: BnF.

On a veu cet audacieux
Hay de la terre et des cieux,
875 On a veu ses palmes fanées
Depuis le cours de trois années,
Dieu ne reglant plus ses desseins,
Ils ont paru des songes vains,[1]
Car[2] vouloit vaincre l'Allemagne,
880 Et dompter la maison d'Espagne,
En laissant perir nos soldats
Victorieux aux pays bas,
En consumant[3] l'or des finances,
Dans l'esclat des magnificences,[4]
885 En prodiguant pour ses duchesses
De quoy munir ses forteresses,
En amassant de grands tresors
Dedans le havre et autres ports,
En laissant dans les autres villes
890 Des troupes foibles et debiles,
Ayant plus de[5] soing des prisons,
Que des forts[6] et des garnisons,
C'estoit un dessein chimerique
Digne de ce grand politique,
895 D'un heros au dessus des noms
Du Roy des petites maisons,
Ses visions creuses et folles
Ont mis les forces espagnoles
Dans le sein de l'estat françois,
900 Et pres du trosne de nos Roys,
La france a recu mille atteintes,
Ses douleurs esgallent ses craintes,
Tous ses membres sont languissant,

---

[1] *Il trouve que ses songes sont vains*: Ars 2.

[2] *Il*: BnF.

[3] *commuant*: BnF.

[4] Two additional lines follow in Ars 1: 'En faisant des profusions / A toutes ces collations'.

[5] *En ayant plus*: Ars 1 and Ars 2.

[6] *armées*: Ars 2.

La guerre a perclus¹ tous ses sens,
905　Et la viguëur de sa noblesse
N'est plus aujourd'hui que foiblesse
Elle est malade en tout son corps
Ne peut faire de grands efforts,
A besoin que la main divine,
910　Le preserve de sa ruine,
Et ne doit demander à dieu,
Que la perte de Richelieu,
Car si le Ciel benit nos larmes,²
S'il seche le cours de nos armes,³
915　Et qu'Armand possede⁴ Louys,
Par ses mensonges inouis,
Il reprendra sa tirannie,
Il redoublera sa manie,
Il banira les plus puissans,
920　Il perdra les plus innocens,
Il concoit desja des vengeances,
Il prepare des violences,
Ce lyon bat desja son flanc,
Son cœur est alteré de sang,
925　Ses yeux estincellans de rage,
Sa gueulle s'apreste au carnage,
Faut-il que⁵ combattant pour nous,
Nous nous exposions à ses coups,
Et qu'en deffendant nos murailles,
930　Ce serpent ronge nos entrailles,
Faut-il qu'en asseurant nos biens,
Nous nous asseurions nos liens,
Faut-il qu'en gardant nostre maistre,
Nous gardions ce barbare Prestre,
935　Et qu'esclaves comme devant
Nous nous perdions en nous sauvant
Grand Roy banny par ta puissance,

---

¹ *perdu*: BnF.

² *armes*: Ars 2.

³ *larmes*: Ars 2.

⁴ This is followed by *de* in BnF.

⁵ *qu'en*: Ars 1 and Ars 2.

La servitude de la France,
Chasse l'orgueilleux potentat,
940 Et le demon de ton estat,
Ton triomphe sera funeste,
Si ce cruel monstre nous reste,
Ouvre les yeux, arme ton bras,
Pour mettre deux tyrans à bas,
945 Couronne les faicts de la Gloire,
Qu'auroit ceste[1] double victoire,
Faicts punir[2] l'autheur de nos maux,
L'autheur de mille et mille impots,
Faictes[3] que la Justice divine
950 Accable ce neuveau conchine,
Laisse deschirer à Paris,
Le plus meschant des favoris,
Et fuys en sauvant la Couronne,
Cet oracle de la Sorbonne,
955 Son sepulchre en vain sera beau,
Les tyrans n'ont point de tombeau,[4]

Imprimé à Envers,   FIN.

---

[1] *Une*: BnF.

[2] *Fay périr*: Ars 1.

[3] *Fay*: Ars 1.

[4] Gouv contains a supplementary terminal couplet: 'L'on verra qu'en l'air à la fin, / Son grand pouvoir prendra fin.'

NOTES TO THE TEXT

6–7 Three cardinals are named here as exemplars of the Roman purple: Georges d'Amboise (1460–1510) was a leading Renaissance prelate and minister of state to Louis XII; Gil Alvarez Carillo d'Albornoz (1300–1367), was a Spanish-born ecclesiastic who served as papal legate in the Italian peninsula under Popes Innocent VI and Urban V; Francisco Jiménez de Cisneros (1436–1517) was a Spanish reformer and statesman. As well as all three cardinals having been involved closely in political developments, Jiménez was associated with the foundation of the University of Alcalá de Henares, which he funded, much in the same way that Richelieu was the patron of the Sorbonne's new structure. Hay du Chastelet accused Morgues of having shown disrespect towards the Sacred College of Cardinals through unfavourable comparisons of Richelieu with Amboise and Jiménez, which indicates that these two figures were perhaps familiar elements of the polemic against Richelieu (*Jugement sur la Préface et diverse pieces que le cardinal Richelieu prétend de faire servir à l'histoire de son credit* (1635), in *Diverses pieces pour la defense de la Royne Mere du roy tres-chrestien Louis XIII*, pp. 512–90 (p. 578)). Favourable comparisons were also made, such as Adam Scaliger's *La vertu resuscitée, ou la vie du Cardinal Albornoz, surnommé pere de l'Eglise* (Paris: Toussainct du Bray, 1629), which the author dedicates to Richelieu 'Puisqu'il y a donc tant de resemblance et de conformité entre vous deux' ('Epistre', sig. [a8]^r). See also Gilbert Du Verdier, *Histoire des Cardinaux illustres qui ont esté employez dans les affaires d'Estat* (Paris: Jean-Baptiste Loyson, 1653), in particular pp. 200–15 on Amboise; pp. 216–33 on Albornoz; and pp. 307–27 on Jiménez.

12 *trente autheurs celebres*: A hyperbolic allusion to the Cinq Auteurs, a group of five writers handpicked by Richelieu to work under his auspices as a collective. The group consisted of: François Le Métel de Boisrobert, Pierre Corneille, Guillaume Colletet, Jean Rotrou, and Claude de L'Estoile.

15 *vos debiles paupieres*: a likely influence for this imagery comes from a poetic translation of Psalm 138 provided by Marin Mersenne and dating from the same period as the *Miliade*, in which the psalmist speaks of the sun's glare: 'Je baisse en t'admirant mes debiles paupieres', *Harmonie universelle, contenant la theorie de la pratique de la musique* (Paris: Sébastien Cramoisy, 1636), p. 88.

36 *sa clemence*: on Richelieu's conflicting duties as statesmen and ecclesiastic to discipline and absolve, see Françoise Hildesheimer, who concludes 'dans le système de Richelieu, c'est la volonté politique exprimée dans le châtiment qui doit être manifestée, non la clémence comme dans le cas d'Auguste vis-à-vis de Cinna', 'Pardonner ou châtier? Richelieu ou l'impossible clémence', in *Le Pardon*, ed. by Jacqueline Hoareau-Dodinau et al, Cahiers de l'Institut d'Anthropologie Juridique, 3 (Limoges: Presses Universitaires de Limoges, 1999), pp. 425–63 (p. 456).

37 The plural of *freres* refers to Gaston d'Orléans, brother to Louis XIII, as well as to this monarch's illegitimate half-brothers, César de Bourbon, duc de Vendôme (1594–1665) and Alexandre de Bourbon, chevalier de Vendôme (1598–1629), who were arrested and imprisoned in 1626 after plotting against Richelieu. César was released in 1630 but Alexandre died in prison the previous year. Gaston d'Orléans (1608–1660), known as Monsieur, was heir presumptive until the birth of the future Louis XIV in 1638; his two half-brothers had aligned themselves with his cause against Richelieu. Tallemant des Réaux comments that the prelate 'haïssoit Monsieur; et craign[oit], veû le peu de santé que le Roy avoit, qu'il ne parvinst à la couronne', *Hist*, I, 236.

38 'Mr de Marillac', Tall, fol. 23^r. Louis de Marillac (1572–1632) was a distinguished soldier who served under Henri IV and then played a leading role in the taking of La Rochelle for which he was promoted to the rank of *maréchal de France* in 1629. As a result of the close association of both him and his brother, Michel, with the *dévot* party and their allegiances to Marie de Médicis and Monsieur, they became the principal victims of the Day of Dupes, being arrested shortly thereafter. Louis was executed in 1632 after a show trial which drew extensive disapproval and Michel died in confinement at Châteaudun: '[J]e m'asseure que tu ne vivrois pas en repos [...] tant que tu auras la puissance de faire trencher la teste à un Mareschal de France', *L'Esprit bien-heureux du Mareschal de Marillac*, p. 24. Yves-Marie Bercé comments that, in respect to legal process, 'Sans respecter les formes, sans réunir un acte d'accusation convaincant, la commission condamna le maréchal à mort', 'Richelieu: la maîtrise de l'histoire' p. 99. The pluralized *Mareschaux* further alludes to Henri II de Montmorency (1595–1632) who joined the cause of Monsieur in 1632 and headed a rebel army which was defeated at the Battle of Castelnaudary after which he was captured, tried, and executed for *lèse-majesté*. There was

widespread disquiet at the ease with which the Cardinal had two leading soldiers executed in the same year. Moreover, another *maréchal*, François de Bassompierre (1579–1646), had been languishing in the Bastille since 1631.

39 Tallemant lists a total of five women who were exiled because of their scheming against the prelate: 'La R. Mere Me de Conty M^e d'Elbeuf Me de Chevreuse Me de Guise', Tall, fol. 23^r. Marie de Médicis (1575–1642) was forced to flee when her position became untenable after her unsuccessful attempt to remove Richelieu in 1630. She spent the rest of her life in exile from the court, first at Compiègne, and thereafter out of France in Brussels, Amsterdam, and Cologne. Associates of the Queen Mother suffered a similar fate. Louise Marguerite de Lorraine, princesse de Conti (1588–1631), was lady-in-waiting to as well as friend and confidant of Marie de Médicis and loyally followed her into exile. Catherine-Henriette de Bourbon, duchesse d'Elbeuf (1596–1663), was the naturalized daughter of Henri IV and was exiled in 1631 with her husband as a result of their support for Monsieur. Marie de Rohan, duchesse de Chevreuse (1600–1679), was linked to many conspiracies against Richelieu's ministry as well as being staunchly allied to Monsieur and being a former lover of Charles IV, duc de Lorraine, Monsieur's host in exile. The duke obtained her return to France after her involvement in a failed coup to replace Louis XIII with his brother in 1626. Two duchesses of Guise went into exile during the 1630s: Catherine de Clèves, duchesse de Guise (1548–1633), returned to her estates et Eu following the disgrace of her daughter, the princesse de Conti mentioned above. Marie de Lorraine, duchesse de Guise (1615–1688), grand-daughter of Catherine, left France for Florence in 1634 with members of her family. Tallemant does not mention the duchesse de Lesdiguières and the duchesse d'Ornano who were also banished by Richelieu. The fact that there are eight possible candidates for the *Quatre Princesses exilées* sharply demonstrates both the level of opposition to Richelieu at the highest levels of the nobility and within the royal family itself as well as the efficiency with which he was able to defuse their influence.

41 Reynald Abad argues that the revolt of *magistrats* at the Cour des Aides in 1631, ostensibly over the increase in wine duty but in reality concerning their ancient privileges, might be considered a forerunner to the civil war which would break out in the next decade: 'Une première Fronde au temps de Richelieu? L'émeute parisienne des 3–4 février 1631 et ses suites', *DSS*, 218 (2003), 39–70. The

rebellious officials were suspended from office and one of their number, Jean Baudoin, was briefly imprisoned. This allusion could equally refer to the imprisonment of six members of the Parlement in 1636, discussed in the note to line 737.

41–44 With the naming of *magistrats*, *grands Seigneurs*, *gardes des Sceaux*, and *gentil-hommes*, the author encompasses the gamut of the *noblesse d'épée* and the *noblesse de robe*, the traditional structure of the state, in particular the administration of justice, which is being undermined by the Cardinal through unjust means.

43 'Chasteauneuf', Tall, fol. 23ʳ. Charles de l'Aubespine, marquis de Châteauneuf (1580–1653) was appointed *garde des sceaux* in 1630 after a diplomatic career, a position he held until his fall from grace in 1633 when he conspired against Richelieu with the duchesse de Chevreuse and was then imprisoned in the château d'Angoulême for a decade. Tallemant does not mention Michel de Marillac (1563–1632) who held the post before Châteauneuf following the disgrace of Étienne d'Aligre in 1626 because of his fidelity to Monsieur. He lost the office following his arrest in 1630 and died during his imprisonment.

45–46 'In a letter from Châteauneuf to Richelieu dated 19 July 1632, the official complains: 'La Bastille est trop pleine de prisonniers. Il seroit besoin de l'en dellivrer et en mettre quelques'uns au loing. Cela ne se peult faire qu'estant prèz de nous', *La Correspondance du cardinal de Richelieu*, ed. Souleyreau, pp. 339–41 (p. 340). In an ironic twist of fate, Châteauneuf ended up in the prison only six months after making these remarks.

81 'Le Chevallier du Guet', Tall, fol. 24ʳ. Louis Testu, seigneur de Villers-Adam et de Frouville (d. 1637), was *chevalier du guet de la ville de Paris*, whose functions made him responsible for the city's safety, a position which he took over from his father, together with the governorship of the Bastille, in 1603. He was also *conseiller d'État* from 1613 to 1637. The following lines (82–92) refer to his oversight of the prison and the fact that he was delegated to implement the order of execution of Louis de Marillac; it was Testu who accompanied him to the scaffold. See *Le Mercure François*, 18 (1632), 88–92.

82 In a similar vein and published at the same time as the *Miliade*, late in 1636, Mathieu de Morgues declares: 'L'on ne te fera pas tant d'honneur aprés ta mort de te donner la charge de grand Prevost du

diable', *Catholicon Français, ou plaintes de deux chasteaux, rapportées par Renaudot, maistre du bureau d'adresse*, in *Pièces curieuses en suite de celles du sieur de S. Germain*, 3 vols ('Sur la coppie imprimée à Anvers': [n.pub.], 1644), II, 41–116 (p. 110). The *Miliade* takes this further, for if Testu is the *prevost* then it is Richelieu himself who is Lucifer.

94 Charles de Machault, seigneur d'Arnouville (1587–1667) rose to become *maître des requêtes* in 1619 and was appointed *intendant de justice et finances* of Languedoc in 1629. He was 'surnommé coupteste pour avoir esté emploié par le Cardinal de Richelieu à plusieurs procès criminels', *Lettres et mémoires adressés au chancelier Séguier (1633–1649)*, ed. by Roland Mousnier, 2 vols (Paris: PUF, 1964), II, 1217. Isaac de Laffemas (1587–1657) became *maître des requêtes* in 1624 and was appointed *intendant* of Champagne in 1630 and in Limoges in 1634. He was known as the 'bourreau de Richelieu' and Mongrédien glosses that 'Laffemas joue le role de policier dans tous les complots qui vont s'ourdir contre l'Éminentissime', *Isaac de Laffemas*, p. 67. Richard Bonney cites these two men as exemplifying the Cardinal's policy of installing hand-picked *intendants* with the aim of 'discouraging local leagues and policing the lesser nobility', *Society and Government in France under Richelieu and Mazarin, 1624–61* (Basingstoke: Macmillan, 1988), p. 153.

98 Mongrédien remarks that 'Laffemas voit tout, poursuit avec acharnement les ennemis, si nombreux alors, du Cardinal, et les condamne à mort sans sourciller', *Isaac de Laffemas*, p. 77.

111 The Scythians were a byword for savagery and the term regularly features in early modern theatre, both French and English, to epitomize barbarity. One of their reputed customs was to drink the blood of their enemies, which was alleged to keep them focused and sober. See Monica Matei-Chesnoiu, *Early Modern Drama and the Eastern European Elsewhere: Representations of Liminal Locality in Shakespeare and his Contemporaries* (Madison: Fairleigh Dickinson University Press, 2009), p. 89.

119 Next to the name of Castrain, Tallemant adds the following note: 'Je ne scache personne de ce nom qu'un vieil Huguenot qui ayant fait un livre p^r reponse a Mlle de Gournay intitulé remerciement des beurriers ou il disoit quelquechose contre Mr de Luynes, fut pendu plustost p^r cela que pour crime qu'on luy imposa d'avoir deux femmes a la fois. Icy il veut attribuer cela au Card qui lors evesque

de Lusson estoit secret' d'Estat', Tall, fol. 25'. Richelieu headed this diocese from 1606 to 1623 and the work in question is almost certainly Marie de Gournay's *Égalité des hommes et des femmes* ([n.p.]: [n.pub.], 1622). Gournay, Michel de Montaigne's protégé, enjoyed Richelieu's particular protection. The inclusion of this name demonstrates that the author of the *Miliade* had been meticulous in researching Richelieu's background, a fact that would not have been lost on the prelate. The Marillac mentioned in this line is undoubtedly Michel, given the close involvement of Laffemas and Machault in his condemnation. François de Rochechouart, Chevalier de Jars (1595–1670), was incriminated because of his liaison with Châteauneuf and the duchesse de Chevreuse. Laffemas personally supervised his interrogation and trial in his capacity as *intendant* of Champagne in 1633 and Madame de Motteville comments on the severity and intensity of the questioning that he endured under the official: 'il le menace, il l'interroge, et fait tout ce qu'une ame pleine de lâcheté est capable de faire', *Mémoires pour servir à l'histoire d'Anne d'Autriche, épouse de Louis XIII, roi de France*. 5 vols (Amsterdam: François Changuion, 1723), I, 67. He received a stay of execution while on the scaffold and on the verge of receiving his capital sentence. After more time confined in the Bastille, he eventually ended up being rehabilitated under Mazarin's ministry owing in large part to his favour with Anne of Austria.

127 *molocle*: In Greek mythology, Molossus, son of Pyrrhus and Andromache, was the ancestor of the Molossians, an ancient Greek tribe inhabiting Epirus renowned for the fighting dogs they kept and bred.

131 *vieux tyran des Arsacides*: a reference to the Arsacid or Parthinian Empire established in the 3rd century BC. It is unclear which leader is referred to here, though it is possibly a conflation with the Seleucid king Antiochus IV Epiphanes (215–164 BC) who persecuted the Jews and traditional religious practice, looming large in the Book of Machabees.

133 Phalaris was the tyrant of the Sicilian province of Acragas in the 6th century BC. His reputed excesses included cannibalism and disposing of his enemies in a brazen bull.

137 As well as the deadly qualities of its gaze – and one cannot help but think of the steely expression of Richelieu in Philippe de Champaigne's portraits (such as the one used on this book's cover) – the basilisk was a Christian symbol of sin and the Devil; see

Laurence A. Breiner, 'The Basilisk', in *Mythical and Fabulous Creatures: A Source Book and Research Guide*, ed. by Malcolm South (New York: Greenwood, 1987), pp. 113–22 (p. 119).

163 This reference to Judas betraying Christ deftly combines the social custom of kissing with the liturgical kisses of the rite of peace during High Mass and the ceremonial *solita oscula* or customary kisses performed during offices.

186 This may be compared with Beys's 'Sonnet, sur la maladie de Monseigneur le Cardinal de Richelieu', in which the poet alludes to an internal struggle involving Richelieu's body and soul; see *Les Œuvres poétiques de Beys*, p. 22.

190 *Turlupin*: 'On a appellé de ce nom un Comedien fameux de Paris, dont le talent étoit de faire rire par de meschantes pointes et equivoques qu'on a appellées *Turlupinades*', *DU*, III, sig. [eeee4]^v.

194 Mæcenas (70–8 BC) was a favourite of Augustus and famed for his patronage and protection of the arts and artists. Furetière notes that Cesare Caporali wrote a 'joli Poëme burlesque' on this figure (*c.* 1605), which makes him suitable for the *Miliade*'s satirical tone (*DU*, II, sig. nnn3^r). On the Cardinal's sponsorship of artistic endeavour, see Marc Fumaroli, 'Richelieu, patron des arts', in *Richelieu: l'art et le pouvoir*, ed. by Hilliard Todd Goldfarb (Montreal: Musée de beaux-arts de Montréal, 2002), pp. 15–47 (particularly pp. 33–37).

203 *ses comedies*: a reference to *La Comédie des Tuileries* which was published in 1638 but was being performed in 1636; as Couton notes, 'on comprend mal le pluriel "ses comédies"', since only this one play had appeared at that point, *Richelieu et le théâtre*, p. 78n.

207–24 These lines constitute an invective against France's participation in the Thirty Years War. The taxes mentioned in line 209 were levied and raised because of the financial burden of the war. As Bonney remarks, '[t]his increased fiscal burden was one of the crucial factors in opposition to the regime', *Society and Government*, p. xiii. However, while this section speaks of the increase in taxation, Ranum underlines that there is no evidence that Richelieu or the ministers did in actuality introduce new tax schemes: 'they were content to push the old ones to extreme limits and to revive old rights that had been dropped in periods of weak central government', *Richelieu and the Councillors*, p. 137.

228 Pierre Le Messier *dit* Bellerose (1592–1670), was principal actor at the Hôtel de Bourgogne from 1635 to 1647.

231 'Non-seulement il assistoit avec plaisir à toutes les Comédies nouvelles; mais encore il étoit bien aise d'en conférer avec les Poëtes, de voir leur dessein en sa naissance, et de leur fournir lui-même des sujets', Paul Pellisson-Fontanier, *Histoire de l'Académie française*, rev. Pierre-Joseph d'Olivet, 2 vols (Paris: Jean-Baptiste Coignard, 1729), I, 88–89.

232 The minor border fortress of La Capelle in Picardy was captured by joint Spanish and Bavarian forces in July 1636 as part of a successive incursion into French territory, including Soissons and Le Catelet. La Capelle was taken with minimal resistance, leading Morgues to claim that its governor had been deceived by Richelieu's envoys, *Diverses pieces pour la defense de la Royne Mere*, p. 63.

233 François Le Métel de Boisrobert (1589–1662), son of a *procureur* of the Parlement de Rouen, came to Paris under the protection of Cardinal du Perron and took Holy Orders. He met Richelieu in 1623 and came to hold a special place in Richelieu's affections as a trusted confidant; he was a member of the Cinq Auteurs and was one of the founding members of the Académie Française. Tallemant remarks on his ability to help pacify the Cardinal's mercurial moods: 'Il luy prenoit assez souvent des melancolies si fortes, qu'il envoyoit chercher Boisrobert et les autres qui le pouvoient divertir', *Hist*, I, 268.

236–43 On 18 January 1634, Richelieu delivered a *harangue* in the Paris Parlement in the presence of the King during which he attacked Monsieur's disobedience, and thus those members of the body which supported him and, in particular, the marriage that had been contracted without his brother's consent. Richelieu also robustly insisted that neither adversity nor age would make him leave office 'puis qu'il plaist au Roy se servir de moy au gouvernement de son Royaume, comme Dieu faict des causes secondes sans qu'il y en ait aucun besoin', *Harangue de Monsieur le Cardinal Duc de Richelieu, faite en Parlement, sa Majesté y estant presente* ([Paris]: [n.pub.], 1634), p. 15 (the mention of 'causes secondes' is possibly aped in line 803). According to Tallemant this speech 'fut assez longue, [et] fit bien du bruit', *Hist*, I, 269.

251–52 The successful outcome of the Battle of Avein (or Avins), in Liège, on 20 May 1635 was apparently unanticipated by

Richelieu. Tallemant adds: 'Les Espagnols au commencement de la Campagne de Corbie entrerent en faveur de l'Evesque du Liege aussy Archevesque de Cologne et frére du Duc de Baviere dans le Liege. Le C[ardinal] crût qu'ils y auroient de l'occupation p^r tout l'Esté car les Liegeois avoient pris les armes et mis 20000 hommes sur pied, et dans cette croyance songea a la conqueste de la Franche Comté tellement que l'Autheur devoit mettre que l'attaque du Liege fut p^r luy un piége', Tall, fol. 27^v. It was something of a bittersweet and short-lived victory for the French: 'The news of the victory caused huge enthusiasm in Paris, and generated unrealistic optimism about the likely success of the rest of the campaign. In fact the victory at Avein caused a breach between the victor, Brézé, and his co-commander Gaspard III de Coligny, maréchal de Châtillon, who considered that he and his army-corps had deliberately been sidelined to permit Brézé to gain the glory from the engagement. The resulting dissension between the French high command weakened the capacity to influence Frederik Hendrik, prince of Orange, after the meeting of the French and Dutch armies', Parrott, *Richelieu's Army*, p. 113.

255 The pillaging of towns by soldiers on both sides who had not received their wages became one of the war's defining and ugly features, as set out so vividly in many of Callot's etchings. One village on the Danube was pillaged a total of eighteen times within two years; Robert Bireley, *The Jesuits and the Thirty Years War: Kings, Courts, and Confessors* (Cambridge: Cambridge University Press, 2003), pp. 204–05.

283 In Greek mythology, the Nereides are fifty sea-nymphs charged with overseeing the ocean and protecting fishermen and travellers.

286 The Tritones are sea-centaurs or male deities. Together with the female Nereides, the Tritones serve under Poseidon.

296 'Gaulmin, un M[aitr]^e de req[uêtes]. On l'a appellé *virum supra titulos etc.*', Tall, fol. 27^v. This seems to have been a not uncommon contemporary quip, for Gilles Ménage 'dit plus d'une fois à ses amis en raillant, qu'il estoit *vir supra titulos*', *Journal des Savants*, 20 (1692), 545. Gilbert de Gaulmin, sieur de Montgeorges (1585–1665), became *maître de requêtes* in 1631 and eventually *doyen* of this body and was particularly reputed for his erudition.

303 *rodomontade*: according to Furetiére denotes 'Vanterie, ou menace vaine et sans fondement. C'est le proper des Capitans de faire des *rodomontades*', *DU*, III, sig. [2v3]^v.

307 *ses esclaves*: Morgues comments that 'Il faut estre son ennemi, ou son esclave', *La verité defendue*, p. 493.

312 *Riche esperance*: possibly refers to Richelieu's domination of the King, since the formulation is an uncommon one and seems to stem from the symbolism of the white lily, emblem of the monarchy. One commentator notes 'les Lys blancs nous marquent une riche Esperance', George Estienne Rousselet, *Le Lys sacré, justifiant le bon-heur de la pieté par divers Parangons du Lys avec les vertus, et les miracles du Roy S. Louys, et des autres Monarques de France* (Lyon: Louis Muguet, 1631), p. 75. It is not unlikely that this precise wording was used in sermons on the feast of St Louis and St Joseph to elucidate the spiritual meaning of the flower. This would certainly explain why this would exemplify Richelieu's 'plus froide arrogance' (l. 309).

315 These were two failed sieges which had long-term strategic consequences and, as Tallemant judges that they are mentioned 'par derision car on ne les put prendre', Tall, fol. 28^r. The prince de Condé failed to take Dôle in Franche-Comté in 1636 and the siege was lifted on 15 August. This was a heavy blow since its capture had been 'an absolute priority for the ministry, one to which all other military effort was subordinated'; Spanish soldiers advanced as a result and the French forces on the north-east frontier were gravely weakened, Parrott, *Richelieu's Army*, p. 119. Valenza, in Piedmont, was besieged by a French force led by Charles de Blanchefort, maréchael de Créqui, but the siege collapsed after only six days. Again, this failure meant a major reconfiguration of the campaign in north Italy, which had been intended to resist Hapsburg forces and had been carried out by the French in the hope that Italian princes would support the main burden of the war effort. Overall control of coalition forces in Italy was granted to the duke of Savoy, Vittorio Amadeo I, which antagonized Créqui, commander of the French troops, a soldier who did not enjoy the duke's confidence. Créqui would blame the duke for having connived the admission of a Spanish relief force. All in all, this not only necessitated new military planning but also created real and damaging suspicion among allied officers; see Parrott, *op. cit.*, pp. 118–19.

322 A fact of which the Cardinal's apologists were well aware, for example: 'Mais, Muses, un seul qui possede / Les qualitez d'un demy-Dieu, / L'incomparable RICHELIEU', Nicolas Faret, *Ode à Monseigneur le Cardinal duc de Richelieu* (Paris: Sebastien Cramoisy, 1633), p. 4. If Tallemant is to be believed, the potential rhyme was also not lost on the minister himself: 'On m'a assure que dans une epistre liminaire d'un livre qu'on luy desdioit, il avoit rayé *héros* pour mettre *demy-dieu*', *Hist*, I, 272.

328 According to the theory of the four humours, an excess of black bile resulted in a melancholic personality and symptoms included sickness and stomach problems, as was the case with Richelieu.

331 'aux hemoroids', Tall, fol. 28^r.

334 Bucephalus was Alexander the Great's famed stallion, ridden by him in battle and conquest. The image of the ecclesiastic on horseback, yet severely discomforted by haemorrhoids, imagining himself to be this celebrated hero has a decidedly Quixotic echo.

347 After the Battle of Avein, French forces had marched to Brussels but soon decamped to Louvain after meeting strong defences. This city was a symbolic target since it was the seat of the court in the Spanish Netherlands as well as the haven of many French dissenters to Richelieu's ministry, and war had formally been declared with Spain in this city on 19 May 1635 by a French royal herald.

349 The siege of Louvain of 1635 failed because of supply problems to the French forces as well as its robust defences. It had not originally been considered as a target for this very reason, but the failure to make any inroads in capturing Brussels resulted in a swift change of tactics. The naming of this and other sieges in the poem directly tackles the entire rationale of French military policy during the war: 'From 1635 until 1642 the French war-effort was conceived in terms of sieges, and this had a profound effect on strategic thinking and military organization', Parrott, *Richelieu's Army*, p. 58.

353 *Le Moyne* denotes Père Joseph. François Le Clerc du Tremblay (1577–1638) who renounced his noble title of baron de Maffliers and his attendance at Court in order to enter the Capuchin branch of the Franciscan family, subsequently taking the name of Père Joseph on taking his vows. He became a close associate of and personal secretary to Richelieu, re-entering Court from 1624, in order to serve him, becoming *ministre d'État* in 1632. This partnership that has

been termed 'cette vie de couple exemplaire, historique, stupéfiante', Colette Piat, *Le Père Joseph: le maître de Richelieu* (Paris: Grasset, 1988), p. 99. François Sublet de Noyers (1588–1645), had familial associations with the Richelieu clan and was elevated to one of the four *intendants des finances* in 1628, *intendant de l'armée* in 1634–35, becoming *secrétaire d'État à la guerre* in February 1636, a post he held until 1643. There were four *secrétaires d'État* at any time, each one in charge of a separate portfolio: war; the King's household; foreign affairs; and Protestant affairs. Foreign affairs and war were catapulted into greater importance following France's declaration of war. Pierre Séguier (1588–1672) became *garde des sceaux* in 1633 and chancellor in 1635. The description of these three figures as *grands Oracles* in the previous line is piercingly sarcastic, since they were incontrovertibly the three most unpopular members of an unpopular government.

354 The elder Bouthillier referred to here is Claude (1581–1652), who hailed from an ancient aristocratic family in Angoulême. He was named *conseiller d'État* in 1619 and *secrétaire des commandements* de Marie de Médicis. His father, Denis, was *clerc* to François de La Porte, his grandfather, so there was a strong family connection to Richelieu. He became *secrétaire d'État* in 1628 and was named, together with Buillon, *surintendant des finances* in 1632, passing on his charge de secrétaire d'État to his son Léon. Madeleine Haehl judges that his promotion marks the entry of the prelate's creatures into high office: 'ce n'est pas un homme mais tout un clan, celui du cardinal, qui s'est introduit au sein du gouvernement', *Les Affaires étrangères au temps de Richelieu: le secretariat d'État, les agents diplomatiques (1624–1642)* (Brussels: Lang, 2006), p. 122. Léon Bouthillier (1608–1652), succeeded his father as *secrétaire d'État* with the portfolio for foreign affairs in 1632. In an unprecedented move, Claude retained a *droit d'intervention* over his son's post; see Yves Le Guillou, *Les Bouthillier, de l'avocat au surintendant (vers 1540–1650): l'histoire d'une ascension sociale et formation d'une fortune* (Angoulême: Société Archéologique et Historique de la Charente, 1999), pp. 138–39. Léon was known affectionately by Louis XIII and Richelieu as 'le Jeune', Moote, *Louis XIII*, p. 172. This was partly to distinguish him from his father; he was created comte de Chavigny which further helped differentiate the two men.

357 'Le Pere Joseph le Clerc, il estoit de Paris. Les Tremblays sont de cette famille', Tall, fol. 28^v. He is called *Le Moyne* twice in lines

353 and 357 and never by his name, which reinforces the incompatibility of his religious status with his high political influence.

358–60 Père Joseph facilitated and supported, through counsel and diplomacy, Richelieu's policy of alliance with Protestant nations which was anti-Habsburg and not based on any confessional lines. Despite the *Miliade*'s portrayal of the friar having no qualms about this manoeuvre, in reality and in private, the priest was cautious about these links: 'Sans les dénoncer ouvertement, le capuchin se méfiait des alliances que le roi avait contractées avec les princes protestants du Nord, alors que Richelieu cherchait à les entretenir et à les utiliser pour imposer la suprématie française aux autres nations', Benoist Pierre, *Le Père Joseph: l'éminence grise de Richelieu* (Paris: Perrin, 2007), p. 312.

363 An allusion to the stigmata borne by St Francis of Assisi, founder of his order, as well as to the Filles du Calvaires, popularly known as the *Calvairiennes*, a female order that Père Joseph founded in 1617 together with Antoinette d'Orléans-Longueville.

364 Père Joseph enjoyed the popular soubriquet of *Éminence grise* (his religious habit was grey), but Richelieu had actively been attempting to procure the red hat for his close associate since 1633, an effort that was bolstered by Louis XIII's official support in the following year. However, confirmation of the desired promotion did not happen until the friar was on his deathbed in 1638, owing to a combination of tension between the French Crown and the Holy See as well as a dispute about the numbers of Capuchin clergy within the French province who had a vote in the general order. See Raoul J. Mauzaize, 'La promotion cardinalice du Père Joseph de Paris et l'affaire des Custodes', *Études Franciscaines*, 16 (1966), 48–79.

372 *fameux mulet*: 'Il y avoit un Mulet expres p^r porter ses [fards?]. Depuis il eut un carosse', Tall, fol. 28^v. Tallemant expands on this anecdote in the *Historiette*: Père Joseph renounced the use of mules after he witnessed his own animal mounting Père Ange's horse during its rutting season, consequently 'Pour evister ce scandale, on luy donna un carrosse', I, 295.

375–78 'Un Colonel Escossois, fort brave homme. Il disoit Mr Joseph est un brave cavalier. Sur la carte le moine disoit en la monstrant du doit, Nous passerons cette riveriere. Mais vostre doit il n'est pas un pont, Mr Joseph, luy disoit-il. Il disoit encore que chaque balle avoit son [*sic*] commission, il en trouva une qui l'avoit p[lus]', Tall, fol. 28ᵛ. In the *Historiettes*, Tallemant names this colourful Scot as Hailbrun (I, 246). This was James Hepburn (*c.* 1598–1636), known as Hébron in France, who fought for Bohemia and Sweden, joining the French army in 1632. He was well known as a formidable solder and was killed in the siege of Saverne. See A. N. L. Grosjean, 'Hepburn, John (*c.*1598–1636)', in *Oxford Dictionary of National Biography* (Oxford: Oxford University Press, 2004) <http://www.oxforddnb.com/view/article/13005> [accessed 24 April 2010].

380 *cauterre*: Furetière lists this as a surgical term referring to a remedy (*DU*, I, sig. [rr4]ᵛ); it is accordingly used here to indicate that all of Père Joseph's worldly needs are being fulfilled.

386 'Le P Ange son secretaire', Tall, fol. 29ᵛ. A pun on the name of Père Joseph's secretary, Père Ange de Mortagne, who was his constant companion between 1619 and 1638.

392 An allusion to the biblical episode of Jacob's ladder (Genesis 28:10–12) which illustrates the friar's pride in not seeking divine assistance. There was an association with Jacob that is perhaps also raised here: when the General of his order summoned him to Rome in 1617 to clarify some aspects of his increasing involvement in the internal politics of France, the priest's apologists noted that the superior ending up blessing Père Joseph as Jacob had blessed Joseph above his siblings (Genesis 49:22–28); see Piat, *Le Père Joseph*, p. 110.

403 Antoine Adam convincingly proposes that the rumours about Séguier's supposedly humble lineage was based on Tallemant confusing two distinct families of the same name; *Hist*, I, 1218n. This confusion would perpetuate itself: a Mazarinade entitled *Advertissement au sieur Cohon, evesque de Dol et de Fraude: par les cuistres de l'Université de Paris* ([Paris]: Jouxte la Copie imprimée à Doüay, 1649) is dismissive of the statesman since 'Nous voyons le petit fils d'un Procureur du Chastelet tenir la place d'un Chancelier de France' and accuses him of having removed a funeral plaque to his grandfather in the church of saint-Séverin (p. 6). Similarly, the *Catalogue des partisans* (Paris: [n.pub.], 1649) states that 'son bisayeul estoit Apotiquaire' (p. 20).

406 *esclave volontaire*: Tallemant depicted Séguier as 'toujours le très-humble valet du ministre', *Hist*, I, 611. Richard Bonney opines

that the Chancellor's 'servility to Richelieu became notorious', *Political Change in France under Richelieu and Mazarin, 1624–1661* (Oxford: Oxford University Press, 1978), p. 120. The lines that follow present Séguier as the apex of idolatrous sycophancy, contrasting this, as with Père Joseph, with his very public religiosity. An unspoken comparison is also to be drawn with his predecessor, Michel de Marillac.

415 Tallemant notes that Richelieu had assumed the title of *monseigneur*, reserved to princes of the blood until that point (*Hist*, I, 149). The prince de Condé pointedly always referred to Richelieu as Monsieur and, in his turn, the Cardinal took great delight in addressing the prince as Monsieur in official correspondence; Bluche, *Richelieu*, p. 216. However, the late sixteenth and early seventeenth centuries was a period during which the dress and title of cardinals was subject to change as the Sacred College appropriated more privileges, particularly following the pontificate of Pius V (1566–1572) who began a custom that was embraced by all his successors in retaining his white Dominican habit rather than assuming red, which then was used by his cardinals.

420 The vision of Séguier casually, and thus fraudulently, sealing blank state documents in his role as chancellor and *garde de sceaux* not only implies incompetence resulting from his eagerness to please Richelieu but also *lèse-majesté*; see Ranum, *Richelieu and the Councillors*, p. 11.

426 *linotte*: Furetière provides three definitions for this term: a caged bird; someone so drunk that he is senseless; a dimwit (owing to the bird's small head), *DU*, II, sig. 3b^r. Not only does the word itself add to the depiction of Séguier as mentally unbalanced, but the picture of him alone and playing with a caged bird is also a figurative *mise en abyme* as he, in his turn, is treated as a plaything by Richelieu.

426 *solitaire*: the *Miliade* may not be far off the mark here in laying out Séguier's aesthetic personality; in a eulogy delivered to the Académie Française, abbé Pierre Cureau de La Chambre gives prominence to the Chancellor's detachment from worldly affairs and his desire, rather than for vainglory, 'il s'étoit voulu banner du monde pour vivre uniquement à JESUS-CHRIST dans sa solitude', 'Oraison funèbre de Messire Pierre Séguier, Chancelier de France, et Protecteur de l'Académie françoise; prononcée en 1672', in *Recueil des harangues prononcées par messieurs de l'Académie*

françoise, dans leur receptions, et en d'autres occasions differentes, depuis l'establissement de l'Académie jusqu'au present, 2 vols (Amsterdam: Aux dépens de la Compagnie, 1709), I, 237–65 (p. 250).

429 The Carthusians are the strictest order with the peculiarity that monks each live in their own small, detached cottage, thus technically living in community while retaining a large degree of independence. Furetière comments that a monk 'vit fort austerement, et dans une closture et une solitude forte estroite', *DU*, I, sig. [2y3]^v. The satire's comment works on a double level, for Séguier had spent several months as a Carthusian postulant during his teenaged years; the author of the *Miliade* is therefore opining that he should never have returned to the world. Séguier's stay with the order has sometimes been dismissed as a fanciful anecdote made by d'Alembert during the eighteenth century, but it predates his account; see René Pocard du Cosquer de Kerviler, *Le Chancelier Pierre Séguier, second protecteur de l'Académie française: études sur sa vie privée, politique et littéraire et sur le groupe académique de ses familiers et commensaux* (Paris: Didier, 1874), p. 13.

434–35 Tallemant pinpoints this reference: 'Le Maistre en le presentant p^r chancel[ier]', Tall, fol. 29^v. Antoine Le Maistre (1608–1658), *avocat au Parlement* and aligned to the Jansenist movement, delivered the Parlement's formal address to Séguier on formally taking up his chancellorship in his *harangue, prononcée au Parlement, sur la presentation des lettres de Monsieur Seguier* in 1636. In point of fact, Le Maistre does not employ *noblesse de cœur* in this speech but rather 'noblesse de sa race'; 'noblesse non seulement du sang, mais de l'esprit'; and 'noblesse de sa nature', *Recueil de divers plaidoyers et harangues, Prononcez au Parlement par Me Antoine le Maistre* (Paris: Michel Bobin, 1652), pp. 244, 250, and 333.

437 *bastons*: 'On dit que le chancellier estant cogner eut des bastonnades en je ne say quelle avanture', Tall, fol. 29^v.

439 Tallemant comments on the Chancellor's piety, recounting that, on the feast of St Joseph (19 March), he had the statue of St Joseph wrapped in his cloak as a mark of respect in the church of the Mathurins, *Hist*, I, 613. Mousnier devotes a section to religion and the Séguier family in his edition of the Chancellor's correspondence. It was a profoundly devout family: Pierre's mother became a nun when his father died, and in the same year of the *Miliade* some of his

grandfather's theological writings were published; see *Lettres et mémoires adressés au chancelier Séguier*, I, 38–41.

441 This accusation is possibly not mere poetic licence: in a letter from Cardinal Bérulle to Richelieu dated 30 August 1629, Bérulle states that two Jesuit clerics, Fathers Regourg and Suffren, spoke to Séguier's wife with a view to exerting pressure on her to persuade her husband to pursue the office of *premier président*. Regourg was her confessor and Suffren the King's spiritual director, and they both promised to assist his case at Court. In other words, Séguier's prominence and rise to power owed much to the influence of certain priests. *Les Papiers de Richelieu: section politique intérieure, correspondance et papiers d'État*, ed. by Pierre Grillon, 6 vols (Paris: Pedone, 1975–85), IV (1980), 568–69 (p. 569).

442 *il faict du veau*: 'on dit qu'un homme a fait le *veau*, quand il a manqué de faire quelque bonne affaire par sa faute', *DU*, III, sig. 3Ecc^v.

445 'La Sorbonne', Tall, fol. 29^v.

448 Louis XIII was intent on reining in the Paris Parlement and Richelieu relied on Séguier's services to curb its dissentive spirit. See Françoise Hildesheimer, 'Richelieu et Séguier ou l'invention d'une créature', in *Études sur l'ancienne France offertes en hommage à Michel Antoine*, ed. by Bernard Barbiche and Yves-Marie Bercé (Paris: École des Chartes, 2003), pp. 209–26. In Hildesheimer's words, Séguier assumed the mantle of 'l'actif promoteur d'une mise au pas de Messieurs du Parlement, oubliant qu'il avait été l'un des leurs' (p. 222).

453 *faquin*: 'Il ne faudrait pas mésestimer le mépris que ce terme de *faquin* recouvrait au XVIIe siècle', *Les Lettres de Guy Patin à Charles Spon, janvier 1649–février 1655*, ed. by Laure Jestaz, Bibliothèque des Correspondances, Mémoires et Journaux, 21 (Paris: Champion, 2006), p. 60n.

463 Madeleine Fabri (1599–1683), daughter of Jean Fabri, sieur de Champauze, *trésorier de l'Extraordinaire des guerres*, married Pierre Séguier in 1615. Tallemant relates: 'On dit que le grand-pere de Fabri estoit serrurier', *Hist*, I, 612. Her family's humble origins in comparison with Séguier's status explain the vehemence of some of the contemporary gossip: 'La famille, originaire d'Orléans, n'était que de marchands et de practiciens: les contemporains eurent

l'impression d'une mésalliance', Mousnier, *Lettres et mémoires*, p. 31.

464 *Cette laide*: Tallemant judges that 'Cette femme n'a jamais esté belle', *Hist*, I, 612. *cette fripiere*: this relates to the traditional homage paid to the chancellor by his officers of six aulnes of cloth; according to Tallemant she was given this name as she insisted on fine cloth being purchased from specific merchants, *ibid*.

470 'Un *Sergent à verge* a le droit particulier d'estre Juré Priseur et Vendeur de biens', *DU*, III, sig. [3F3]^v.

471 *harpie*: a mythological monster which is half-woman and half-bird. Furetière provides the context in which it is used in this line: 'On dit proverbialement d'une femme criarde et avare, que c'est une vraye *harpie*', *DU*, II, sig. Aa3^v.

476 *cotte*: 'Parite de vestement des femmes, qui s'attache à leur ceinture, et qui descend jusqu'en bas', *DU*, I, sig. [3q4]^r. The entry also specifies that the term is only applied to peasants' dress, so the poet denigrates her humble origins at the same time as her lasciviousness.

480 'Un chanoine de Nostre dame nommé Tevenin qui auroit eu de l'attachement avec le chancellier estant presid[ent] au mortier ou on medisoit avec elle', Tall, fol. 30^r (a rumour also mentioned in his *Historiettes*, I, 612–13). Claude Thévenin (1595–1665) also held the office of *conseiller du Roy*; see Paris, Archives Nationales du Caran, ET/XCIX/133. Similar rumours concerning her predilection for romantic liaisons with clergy are voiced in *Le Silence au bout du doigt* ([Paris]: [n.pub.], 1649?): 'elle a plus de galands que de chappelets, bien que'elle en ait une infinite, et que tous les Religieux soient ses favoris'.

483 'Sublet des Noyers', Tall, fol. 30^v.

485 Tallemant judges that 'M. de Noyers avoit une vraye ame de valet', perhaps inspired by this verse of the *Miliade*, *Hist*, I, 298.

486 *un triboulet*: Triboulet was court jester to Louis XII and François I. The popular usage of his name as a generic term for a buffoon is not recorded until the 1727 edition of Furetière, which notes 'On dit, proverbialement, Servir de *triboulet*; pour dire, Servir de fou, faire rire la compagnie', *Dictionnaire universel, Contenant generalement tous les mots François, tant vieux que modernes, et les termes des sciences et des arts*, 4 vols (The Hague: Pierre Husson et

al, 1727), IV, sig. [4v3]^v. This appears to be the first recorded use of the term within this context, almost a century before the dictionary definition. Triboulet is encountered by Panurge in Rabelais's *Cinq Livres*, when he consults him on Pantagruel's urging to discover the cause of his 'perplexité' as to whether he should marry, a fitting allusion given Séguier's alleged subservience to his spouse (François Rabelais, *Tiers Livre*, ed. by M. A. Screech, Textes Littéraires Français, 102 (Geneva: Droz, 1964), pp. 303–12 (Chaps 45 and 46)).

498 'Brienne et La vrilliere', Tall, fol. 30^v. Henri-Auguste de Loménie, comte de Brienne (1595–1666) and Louis Phelypeaux d'Herbault, marquis de la Vrillière (1599–1681) shared the oversight of the Départment des affaires étrangères from 1624 together with Nicolas Potier d'Ocquerre and Charles de Beauclerc. A *règlement* of 1624 gave Loménie the care of England, Turkey, and the Levant, whereas Phélypeaux dealt with Spain, Piedmont, Italy, and Switzerland.

507 *Servient*: Abel Servien, marquis de Sablé et de Boisdauphin (1593–1659) served Richelieu on diplomatic missions, notably with Savoy, and was created *sécretaire d'État à la guerre*, forfeiting the office to Sublet de Noyers in 1636 when he was disgraced. This is the flight referred to in the following two lines.

525 Chavigny (Léon Bouthillier) was delegated by the Cardinal to supervise Gaston d'Orléans after his return from exile in 1634 and during the period in which the question of his clandestine marriage's legal and canonical status was being negotiated: 'Chavigny, qui faisoit agir les autres, avoit son ordre particulier, d'abandonner rarement son Altesse, mais dans cette subjection, comme il estoit jeune et mois moderé, qu'il ne la paru depuis, il ne gardoit pas le respect qui estoit deu à Monsieur', *Mémoires de Monsieur de Montresor*, I, 62–63. Montrésor details how both the Cardinal and Chavigny manipulated Monsieur and the King in order to to ensure that the annulment would be realized (I, 65–70).

531 Not without a tinge of irony, one Mazarinade observes that '[Chavigny] a estudié la Politique dans l'Escole la plus rafinée de nostre Siecle, qui a esté celle du Cardinal de Richelieu', *Les Contretemps su sieur de Chavigny, premier ministre de monsieur le prince* ([Paris]: [n.pub.], 1652), p. 3.

533 Retz dryly notes that Chavigny enjoyed the unofficial status of 'confidentissime du cardinal', *Œuvres*, p. 143.

534 Châteauneuf used the pseudonym of 'cul pourri' in intimate letters to the duchess of Chevreuse to denote the Cardinal. When these letters were intercepted, the minister was so infuriated that it is no exaggeration to note that this term directly precipitated Châteauneuf's disgrace and imprisonment; see Abraham-Nicolas Amélot de La Houssaie, *Mémoires historiques, politiques, critiques, et littéraires*, 3 vols (Amsterdam: Zacharie Chatelain, 1737), I, 157–58. A libel penned during the last illness of the prelate referred to this medical problem claiming that his room was always kept heavily scented '[Pour] moderer un peu l'odeur puantissime, / Qui sort du cul poury de l'Eminentissime', *Sur L'Enlevement des reliques de sainct Fiacre*, p. 8.

545 The poet mocks the creation of Léon Bouthillier as a *comte* at a very young age which meant that he outranked his own father. Tallemant adds: 'on vit un vaudeville: *Et qu'on face Chavigny, De ces ducs a la moderne*', Tall, fol. 31^r. Richelieu's rewarding of his creatures with seemingly undeserved and unseemly advancement is also satirized with the mention of the Ordre de Saint-Esprit in line 746.

545 'on a dit qu'il estoit son fils et qu'estant encore escollier, le Card[inal] en avoit conté a Me Boutellier', Tall, fol. 31^r.

557 The poet unfavourably compares the present state of the government with that of Henri IV and the minority of Louis XIII. Pierre Jeannin (1540–1622) was a diplomat under Henri IV and then under the regency and held the post of *surintendant des finances* from 1616 to 1619. Maximilien de Béthune, duc de Sully (1559–1641) was *surintendant des finances* and a minister under his close friend Henri IV. While he lost power after Henri IV's death, he was elevated to the rank of *maréchal* in 1634 at the age of 75 years old, which underlines the esteem in which he was still held, over two decades since last having enjoyed any real power.

558 Nicolas de Neuville, seigneur de Villeroy (1542–1617) was *sécretaire d'État aux affaire étrangères* under Henri IV. Nicolas Brûlart de Sillery (1544–1624) became *garde des sceaux* in 1604, and was Henri IV's chancellor from 1607.

563 The two names that are mentioned here accentuate Richelieu's nepotism as well as reiterating the fact that two major figures involved in the war were had close family ties to him. Urbain de Maillé, marquis de Brézé (1597–1650) married Richelieu's sister,

Nicole, in 1617. He was French ambassador extraordinary to Sweden in 1632, and became a field marshal and governor of Calais on his return, commanding the French army in Germany during the campaign of 1634 to 1635. Charles de La Porte, marquis de La Meilleraye (1602–1664) was Richelieu's first cousin and played a leading role in the war effort after having distinguished himself during the siege of La Rochelle in 1629. He became *grand maître de l'artillerie* in 1632.

567 Pierre-César de Camboust, marquis de Coislin (1613–1641). He married Pierre Séguier's daughter, Marie, in 1634, so the referencing of this figure once again parodies the highly nepotistic and close-knit nature of Richelieu's ministry. He was *colonel général* of the Swiss regiments from 1635.

569 François de Vignerot, marquis du Pont de Courlay (1609–1646) was appointed *général des galères du roi* in 1635. He was Madame de Combalet's brother.

571 '2 bossus', Tall, fol. 31^v. Antoine Adam mentions that '[c]es bossus qui entouraient Richelieu fournissaient une matière facile aux libellistes', *Hist*, I, 1005n. Both Coislin and Pont de Courlay were nephews of Richelieu.

580 Claude de Bullion, marquis de Gallardon (1580–1640) became *surintendant des finances* with Chavigny in 1632 and *garde des sceaux* in 1633. He negotiated the formal reconciliation between Louis XIII and his brother in 1635

586 'Bullion avoit tousjours six millions chez le trezorier de l'Espagne Fieubet; car c'estoit celuy à qui il se fioit le plus', *Hist*, I, 248. In the context of a war against Spain, this was viewed as particularly discreditable. His fortune was enormous; he left almost 8 million livres in his will and Jean-Pierre Labatut concludes that the extent of this, particularly from 1628 onwards, points to 'une participation plus ou moins honnête aux benefices de l'État', 'Aspects de la fortune de Bullion', *DSS*, 60 (1963), 11–37 (p. 36).

601 Bernard, duke of Saxe-Weimar (1604–1639) was a Protestant general commanding Swedish forces during the Thirty Years War who entered the service of France in 1635, bringing his troops with him. Hildesheimer sees him as a '[t]alentueux entrepreneur de guerre' (*Richelieu*, p. 380) and Parrott similarly designates him 'France's ally-entrepeneur', *Richelieu's Army*, p. 80.

610 The repeated mention of *magistrats* in the poem not only reinforces the arbitrary nature of the decisions that were taken during Richelieu's ministry that effectively circumvented and bypassed the Parlement de Paris but also underscores the fact that this had an impact upon the capital itself: 'Les magistrats du Parlement tiennent la première place dans la ville. Ils y dépensent leurs revenues. Ils détiennent le monolope du magistrat municipal. Ils aliment les institutions charitables, dominent l'Université, sont membres des fabriques paroissiales', Roland Mousnier, *Les Institutions de la France sous la monarchie absolue, 1589–1789*, 2 vols (Paris: PUF, 1974–80), II, 334.

617 'Intendant des finances après Controoller general', Tall, fol. 32^r. Claude Cornuel (d. 1640) was *intendant des finances* and *président en la Chambre des Comptes de Paris* from 1635.

621 'On appelloit Bullion *le gros Guillaume raccourcy*', *Hist*, I, 266. Antoine Adam suggests that Tallemant lifted this expression from the *Miliade* (*Hist*, I, 940n). He also adds that the name was that of 'un farceur de l'hostel de Bourgogne. Bullion estoit fort petit', Tall, fol. 32^r.

625 *Le gros coquet*: a pun on François Coquet (d. 1645), *contrôleur general des finances* and 'confident de Bullion' (*Hist*, I, 304). La Houssaie comments that Cornuel used the services of Coquet in more ways than one, for this man 'entendoit assez bien les Finances, mais encore mieux l'art de négocier en Amour. Cornuel lui vendoit sa femme, et Coquet des maîtresses', *Mémoires historiques*, II, 429, though relies on the *Miliade* as the source of this rumour.

629 *pifre*: 'Terme injurieux dont on se sert pour reprocher à un homme qu'il est trop gras et replet', *DU*, III, sig. N2^r.

638 The gibbet at Montfaucon, situated to the north of Paris, was celebrated for its staggering dimensions. The *pilliers* refers the stone structure of sixteen pillars which allowed several convicts to be hanged at the same time on three different levels. See Freddy Joris, *Mourir sur l'échafaud: sensibilité collective face à la mort et perception des executions capitals du Bas Moyen Âge à la fin de l'Ancien Régime* (Liege: Céfal, 2005), p. 53.

640 'Lieutenant Civil, il voloit hardiment. On disoit de luy qu'il sacquittoit bien de sa charge. Il avoit emprunté de l'argent p^r l'a[iguillon?]', Tall, fol. 32^v. Moreau was involved in misleading the Cardinal's niece to his own financial advantage by a grossly

inaccurate valuation of the duchy of Aiguillon in 1645 (*Hist*, I, 309. Michel Moreau, *conseiller au Grand Conseil, maître des requêtes*, and *lieutenant civil du Châtelet* (d. 1637). His son, Michel-Jérôme, enjoyed the friendship of Paul Scarron and Madeleine de Scudéry; see Alain Niderst, *Madeleine de Scudéry, Paul Pellisson et leur monde* (Paris: PUF, 1976), pp. 227–28.

645 'Martin, un financier qui tenoit si bonne table', Tall, fol. 32^v. The identity of this Martin remains mysterious; Tallemant mentions 'trois Martin à Paris', one of whom was known as 'Martin mangé, un qui s'estoit ruiné à tenir table', *Hist*, II, 798.

646 *fils de putain*: Moreau was in charge of policing prostitution in the capital and reinforced and tightened existing statutes against soliciting in 1635 with the issue of a new *réglement général* for the capital's police.

647 A pun on the twin role of Moreau as *lieutenant civil* as well as *prévôt des marchands*.

651 'Le Grand senat pour l'auguste Senat n'est pas heureusement dit', Pierre Richelet, *La Versification françoise, ou l'art de bien faire et de bien tourner les vers* (Paris: Estienne Loyson, 1671), p. 165.

652 Nicolas Le Jay, baron de Tilly, Maison-Rouge et Saint-Fargeau (1575–1640) was a career parliamentarian who became *premier president* of the Parlement de Paris in 1630 as well as *garde des sceaux* in February 1636.

653 'le p^r President', Tall, fol. 32^v. The author of an unpublished poem in manuscript, 'Sur la mort de M. le Prémier Président. Sonnet' is of the opinion that, while Le Jay governed 'un auguste Parlement', he also showed 'Qu'il savoit bien aveuglement / Obëir au commandement / De ceux desquels il tenoit l'estre', Arsenal MS 4126, fol. 1092.

656 *sans naissance*: while Le Jay may not have hailed from the *noblesse d'épée*, his family produced a distinguished line of royal administrators going back to the fourteenth century; see Louis Moreri, *Le Grand dictionnaire historique, ou le mélange curieux de l'histoire sacrée et profane*, 2 vols, 3rd edn (Lyon: Jean Girin and Barthélemy Rivière, 1683), II, 233.

660 *Rosse*: 'Meschant cheval usé et éréne, qui n'est point sensible à l'esperon, ni à la gaule', *DU*, III, sig. xx2^v–xx3^r.

661 *harats*: 'Lieu destiné à mettre des juments poulinieres avec des estalons pour faire race', *DU*, II, sig. aa2ʳ.

663 *maison rouge*: this was his famously lavish château at Tilly, near Fontainebleau.

664 Tallemant identifies this mistress: 'aupres de Fontainebleau avec la femme d'Herbelay, le M[aîtr]e de req[uêtes]', Tall, fol. 33ʳ. The official's wife was named Marie Sanguin.

679 Jacques Le Prévost, seigneur d'Herbelay (d. 1653), whose wife is already mentioned in l. 663, was *conseiller d'État* and *maître de requêtes* as well as *intendant* for Champagne. He was hand-picked as one of the judges of the maréchal de Marillac and voted for his death; see Jean Le Clerc, *La Vie du Cardinal, Duc de Richelieu*, 5 vols (Amsterdam: Aux dépens de la Compagnie, 1753), IV, 356. For Courville, Tallemant adds 'son Intendant'. Elsewhere, he mentions a sexually voracious baronne de Courville, namely Anne de Formentières, *Hist*, II, 119–20.

685 Frédéric-Maurice de la Tour d'Auvergne, duc de Bouillon (1605–1652) came from a family with a reputation of rebellion. He converted to Catholicism in 1634 and arrived at the French court in 1635, being given command of the cavalry in the French army in Flanders. He detested Richelieu and secretly corresponded with Gaston d'Orléans, giving a haven to the exiled comte de Soissons in 1636. The sense of this line, then, is that Le Jay is indiscriminate in his conquests: he cuckolds both loyal servants such as d'Herbelay as well as anti-Richelieu subversives such as La Tour.

689–90 'Cestoit un marchand de bois abastus qui estoit fort riche. Il estoit cap[itain]e de son quartier et on le nommoit toujours le Cap[itai]ne Marchand. Ce Marchand fit bastir le pont aux oyseaux qui, ayant esté bruslé, le Roy donna a son gendre les places du costé de la rüe neufve Sᵗ Louys dont les maisons avancent dans l'eau. Il estoit cogner quand il espousa la fille de cet homme après il fut lieutenant civil en suite preside[nt] au mortier puis p[remie]r Preside[nt] et il fut surnommé le Pont Marchand et avant cela sappel[loit] le point aux Meusniers, depuis le pont aux oyseaux. Cet homme mourut de regret de la mort d'Henry 4', Tall, fol. 33ʳ. Le Jay's wife, Madeleine Marchand, was the daughter of Charles Marchand a notable bridge constructor and entrepreneur, though he died some time after Henri's death in 1610, as he rebuilt the Pont au

Change and Pont Marchand after fire ravaged them in 1621, as noted by Tallemant.

695 'On appelle figurément un vieux *bouquin*, un homme puant et lascif qui a passé sa vie dans la débauche', *DU*, I, sig. hh2^v.

702 Le Jay had no legitimate children but left an impressive number of illegitimate issue; decades later, Saint-Simon would observe, in passing, 'il laissa une troupe de bâtards', 'Grand officiers de l'ordre du Saint-Esprit', in Louis de Rouvroy, duc de Saint-Simon, *Mémoires*, ed. by Arthur de Boislisle, 11 vols (Paris: Hachette, 1890–1930), XI (1924), 439–85 (p. 471).

709 *Rollet*: 'Petit rôle. Il n'est plus guere en usage qu'au figuré dans ces deux phrases proverbiales, *Jouer bien son rôlet*, pour dire, Joüer bien son personnage. *Estre au bout de son rôlet*, pour dire, Ne sçavoir plus que dire ni que faire', *AF*, II, 423. The sense in the context is of Bullion performing the role of a pedantic and bizarre character.

710–16 these lines, which extol Le Jay's interest in horticulture, probably reflect the fact that he acquired the estate of Conflans in 1634, whose gardens were a byword for natural beauty and had been lauded by Ronsard; see 'A très-vertueux Seigneur N. de Neufville', in *Œuvres complètes*, ed. by Jean Céard et al, 2 vols (Paris: Gallimard, 1993–94), I, 439–43 (particularly ll. 153–60).

715 This line alludes to the *roi vigneron*, a Carnavelesque tradition of the *fête des fous*. As well as the implied disrespect there is also an echo of a popular legend about Henri IV that he conversed with a winegrower without revealing his identity in order to discover what the common man thought about the state of the country; see Louis-Laurent Prault, *L'Esprit d'Henri IV, ou anecdotes les plus intéressantes, Traits sublimes, Reparties ingénieuses, et quelque Lettres de ce Prince* (Paris: Prault, 1775), pp. 220–21. Both these possible allusions craft a *monde à l'envers* in which the King is not only lacking in leadership but is also unaware of the state of affairs in his kingdom.

720 *follet*: 'Qui est un peu fou ou gaillard', *DU*, II, sig. H3^v.

723 *anter*: a homophonic mispelling of *enter* which propagates the horticultural theme of the surrounding lines.

727 *gorge ouverte*: 'il l'avoit tousjours ainsy par trop de cuisine', Tall, fol. 34^r.

737 On 8 January 1636, the King had six *conseillers* of the Parlement arrested and incarcerated after they had rebelled against his creation of twenty-four new *charges*, a measure which served to dilute the body's authority. In forbidding the Parlement to discuss the question or send delegations to him, 'Le roi avait manifestement abusé de son autorité en defendant au Parlement de tenir des assemblées. C'était en réalité lui enlever le droit de remonstrance', Glasson, *Le Parlement de Paris*, I, 159.

738 *cire verte*: green wax was used to seal *actes perpétuels* whereas yellow ink was used for any temporary legislation or correspondence. See Pierre-Camille Lemoine, *Diplomatique-pratique ou traité de l'arrangement des archives et trésors des chartes* (Metz: Joseph Antoine, 1765), pp. 74–77. This insertion adds to the sense of the permanency of this erosion of liberties.

740 *leze Eminence*: 'Prosecution for lese majesty was one of the main devices used by Richelieu to quash opposition to the central administration', Ralph E. Giesey, Lanny Haldy, and James Millhorn, 'Cardinal Le Bret and Lese Majesty', *Law and History Review*, 4 (1986), 23–54 (p. 24). On Richelieu's exploitation of *raison d'État* to encompass attacks against his person or politics, see Laurie Catteeuw, 'Censure, raison d'État et libelles diffamatoires à l'époque de Richelieu', *Papers on French Seventeenth-Century Literature*, 71 (2009), 363–75.

746 *cordon bleu*: 'signe extérieur de "princérie", le cordon bleu était la plus haute récompense d'un Français', Hervé Pinoteau, 'Ordre du Saint-Esprit', in *Dictionnaire du Grand Siècle*, ed. by François Bluche (Paris: Fayard, 1990), p. 1384. Le Jay received his insignia in 1636. Not without reason, Richelieu's detractors accused him of degrading the order. Richelieu received the honour in 1633 together with four members of his family (his brother-in-law, his first cousin, and two nephews). Since his brother had already been admitted to the order in 1632, this meant that there were six recipients from his family.

749 *roue*: being broken at the wheel was reserved for particularly heinous crimes, including parricide, which makes it apt for Le Jay who is depicted as having been serially unfaithful to service to his sovereign and country, his allegorical parents. This method of execution was rarely carried out on nobility and almost always commuted to another means if contained in the terms of a sentence;

see Stuart Carroll, *Blood and Violence in Early Modern France* (Oxford: Oxford University Press, 2006), pp. 209–10.

757 *sourcilleux*: 'Terme poëtique, qui ne se dit que des montagnes et des rochers forts élevé, et qui semblent être orgueilleux par leur élevation', *DU*, III, sig. LII3^v.

759 *jeune hercule*: Richelieu turned 51 years old on 8 September 1636. As well as mocking his vanity, this description once again suggests Richelieu's appropriation of regal imagery since the mythical hero regularly personified royal prowess in seventeenth-century literature. See Carine Barbafieri, 'Hercule et Achille, héros français au XVIIe siècle: de la vraisemblance à l'âge classique', *L'Information littéraire*, 60.3 (2008), 43–54 (p. 43).

787 After the capture of La Rochelle, French troops marched to relieve Casale. Savoyard and Spanish forces were attacked at Susa with the French losing more men to avalanches than to enemy action; see Peter H. Wilson, *The Thirty Years War: Europe's Tragedy* (London: Penguin, 2009), p. 442.

791–4 It is not difficult to find such acclaim, for example Nicolas Frenicle waxes: 'Si quelqu'un dans ses Vers parle de RICHELIEU, / Que sous l'habit d'un homme il nous décrive un Dieu; / Vous n'estes point sujet à l'humaine impuissance; / Votre rare Vertu vous donne une autre essence', 'Hymne de la victoire apres la reduction de La Rochelle. A Monseigneur le cardinal duc de Richelieu', in *Le Sacrifice des Muses*, pp. 92–106 (p. 105). This type of eulogy is seen to sit uneasily with Richelieu's subservience to God and the King.

808 'Le jour mesme que La R[ochelle] fut reduitte, la mer rompit la digue', Tall, fol. 35^r. Bluche comments that the taking of the the city in 1628 was a seminal moment in the prelate's career: 'Tout change avec le siège de La Rochelle. La conduite des opérations, leur succès, gagnent au Cardinal-Ministre la confiance entière d'un monarque ombrageux', *Richelieu*, p. 216. The poet is implying that malevolent forces have assisted Richelieu's rise (already intimated by 'les avantures sinistres' in line 771).

810 Morgues rails against the prelate's defenders, in particular Paul Hay du Chastelet, for not crediting Marshals de Schomberg, de Thoiras, de Marillac, and the commandeur de Valencé for their role in the taking of La Rochelle from Protestant hands in 1629 (*La verité defendue*, p. 455). French forces remain equally uncredited for the French defence of Casal and Mantua in 1629 and 1630. Morgues

comments that hostile tracts against Richelieu called him Cardinal de La Rochelle after the victory over the city, *La verité defendue*, p. 449. Morgues negates the victories of the French forces by stressing the indecorum of a subject taking the entire credit for this action, even though three monarchs were involved in the conflict (pp. 454–55).

811 The three towns mentioned in this line refer to successful military developments after the fall of La Rochelle (the *Ré* being the île de Ré, to which the Duke of Buckingham and his troops had retreated after having been prevented from entering La Rochelle to aid the Protestant population). With the war of succession in Mantua (1628–1631), Richelieu planned a rapid intervention through Piedmont following the surrender of La Rochelle in order to relieve the siege of Casale. The Spanish retreated and the French garrisoned Casale.

821 A parody of Joshua 10:12 where Joshua calls on God to halt the course of the sun in order to ensure the Israelites' victory over the Amorites. This is one of several biblical episodes which are brought into service, together with mythological episodes, in order to represent Richelieu's hubris, notably David and Goliath in line 818.

843 After Charles IV had reneged on his obligations to France under the treaties of La Neuveville and Charmes, together with his intrigues with Gaston d'Orléans and with the Spanish allies, Richelieu invaded Lorraine after he had received proof of the prince's complicity with the House of Habsburg in December 1633. Richelieu subsequently forced his abdication in favour of his brother on 19 January 1634, the usurpation to which the author refers. On the Cardinal's intervention in matters of Lorraine sovereignty, see Marie-Catherine Vignal Souleyreau, *Richelieu ou la quête d'Europe* (Paris: Pygmalion, 2008), pp. 233–43, which the same author has termed elsewhere 'la mise en œuvre de la saisie féodale', *Richelieu et la Lorraine* (Paris: L'Harmattan, 2004), p. 198. For a justification of the invasion of Lorraine, see the section 'Souveraineté du Roy sur la Lorraine' in Charles Vialart, *Histoire du ministère d'Armand Jean du Plessis Cardinal Duc de Richelieu, sou le règne de Louis le Juste XIII. du nom. Roy de France et de Navarre* (Paris: Gervais Alyot et al, 1649), pp. 712–13.

844 *sa souveraine*: 'La R[eine] Mere', Tall, fol. 35^v.

845 'M^r et M^e', Tall, fol. 35^v. On 3 January 1632, Gaston d'Orléans whose wife Mme de Montpensier had died, secretly married Marguerite de Lorraine Vaudémont, the young sister of Charles, duc de Lorraine, in a small convent chapel at Nancy. This was an astonishingly defiant act. However, with no successor and a monarch who was frequently ill, assuring future offspring from the heir presumptive seemed prudent. Moreover, the marriage was celebrated in the presence of a delegate from the Cardinal Bishop of Toul, and the union thus not only was a disruptive political act during the Thirty Years War but it also brought the French monarchy into conflict with the Church yet again over the recurring question of the validity of marriages conducted without parental (or royal) consent. On the vast diplomatic efforts that were necessitated in order to resolve the question of the match's validity, involving canonists, papal legates, diplomats, the Sorbonne, and the Vatican, see Pierre Blet, *Richelieu et l'Église* (Versailles: Via Romana, 2007), pp. 145–84. Only on his deathbed and after having received Viaticum, Louis XIII did finally agreed to grant Marguerite de Lorraine a passport to enter France and be reunited with Gaston, which does seem to indicate that this had long troubled his conscience (Blet, p. 184).

851 'de M^r et M^e p^r le marier avec sa niece', Tall, fol. 35^v. The verses that follow repeat the allegation that the prelate desired the marriage of his niece with Gaston d'Orléans. This might seem far-fetched, particularly in light of the fact that Louis XIII was then childless and Monsieur was heir presumptive. There is, however, a direct witness to these events, namely Monsieur's daughter who relates overhearing conversations about her father's rehabilitation. While she took little notice since she preferred playing with her toys, Richelieu came one day to speak with her directly: 'Il faisait dire que, pour faire la paix de Monsieur avec le roi, il fallait rompre son mariage avec Marguerite de Lorraine et lui faire épouser Mlle [*sic*] de Combalet, nièce du cardinal, qui est aujourd'hui Mme d'Aiguillon. Je ne pouvais m'empêcher de pleurer dès qu'on m'en parlait et, dans ma colère, je chantais, pour me venger, toutes les chansons que je savais contre le cardinal et sa nièce', *Mémoires de la Grande Mademoiselle*, ed. by Bernard Quillet (Paris: Mercure de France, 2005), p. 39. The princess's credibility might, however, be called into question in light of the fact that she wrote this account in 1653 after almost certainly acquainting herself with the claims made in the *Miliade*.

854 This line contains two puns of a floral nature to accompany the royal lilies mentioned in the previous line: *grate-cul*, dog rosehip, deftly alludes to Richelieu's haemorrhoidal irritation resulting in his becoming a *grate-cul* whereas *seps vieillis* is at the expense of Combalet's maiden name of Vignerot.

857 'Le Roy n'avoit point d'enfants, cestoit en [1633?]', Tall, fol. 35^v. Marie-Madeleine de Vignerot de Pont-Courlay (1604–1675) was the daughter of Richelieu's sister, Françoise, and married to Antoine de Beauvoir du Roure, sieur de Combalet in 1620. On Richelieu's trust in his niece, Morgues criticizes the fact that 'le Cardinal veut faire passer la Royne pour un esprit infame', *La verité defendue*, p. 454.

858 'On dit aussi par raillerie, qu'un homme n'est qu'un chetif *Argoulet*, un pauvre *Argoulet*, pour dire, que c'est un homme de neant, et pour le mespriser', *DU*, I, P^v.

860 *hermaphrodite voluntaire*: 'hermaphrodites came to stand for all kinds of sexual ambiguity, including the associated transgressions of sodomy and cross-dressing', Lorraine Daston and Katharine Park, 'The Hermaphrodite and the Orders of Nature: Sexual Ambiguity in Early Modern France', *GLQ: A Journal of Lesbian and Gay Studies*, 1 (1995), 419–38 (p. 428). Here, and in the following line, hermaphrodism is an uncomplicated circumlocution for bisexuality.

861 'M^e du vigean', Tall, fol. 35^v. Anne de Neufbourg, wife of François Poussart, baron du Vigean. Tallemant recounts that Mme de Vigean had a close friendship with Mme de Sablé, and that 'Mme d'Aiguillon l'emporta sur elle'. The *Miliade* goes further in the insinuation of a same-sex liaison with this couplet; see Marie-Jo Bonnet, *Les Relations amoureuses entre les femmes du XVIe au XXe siècle: essai historique* (Paris: Jacob, 1995), pp. 79–80.

861 *teint de saffron*: Furetière defines the near-homophonic *safran* as a piece of wood used in shipbuilding for the rudder, *DU*, III, sig. [3m4]^r. Given that Tallemant describes her husband's generous endowment as 'le plus grand abatteur de bois' (*Hist*, I, 305), there is the possibility of some lewd wordplay here that denigrates Combalet's virginity: if she has a woody hue, then it follows that she has been into close contact with wood. This equivocation is fortified by the bawdy potential of the *fontaine* in her bedroom (l. 863) and the heady blend of the sensual and exotic ingredients of saffron, amber, and jasmine.

863 the reference to the Naiades and the mythological elements that follow until line 869 resonate with the air of a *conte* or a thus undermining the idea of Combalet's purity.

869 After her husband died in 1622, Combalet took annual vows in the Carmelite order, though the speculation about her alleged virginity seems to have been relentless and was often tied to speculation about her sexuality. A popular name for her was 'demi-vierge' (Bluche, *Richelieu*, p. 106). Montglat echoes contemporary tittle-tattle with his nonchalant assessment: 'la Veuve de Combalet sa niéce depuis peu redevenuë pucelle', *Mémoires de François de Paule de Clermont, marquis de Monglat*, ed. by Guillaume-Hyacinthe Bougeant, 4 vols (Amsterdam: [n.pub.], 1727), I, 73. She adamantly refused to countenance a second marriage, despite her uncle's entreaties, and was created duchesse d'Aiguillon in her own right in 1638, being known thereafter as 'princesse nièce' (Hildesheimer, *Richelieu*, p. 155). Tallemant explains here that Combalet was the nephew of the connétable de Luynes: 'parent de Mrs de Luynes', Tall, fol. 36^r.

870 *maistre mullet*: 'on disoit qu'il en estoit bien pourveû', Tall, fol. 36^r, in other words: he possessed particularly generously proportioned genitalia. Tallemant considers that the possibility that Richelieu's niece did not consummate her marriage was especially odd since 'il passoit pour l'homme le mieux fourny de la Cour'; see *Hist*, I, 305–06 (p. 305).

875 *palmes fanées*: a biblical image: 'The vineyard is confounded, and the fig tree hath languished: the pomegranate tree, and the palm tree, and the apple tree, and all the trees of the field are withered: because joy is withdrawn from the children of men', Joel 1:12. The prophet laments the locust plague and desolation of Israel just as the poet sees devastation across the political and geographical landscape of France.

885 *ses duchesses*: 'M^e de chaune ou M^e d'Aiguillon sa niepce devant Me de Combalet', Tall, fol. 36^r. Claire-Charlotte d'Ailly de Picquigny, duchesse de Chaulnes was rumoured to be Richelieu's mistress, though it is more likely that the poet is referring to his nieces. Since Combalet did not become a duchess until 1638, Tallemant is mistaken in his suggestion. It is more likely to refer to Marie du Camboust, who married Jean-Louis de Nogaret de La Valette, duc d'Épernon in 1634 as well as Claire-Clémence de Maillé-Brézé. While the latter niece did not marry the duc d'Enghien

(the future Grand Condé) until 1641, the match was formally drawn up when she was aged five years old in 1633.

888 *le havre et autres ports*: as part of his maritime ambitions, Richelieu acquired the governorships of Le Havre, Brest, and Brouage. Richelet condemns the use of *et autres* as found in this line: 'Le *t* ne se prononçant jamais dans la conjonction *et*, c'est une faute que de placer cette conjonction devant une voyelle', *La Versification françoise*, p. 114. However, this is the sole such occurrence in the poem and directly follows the aspirate *le havre*.

896 *petites maisons*: 'On appelle à Paris, Petites Maisons, l'Hospital où l'on enferme ceux qui ont l'esprit aliené', *AF*, II, 11. Malherbe used the expression 'Empereur des petites maisons' to castigate Racan for being besotted with a woman who mocked him in return: 'À un Gentil-homme de ses amys. *Il le dissuade de sa recherche*', in *Recueil de lettres nouvelles*, ed. by Nicolas Faret (Paris: Toussainct du Bray, 1627), pp. 87–99 (p. 99). Voltaire observed that Louis XV 'me parait tres sage, mais il me parait le Roi des petites maisons', a description which might well be lifted from the *Miliade* (Letter to Étienne Noël Damilaville, 1 February 1764 (D11679), *Correspondence and Related Documents*, ed. by Theodore Besterman, *The Complete Works of Voltaire*, LXXXV–CXXXV (Oxford: Voltaire Foundation, 1968–77), CXI (1973), 204–05 (p. 204)).

904 *perclus*: as well as the usual meaning of paralysis, Furetière notes that the word is applied figuratively 'de l'esprit, d'un homme qui ne raisonne plus', *DU*, III, sig. K^r.

910 *ruine*: the word is versatile in the seventeenth-century, indicating the demolition of buildings, as well as moral, personal or financial destruction, making it particularly appropriate to describe the consequences of a costly and brutal war. See *DU*, III, sig. LII3^v.

923–26 an allusion to St Peter's admonition: 'Be sober and watch: because your adversary the devil, as a roaring lion, goeth about seeking whom he may devour', 1 Peter 5.7.

950 Concino Concini (1575–1617) was a favourite of Marie de Médicis during Louis XIII's minority and was widely unpopular for having abandoned the direction of Henri IV's policies. It was Louis's decision to have him murdered which marked the end of the regency and was a symbolic blooding for the young man. There is a direct ministerial succession at play for Richelieu became a minister

on 25 November 1616 and his entry into politics was at Concini's behest. As the government was popularly called the 'Ministère Concini', Richelieu can be said to have been the 'ministre de Concini'; see Michel Carmona, *Richelieu: l'ambition et le pouvoir* (Paris: Seine, 1990), p. 259.

954 On Richelieu's patronage of the university, see *La Sorbonne en gloire et en deüil, ou discours historique de sa fondation, de son accroissement, des grands fruits qu'elle a causez tant dans l'Eglise que dans l'Estat; et des regrets sur la mort de son Restaurateur Monseigneur le Cardinal Duc de Richelieu, qui y a choisi son Tombeau* (Paris: Jean Paslé, 1643).

956 This provides a robust, and possibly purposeful, counterpoint to Faret's *Ode à Monseigneur le Cardinal duc de Richelieu*, at the end of which the poet reflects: 'RICHELIEU, quel triomphe adorable aux Mortels, / Et quelle pompe magnifique / D'illustres monuments ornera tes Autels?' (p. 14).

APPENDIX

Poems by Authors Suspected of the *Miliade* Relating to this Work

1. CHARLES DE BEYS

Stances, contre l'autheur inconnu d'un libelle dont je fus soupçonné[1]

ENNEMY conjuré des vertus de la France,
Effroyable Imposteur, dont l'enorme assurance
A porté le mespris jusques aux plus saints lieux;
Monstre qui t'eslanças des gouffres de la Terre;
Impie, osas-tu bien sans craindre le Tonnerre,
Medire insolement du pouvoir de nos Dieux?

Sans doute, en meditant un si damnable ouvrage,
Tu sentis en horreur se convertir ta rage;
Ton esprit se troubla, ton front sua d'effroy;
Ta main s'appesantit, ta couleur devint blesme;
Et demeurant perclus dés le premier Blasphême,
Ton Demon enragé les acheva pour toy.

Lumieres de nos jours, dont la vertu feconde
Conserve le plus beau des Empires du monde;
Astres, qui me donnez de si vives ardeurs;
Grand Soleils des François, Divinitez visibles,

---

[1] This poem and the three following ones are taken from Beys's *Œuvres poétiques*, pp. 177–86, 187–94, 195–97, 243, 244 respectively.

Le Gouvernement Present

Se peut il rencontrer des ames insensibles,
Qui contemplant vos faits, mesprisent vos Grandeurs.

Ouy; ce Dieu qui vous fit ses vivantes Images,
Qui receut en naissant tant des müets hommages;
Qui des ses premiers ans fit taire les Docteurs;
Qui par tant de discours, et par tant de Miracles,
Estoffa la parole aux plus fameux Oracles,
Ne pût fermer la bouche à ses Blasphemateurs.

Ce n'est pas d'aujourd'huy, RICHELIEU, que l'envie,
Expose à sa fureur la plus illustre vie;
Rien que le grand esclat ne la peut provoquer;
Plus on est Eminent, plus elle est outragée;
Et des lieux eslevez, sa colere enragée,
N'abbat point les vertus, mais les fait remarquer.

Ayant oüy ton nom jusqu'aux bords du Cocyte,
Elle se leve, et court ou sa haine l'incite;
Son long crin de serpens en desordre la suit,
Qui degoutte de l'eau du fleuve qu'elle a veüe,
Aux lieux ou t'on merite esleve plus de bruit.

Là te voyant assis au dessus des tempestes,
Que forment contre toy ses serpens estouffer;
Elle pousse en criant la derniere parole;
Et comme une victime elle mesme s'immole,
Pour signaler le jour qui te voit triompher.

FRANCE, leve tes yeux vers ce puissant Genie,
Qui durant le grand bruit qu'a fait cette manie,
Ne s'est pas detourné de l'oreille du Roy;
Voy comme cette haute et pure Intelligence
Montre sans s'émouvoir la mesme diligence,
A gouverner toûjours les Astres dessus toy.

Peux-tu rien remarquer dans ce Divin visage,
Qui mesme aux Imposteurs soit de mauvais presage;
On y voit la Douceur avec la Majesté,
Que Dieu dans tous ses traits, a si bien confonduës;
Qu'au moment qu'à nos yeux elles sontrespanduës,
Il s'acquiert de l'Amour, et de l'Authorité.

Malgré tant de Rayons, faut-il que l'Impudence,
Blasme l'heureux Estat, ou t'as mis sa prudence,
Tasche d'esteindre un feu si brillant et si saint;
Interprete si mal des actions si pures;
Et poursuivre en fureur avec tant d'impostures,
L'Esprit qui te conserve, et que l'Espagne craint.

Requeste à Monsieur de Laffemas, Composée dans la Bastille. Stances.

Toy qui par des ressorts cachez.
Apprends les actions secrettes;
Et devant qui les noirs pechez,
Cherchent d'inutiles retraittes;
LAFFEMAS, dont l'Esprit perçant,
Voit le Coupable, et l'Innocent
Dans le fond de la Conscience
Et trouve avec facilité,
Le Mensonge, et la Verité,
De la plus subtile Science.

Tu peux connaistre qu'avec fruit,
J'ay vû ces Rimes satiriques;
Comme un fidelle bien instruit,
Peut voir les Livres Heretiques;
Mon aversion dans mon sein,
Fit naistre un genereux dessein,
Je ne pûs garder le silence,
Ma Muse sçais bien ce que'elle fit,
Pour en reprimer l'Insolence.

Tous ceux qui m'ont entretenu,
De cette piece criminelle,
Avoüeront qu'ils ont reconnu,
Et mon Jugement, et mon Zele;
On a mis des tesmoins icy,
Par qui tu peux estre esclaircy;
S'ils m'accusent de l'avoir veuë,
Je t'assure que pour le moins,
Ils me serviront de tesmoins,

Le Gouvernement Present

De l'horreur que j'en ay conceuë.

Si j'avois perdu la raison,
Au point d'avoir fait tant de crimes;
Sçachant qu'un tesmoin en prison,
M'accusoit d'avoir vû ces Rimes;
Libre dans un Monde nouveau,
L'eusse pû creusant mon tombeau,
Eviter les traits de ton ire;
Je me fusse privé des yeux,
Indigne de revoir les Dieux,
De qui ce Monstre osa mesdire.

Et vrayment, j'eusse esté Brutal,
Si connaissant bien quel supplice,
Merite un crime sans égal,
Je n'eusse pas craint ta Justice!
O Ciel, avec combien d'effroy,
Eussé-je parû devant toy;
Ma langue eust perdu son usage,
Un feu secret m'eust bourrelé,
Et ce que mon cœur t'eust celé,
Tu l'eusses vû sur mon visage.

Mais j'ay condamné cét Escrit,
Et la douceur de ma nature,
N'a pas permis à mon Esprit,
De digerer une Imposture;
J'ay pour les vertus un respect,
Qui me fait trembler à l'aspect,
De tant de personnes Insignes;
Et veux poursuivre en Liberté,
Cét ouvrage dont ta Bonté
A souffert les premieres lignes.

Là milles serpens abbatus,
Rejetteront les venims mesmes,
Au Monstre, à qui tant de vertus
Ont fait vomir tant de Blasphesmes;
Mes vers le rendront odieux,
A tous ces foibles envieux,
Partisans de sa calomnie;

Je me sens inspiré d'un Dieu,
Pour qui mon amour en ce lieu,
Parlera mieux que mon Genie.

GRAND ESPRIT, l'estime qu'il fait,
De ta profonde connaissance,
Donne de la peur au forfait,
Et de l'Espoir à l'Innocence;
Par là j'appaise mes ennuis,
Et voyant de combien je suis
Esloigné d'un si lasche vice;
J'espere d'estre promptement,
Reconnu par ton Jugement,
Et renvoyé par ta Justice.

Stances, à Monseigneur le cardinal de Richelieu; Commencées dans la Bastille. Fragment.

Toy qui du plus haut lieu jusqu'au sacré valon,
Fais descendre souvent le char de la fortune;
GRAND DUC, à qui le soin de soûmettre Neptune,
N'osta pas le desir d'embrasser Apollon;
Qui triomphant encor apres tant de conquestes,
Des Poëtes fameux viens Couronner les Testes;
Et pour te delasser d'un plus solide employ,
Donnes à l'entretien des neuf doctes Pucelles,
De ces heureux momens, qui servent à ton Roy,
Pour ayder ses voisins, et dompter ses Rebelles.

Il est vray que je suis un de ces criminels,
A qui les Deitez, n'ont pas esté propices;
Qui durant les grands feux de tant de sacrifices,
N'osa pas s'approcher du pied de tes Autels;
Mais le Respect a fait mon malheur et mon crime;
Je crûs en ne t'offrant qu'une maigre victime,
Entre mille Devots si bien parez de fleurs,
Que mon Humilité feroit tort à mon Zele;
Et j'eus peur que mon vœu bien different des leurs,
Pour estre moins subtil, ne parût moins fidelle.

Lors que ces grands Esprits taschent à concevoir,

Dans l'estat Glorieux ta Sagesse infinie,
Je demeure confus, et mon foible Genie,
En ta seule conduite admire ton pouvoir;
Aveugle que je suis, je n'ay pas l'Impudence,
De chercher les secrets de cette Providence,
Qui nous est si visible en ton Gouvernement;
Je sçay que le hazard ne regle point ces choses,
Et souvent je m'escrie avec estonnement,
Que je voy des effets dont j'ignore les causes.

A Monseigneur le Prince, sur sa Prison. Sonnet

Grand Prince, ta raison ne fut point estonné,
Lors que l'on t'esloigna du celeste flambeau,
Et le regret de voir ta puissance enchaisnée,
Te donna peu de peine en ce fatal Tombeau;

Ce qui t'aigrit le plus contre la destinée,
Et blessa ton esprit si solide et si beau,
Ce fut le desplaisir de passer une année,
Sans pouvoir emporter un triomphe nouveau.

Mais ne t'en fasches point: La prison la plus noire
Te servit à gagner la plus belle victoire;
Ton courage en ce lieu tes soupirs estouffa;

N'ayant rien à dompter par le fer et la flamme:
CONDÉ, tu te vainquis par la force de l'ame,
Et de tes passions, ta vertu triompha.

Epigramme

QUEL changement! Ils current faire,
D'un Havre ta prison, mais, GRAND PRINCE,
Je voy qu'ils firent le contraire,
Puisque cette prison fut un Havre pour toy.

LE GOUVERNEMENT PRESENT

2. COMTE D'ÉTELAN

Stances[2]

Celuy dont l'innocence assure le courage,
Ne se voit étoné par l'insolente rage,
D'un peuple furieux au desordre porté
Le severe sourcil des tirans il meprise,
      et leur orgueil se brise
Comme un foible cristal contre sa fermeté.

Bien que soubs son vaisseau toute la mer s'irrite
Du vent impetueux qui les vagues agite,
Il voit les flots esmeus sans jamais esmouvoir,
Et bien que Jupiter avecques son tonnerre,
      fasse trembler la terre
desbranler sa constance il n'a pas le pouvoir.

Ce cœur audacieux maistre de tout le monde,
Mesprisans les plaisirs de la terre et de l'onde,
D'un visage asseuré affronte le trespass,
Mesme tout l'univers brisé de la tempeste
      Tomberoit sur sa teste.
Que la peur du danger ne le toucheroit pas.

C'est avec ces vertus que le fils de Semele,
Des Tigres furieux dont son char il attele,
Fist ployer soubs le joug le courage indomté;
Et c'est par ces vertus que le pere de Rome
      S'il est mort comme un homme,
A comme un demy Dieu le trespass surmonté.

Par cet art merveilleux le jeune Tyndaride
Et ce fameux heros le vagabond Alcide

---

[2] This unpublished poem is found in Arsenal MS 4129, fols 739–40, a manuscript in Valentin Conrart's hand.

LE GOUVERNEMENT PRESENT

Ont acquis justement place dedans les cieux
Et c'est ainsy qu'auguste en splendeur nompareille,
      D'une merveille
Gouttera le Nectar parmy les demy dieux.

3. BRUC DE MONTPLAISIR

Contre la satyre Qu'on appelle vulgairement la piece de mille vers. Sonnet.[3]

Laissez lasches Esprits parler la renommée
Et ne pretendez point par nos prophanes vers
Interrompre la voix de cent peuples divers,
Qui du beau nom d'Armand sans cesse est animée.

Son illustre vertu dont la gloire est semée,
Jusqu'aux derniers clymats où s'estend l'univers
Confondre vos erreurs, et vos desseins couverts
Comme ceux des Titans s'en iront en fumée.

Ainsi la terre en vain escale en divers lieux,
Ses nuages espais vers le flambeau des Cieux,
Et jamais ne ternit l'Esclat de sa lumiere.

Elle saveugle seule en cachant ce bel œil,
Et ses noires vapeurs fournissent la matiere
Des foudres dont le Ciel doit punir son orgueil.

---

[3] I have transcribed this from the handwritten version of Conrart in Arsenal MS 4129, fols 723–24. This poem was subsequently published in *Poesies du marquis de Montplaisir* (Amsterdam: [n.pub], 1759), p. 34 under a different title (*Contre ceux qui médisoient du* Cardinal DE RICHELIEU) and with different punctuation and capitalization.

BIBLIOGRAPHY

A: EARLY VERSIONS OF THE *MILIADE*

MANUSCRIPTS

'Le tableau du gouvernement de Mr le Car. de Richelieu', Paris, Bibliothèque nationale, MS fonds français 13641, pp. 1–49. [This is written in an identical hand to documents alluding to Richelieu's death within the same collection (pp. 58 and 88)]

'Le Tableau du gouvernement present ou eloge de Monsieur le Cardinal de Richelieu', fols 23^r–37^r. Paris, Bibliothèque nationale, MS fonds français 19145. [This is Tallemant's annotated copy]

'Les mil vers', Paris, Bibliothèque nationale, MS fonds français 19146, pp. 4–19. [This is in the same hand as a legal document dated 13 May 1642 in the same collection (p. 26)]

'Le Tableau du gouvernement present ou Eloge de Son Eminence Monseigneur le Cardinal Duc de Richelieu. Satyre de mille vers', Paris, Bibliothèque nationale, MS fonds français 22579, fols 46^r–62^v. [This manuscript has the handwritten mention 'par Bussy Pasquier' at its end]

'LE TABLEAU DU GOUVERNEMENT PRÉSENT. OU ELOGE DE MONSIEUR LE CARDINAL DE RICHELIEU', Paris, Bibliothèque de l'Arsenal, MS 3135, fols 1115–41. [This is in Valentin Conrart's hand with some brief annotations]

'Le Tableau du Gouvernemen presen ou Eloge du Cardinal de Richelieu', Paris, Bibliothèque de l'Arsenal, MS 3307, fols 40^r–47^r. [part of the Recueil Faret de Fontette]

'Le Tableau du Gouvernement présent ou Eloge du C', Paris, Bibliothèque Sainte Geneviève, MS 1135, fols 41^r–54^v. [This copy is incomplete, ending with line 842 'De voler toutes les Citez']

PRINTED WORKS

Octavo Editions

LE GOVVERNEMENT PRESENT OV ELOGE DE SON EMINENCE. SATYRE OV LA Miliade ('Imprimé à Envers': [n.pub.], 1636?). Aix-en-Provence, Bibliothèque Municipale Méjanes, Patrimoine fonds ancien C 3077.

LE GOVVERNEMENT PRESENT OV ELOGE DE SON EMINENCE. SATYRE OV LA Miliade ('Imprimé à Envers': [n.pub.], 1636?). Yale University, Beinecke Rare Book and Manuscript Library, 2009 2144.

LE GOVVERNEMENT PRESENT OV ELOGE DE SON EMINENCE. SATYRE OV LA Miliade ('Imprimé à Envers': [n.pub.], 1636?). Duke University, Rare Book, Manuscript, and Special Collections Library, D-6 Pam 1639 c.1.

LE GOVVERNEMENT PRESENT OV ELOGE DE SON EMINENCE. SATYRE OV LA Miliade ('Imprimé à Envers': [n.pub.], 1636?). The Hague, Koninklijke Bibliotheek, KW 757 D26.

LE GOVVERNEMENT PRESENT OV ELOGE DE SON EMINENCE. SATYRE OV LA Miliade ('Imprimé à Envers': [n.pub.], 1636?). Paris, BN, Ye 4086.

LE GOVVERNEMENT PRESENT OV ELOGE DE SON EMINENCE. SATYRE OV LA Miliade ('Imprimé à Envers': [n.pub.], 1636?). Paris, BN, Ye 23474.

LE GOVVERNEMENT PRESENT OV ELOGE DE SON EMINENCE. SATYRE OV LA Miliade ('Imprimé à Envers': [n.pub.], 1636?). Paris, BN, 1518.72.30.

Quarto Editions

LE TABLEAV DV GOVVERNEMENT PRESENT, OV ELOGE DE SON EMINENCE. SATYRE DE MILLE VERS. Nouvelle edition reveuë, et exactement corrigée (Paris: [n.pub.], 1649). Paris, BN, 8-Z Le Senne 10562.

LE GOVVERMENT PRESENT, OV ELOGE DE SON EMINENCE, SATYRE, OV LA MILIADE ([Paris]: [n.pub.], 1650?). Paris, Bibliothèque de la Mazarine, A11557-8.

LE GOVVERNEMENT DE L'ESTAT PRESENT, Où l'on void les fourbes et tromperies de Mazarin (Paris: [n.pub.], 1652). Paris, Bibliothèque de l'Arsenal, 8 H 7850 and Auxerre, Bibliothèque municipale, C 2560 4 V.5 p.22°.

Anthology

'LE TABLEAU DU GOUVERNEMENT de Mr. Le Cardinal de Richelieu', in *LE TABLEAU de la Vie et du Gouvernement de Messieurs les Cardinaux RICHELIEU et MAZARIN, et de Monsieur COLBERT, représenté en diverses Satyres et Poësies ingenieuses; avec un Recueil d'Epigrammes sur la vie et la mort de Monsieur FOUQUET, et sur diverses choses, qui sont passées à Paris en ce temps-là* (Cologne: Pierre Marteau, 1693), pp. 1–37.

'LE TABLEAU DU GOUVERNEMENT de Mr. Le Cardinal de Richelieu', in *LE TABLEAU de la Vie et du Gouvernement de Messieurs les Cardinaux RICHELIEU et MAZARIN, et de Monsieur COLBERT, représenté en diverses Satyres et Poësies ingenieuses; avec un Recueil d'Epigrammes sur la vie et la mort de Monsieur FOUQUET, et sur diverses choses, qui sont passées à Paris en ce temps-là* (Cologne: Pierre Marteau, 1694), pp. 1–37.

B: OTHER PRIMARY TEXTS

MANUSCRIPTS

Ételan, 'Passage de Somme', Paris, Bibliothèque de l'Arsenal (Ars), MS 4145, fols 545–54 and Paris, Bibliothèque nationale (BN), MS fonds français 19115, fols a–b.

–'Stances' ('Celuy dont l'innocence'), Bibliothèque de l'Arsenal MS 4129, fols 739–40.

–'Stances de Monsieur le Comte d'Estelan pour Madame la Marquise de Sablé en lui envoyant son Roman de l'Inconnu', Paris, Bibliothèque nationale, MS fonds français 6712, fols 53^v–54^r.

–'Sur l'oppium', Bibliothèque de l'Arsenal, MS 4126, fol. 1086.

Favereau, Jacques, 'La satyre Ménippée de Caresme prenant Autrement les Visions Amoureuses du Berger Amynthe, surnommé le Pasteur fidèle', Paris, Bibliothèque nationale, MS fonds français 19142, fol. 120^r–25^v.

Montplaisir, René de Bruc, marquis de, 'Contre la satyre Qu'on appelle vulgairement la piece de mille vers. Sonnet', Bibliothèque de l'Arsenal MS 4129, fols 723–24.

PRINTED WORKS

Anon., *Advertissement au sieur Cohon, evesque de Dol et de Fraude: par les cuistres de l'Université de Paris* ([Paris]: Jouxte la Copie imprimée à Doüay, 1649).

–*Le Catalogue des partisans* (Paris: [n.pub.], 1649).

–*Le Constipé de la cour. Avec une prophétie burlesque* ([n.p.]: [n.pub.], 1649?).

– *Les Contre-temps su sieur de Chavigny, premier ministre de monsieur le prince* ([Paris]: [n.pub.], 1652).

–*Le créve coeur, et les sanglots de Monsieur le Prince. Addressez à la France* ('A Envers': [n.pub.], 1649?).

–*L'Esprit bien-heureux du Mareschal de Marillac, à l'esprit mal-heureux du Cardinal de Richelieu* ([Paris]: [n.pub.], 1632?).

–*La Miliade ou l'Eloge burlesque de Mazarin, pour servir de piece de carnaval* ([Paris]: [n.pub.], 1651).

–*La Pure vérité cachée et autres Mazarinades rares et curieuses*, ed. by Pierre-Gustave Brunet (Amsterdam: [n.pub.], 1867).

–*La Sorbonne en gloire et en deüil, ou discours historique de sa fondation, de son accroissement, des grands fruits qu'elle a causez tant dans l'Eglise que dans l'Estat; et des regrets sur la mort de son Restaurateur Monseigneur le Cardinal Duc de Richelieu, qui y a choisi son Tombeau* (Paris: Jean Paslé, 1643).

–*Sur L'Enlevement des reliques de sainct Fiacre, apportées de la ville de Meaux, pour la guerison du cul de M^r le Cardinal de Richelieu* ('En Envers': [n.pub.], 1643).

Aldrovandi, Ulysse, *Serpentum et draconum historiæ* (Bologna: Clement Ferroruium, 1640).

Aubery, Antoine, *Histoire du Cardinal duc de Richelieu* (Paris: Antoine Bertier, 1660).

Bassompierre, François de, *Journal de ma vie: memoires du maréchal de Bassompierre. Première édition conforme au manuscrit original*, ed. by Audoin de Chantérac, 4 vols (Paris: Renouaurd, 1870–77).

Beys, Charles de, *L'Hospital des fous, tragi-comédie* (Paris: Thomas Quinet, 1636).

—*Les Illustres Fous of Charles de Beys*, ed. by Merle I. Protzman (Baltimore: Johns Hopkins Press, 1942).

—*Les Œuvres poétiques de Beys* (Paris: Toussainct Quinet, 1651).

Boaistuau, Pierre, *Histoires prodigieuses extraictes de plusieurs fameux autheurs grecs et latins, sacrez et prophanes, mises en notre langage* (Paris: Jacques Macé, 1567).

Boucher, Jean, *De Justa Henrici Tertii abdicatione e Francorum regno, libri quatuor* (Paris: Nicolas Nivelle, 1589).

Brienne, Louis-Henri de Loménie, comte de, *Mémoires de Louis-Henri de Loménie, comte de Brienne, dit le jeune Brienne*, ed. by Paul Bonnefon, 3 vols (Paris: Laurens, 1916–19).

Chapelain, Jean, *Lettres de Jean Chapelain, de l'Académie française*, ed. by Philippe Tamizey de Larroque, 2 vols (Paris: Imprimerie Nationale, 1880).

—'Lettre ou discours de M. Chapelain, en forme de poëme, à M. Favereau, Conseiller du Roy en sa Cour des Aydes, portant son opinion sur le poëme d'Adonis du Cavalier Marino' in Giambattista Marino, *L'Adone* (Venice: Oliviero di Varano, 1623), p. i–xvi.

Charpentier, François, *Carpentariana ou remarques d'histoire, de morale, de critique, d'érudition, et de bons mots de M. Charpentier, De l'Academie Françoise*, ed. by M. Boscheron (Paris: Nicolas Le Breton, 1724).

Cinq Auteurs, *La Comédie des Tuileries; et, L'Aveugle de Smyrne*, ed. by François Lasserre, Sources Classiques, 87 (Paris: Champion, 2008).

Clavaret, Jean, 'Lettre du Sr Clavaret au Sr Corneille, soy disant autheur du Cid', in *La Querelle du* Cid *(1637–1638)*, ed. by Jean-

Marc Civardi, Sources Classiques, 52 (Paris: Champion, 2004), pp. 537–43.

Colletet, François, 'Beys au tombeau', in *La Muse coquette; ou, les delices de l'honneste Amour et de la belle Galanterie*, 3 vols (Paris: Jean-Baptiste Loyson, 1665), III, 220–21.

Colomby, François de, *De l'Autorité des roys, premier discours* (Paris: Toussainct Du Bray, 1631).

Dictionnaire de l'Académie française, 2 vols (Paris: Pierre Coignard, 1694).

Du Verdier, Gilbert Saulnier, *Histoire des Cardinaux illustres qui ont esté employez dans les affaires d'Estat* (Paris: Jean-Baptiste Loyson, 1653).

Faret, Nicolas, *Ode à Monseigneur le Cardinal duc de Richelieu* (Paris: Sebastien Cramoisy, 1633).

Favereau, Jacques, *La France consolée, epithalame pour les nopces du tres chrestien Louys XIII Roy de France et de Navarre et d'Anne d'Autriche Infante d'Espagne* (Paris: Jean Petit Pas, 1625).

Fournier, Édouard (ed), *Variétés historiques et littéraires: recueil de pièces volantes rares et curieuses en prose et en vers*, 10 vols (Paris: Pagnerre, 1855–63).

Furetière, Antoine, *Dictionaire universel, Contenant generalement tous les mots François tant vieux que modernes, et les Termes de toutes les Sciences et des Arts*, 3 vols (The Hague and Rotterdam: Arnout and Reinier Leers, 1690).

Garasse, François, *Mémoires de Garasse (François) de la Compagnie de Jésus*, ed. by Charles Nisard (Paris: Amyot, 1860).

Géliot, Louvan, *Indice armorial ou Sommaire Explication des mots usitez au Blason des Armoiries* (Paris: Pierre Billaine, 1635).

Godeau, Antoine, *La Sorbonne, poëme* (Paris: Pierre Le Petit, 1653).

Gournay, Marie de, *Égalité des hommes et des femmes* ([n.p.]: [n.pub.], 1622).

Guarini, Giambattista, *Il compendio della poesia tragicomica / De la poésie tragi-comique*, ed. by Laurence Giavarini, Textes de la Renaissance, 140 (Paris: Champion, 2008).

Harangue de Monsieur le Cardinal Duc de Richelieu, faite en Parlement, sa Majesté y estant presente ([Paris]: [n.pub.], 1634).

Jansen, Cornelius, *La Mars françois ou la guerre de France, En laquelle sont examinées les raisons de la Justice pretendu des Armes, et des Alliances du Roi de France* ([Paris?]: [n.pub.], 1637).

Joliat, Eugène, Saint-Évremond's *Les Académistes*, succès de scandale', *Studi Francesi*, 28 (1984), 286–89.

Journal des Savants, 20 (Amsterdam: Wolfgang et al, 1693).

La Croix, Antoine Phérotée de, *L'Art de la poësie françoise. Ou la methode de connoitre et de faire toute sorte de Vers* (Lyon: Thomas Amaulry, 1675).

La Fontaine, Jean de, 'Les Frères de Catalogne', in *Contes et nouvelles érotiques*, ed. by Jean-Paul Morel (Paris: Séguier, 1995), pp. 60–66.

La Houssaie, Abraham-Nicolas Amélot de, *Mémoires historiques, politiques, critiques, et littéraires*, 3 vols (Amsterdam: Zacharie Chatelain, 1737).

La Porte, Pierre de, *Mémoires de M. de La Porte, premier valet de chambre de Louis XIV* (Paris: Volland, 1791).

La Vicane, Sieur de, *Lettre au Roy, Sur les Vertus Eminentes de Monseigneur le Cardinal Duc de Richelieu, Dans les heureuses Conduittes et Succez des Affaires de sa Majesté* (Paris: Pierre Mettayer, 1633).

Le Clerc, Jean, *La Vie du Cardinal, Duc de Richelieu*, 5 vols (Amsterdam: Aux dépens de la Compagnie, 1753).

Lefèvre, Nicolas, *La Vie de Michel de Marillac (1560–1632): garde des sceaux de France sous Louis XIII*, ed. and trans. by Donald A. Bailey (Laval: Presses Universitaires de Laval, 2007).

Lelong, Jacques, *Bibliothèque historique de la France, contenant Le Catalogue des Ouvrages, imprimées et manuscrits, qui traitent de l'Histoire de ce Royaume, ou qui y ont rapport*, rev. edn by Fevret de Fontette, 5 vols (Paris: Jean-Thomas Herissant, 1759).

Le Maistre, Antoine, *Recueil de divers plaidoyers et harangues, Prononcez au Parlement par Mr Antoine le Maistre* (Paris: Michel Bobin, 1652).

Lemoine, Pierre-Camille, *Diplomatique-pratique ou traité de l'arrangement des archives et trésors des chartes* (Metz: Joseph Antoine, 1765).

L'Estoile, Claude de, 'Ode à Monseigneur le cardinal de Richelieu, in *Le Sacrifice des Muses, au grand cardinal de Richelieu* (Paris: Sebastien Cramoisy, 1635).

Malherbe, François de, 'À un Gentil-homme de ses amys. Il le dissuade de sa recherche', in *Recueil de lettres nouvelles*, ed. by Nicolas Faret (Paris: Toussainct du Bray, 1627).

Marais, Mathieu, *Journal et mémoires de Mathieu Marais, avocat au Parlement de Paris, sur la régence et le règne de Louis XV (1715–1737): publiés pour la première fois d'après le manuscrit de la Bibliothèque impériale*, ed. by Adolphe Mathurin de Lescure, 4 vols (Paris: Firmin-Didot, 1863–68).

Marolles, Michel de, *Mémoires de Michel de Marolles, abbé de Villeloin*, ed. by Claude Pierre Goujet, 3 vols (Amsterdam: [n.pub.], 1755).

—*Tableaux du Temple des Muses Representant les Vertus, et les vices, sur les plus illustres fables de l'Antiquité* (Paris: Antoine de Sommaville, 1655).

Le Mercure François, 25 vols (Paris: Jean Richer, 1617–48).

Mersenne, Marin, *Harmonie universelle, contenant la theorie de la pratique de la musique* (Paris: Sébastien Cramoisy, 1636).

Molière, Jean-Baptiste Poquelin de, *Œuvres complètes*, ed. by Georges Forestier and Claude Bourqui, 2 vols (Paris: Gallimard, 2010).

Montglat, François de Paule de Clermont, marquis de, *Mémoires de François de Paule de Clermont, marquis de Monglat*, ed. by Guillaume-Hyacinthe Bougeant, 4 vols (Amsterdam: [n.pub.], 1727).

Montpensier, Anne Marie Louise d'Orléans, duchesse de, *Mémoires de la Grande Mademoiselle*, ed. by Bernard Quillet (Paris: Mercure de France, 2005).

Montplaisir, René de Bruc, marquis de, *Poesies de Lalanne et du marquis de Montplaisir*, ed. by Charles Hugues Lefebvre de Saint-Marc (Amsterdam and Paris: Pierre Alexandre Leprieur, 1759).

Montrésor, Claude de Bourdeille, comte de, *Mémoires de Monsieur de Montresor. Diverse Pieces durant le Ministere du Cardinal de Richelieu*, 2 vols (Cologne: Jean Sambix le jeune, 1663).

Moreri, Louis, *Le Grand dictionnaire historique, ou le mélange curieux de l'histoire sacrée et profane*, 2 vols, 3rd edn (Lyon: Jean Girin and Barthélemy Rivière, 1683).

Morgues, Mathieu de, *Abrege de la vie du cardinal de Richelieu pour luy server d'epitaphe* ([Antwerp]: [n.pub.], 1643).

>–*Catolicon François, ou plainctes de deux chasteaux, rapportées par Renaudot, maistre du bureau d'adresses* ([Antwerp?]: [n.pub.], 1636).

>–*Catholicon Français, ou plaintes de deux chasteaux, rapportées par Renaudot, maistre du bureau d'adresse*, in *Pièces curieuses en suite de celles du sieur de S. Germain*, 3 vols ('Sur la coppie imprimée à Anvers': [n.pub.], 1644).

>–*Jugement sur la Préface et diverse pieces que le cardinal Richelieu prétend de faire servir à l'histoire de son credit*

(1635), in *Diverses pieces pour la defense de la Royne Mere du roy tres-chrestien Louis XIII*, pp. 512–90.

–*La verité defendue: ensemble quelques observations sur la conduite du Cardinal de Richelieu*, in *Diverses pieces pour la defense de la Royne Mere du roy tres-chrestien Louis XIII* ([Antwerp]: [n.pub.], [1637]), pp. 435–511.

Motteville, Françoise de, *Mémoires pour servir à l'histoire d'Anne d'Autriche, épouse de Louis XIII, roi de France*, 5 vols (Amsterdam: François Changuion, 1723).

Mourgues, Michel, *Traité de la poësie françoise*, rev. edn (Paris: Jacques Vincent, 1724).

Naudœana et Patiana, ou singularitez remarquables prises des conversations de Mess. Naudé et Patin (Paris: Florentin and Pierre Delaulne, 1701).

Navarre, Marguerite de, *Heptaméron*, ed. by Simone de Reyff (Paris: Garnier Flammarion, 1982).

Pasquier, Étienne, *Pourparlers*, ed. by Béatrice Sayhi-Périgot, Textes de la Renaissance, 7 (Paris: Champion, 1995).

Patin, Guy, *Les Lettres de Guy Patin à Charles Spon, janvier 1649–février 1655*, ed. by Laure Jestaz, Bibliothèque des Correspondances, Mémoires et Journaux, 21 (Paris: Champion, 2006).

Pellison-Fontanier, Paul, *Histoire de l'Académie française*, rev. edn Pierre-Joseph d'Olivet, 2 vols (Paris: Jean-Baptiste Coignard, 1729).

Pereisc, Nicolas-Claude Fabri de, *Les Correspondants de Peiresc: lettres inédites*, ed. by Philippe Tamizey de Larroque, 2 vols (Paris, 1879–97; Geneva: Slatkine, 1972).

Prault, Louis-Laurent, *L'Esprit d'Henri IV, ou anecdotes les plus intéressantes, Traits sublimes, Reparties ingénieuses, et quelque Lettres de ce Prince* (Paris: Prault, 1775).

Rabelais, François, *Tiers Livre*, ed. by M. A. Screech, Textes Littéraires Français, 102 (Geneva: Droz, 1964).

Recueil des harangues prononcées par messieurs de l'Académie françoise, dans leur receptions, et en d'autres occasions differentes, depuis l'establissement de l'Académie jusqu'au present, 2 vols (Amsterdam: Aux dépens de la Compagnie, 1709).

Renaudot, Théophraste, *Mémoires de Théophraste Renaudot*, ed. by Christian Bailly (Paris: Albatros, 1981).

Retz, Jean-François Paul de Gondi, Cardinal de, *Œuvres*, ed. by Marie-Thérèse Hipp and Michel Pernot (Paris: Gallimard, 1984).

Richelet, Pierre, *La Versification françoise, ou l'art de bien faire et de bien tourner les vers* (Paris: Estienne Loyson, 1671).

Richelieu, Armand Jean du Plessis, Cardinal de, *La Correspondance du cardinal de Richelieu: au faîte du pouvoir, l'année 1632*, ed. by Marie-Catherine Vignal Souleyreau (Paris: L'Harmattan, 2007).

—*Europe, comédie héroïque. Attribuée à Armand du Plessis, Cardinal de Richelieu et Jean Desmarets Sieur de Saint-Sorlin*, ed. by Sylvie Taussig (Turnhout: Brepols, 2006)

— *Les Papiers de Richelieu: section politique intérieure, correspondance et papiers d'État*, ed. by Pierre Grillon, 6 vols (Paris: Pedone, 1975–85).

—*Testament politique*, ed. by Louis André (Paris: Laffont, 1947).

Ronsard, Pierre de, *Œuvres complètes*, ed. by Jean Céard et al, 2 vols (Paris: Gallimard, 1993–94).

Rou, Jean, *Mémoires inédits et opuscules de Jean Rou (1638–1711)*, ed. by Francis Waddington, 2 vols (Paris: Agence Centrale de la Société, 1857).

Rousselet, George Estienne, *Le Lys sacré, justifiant le bon-heur de la pieté par divers Parangons du Lys avec les vertus, et les miracles du Roy S. Louys, et des autres Monarques de France* (Lyon: Louis Muguet, 1631).

Saint-Amant, Marc Antoine Girard de, *Saint-Évremond et comte d'Ételan, La Comédie des Académistes et Saint-Évremond, Les Académiciens*, ed. by Paolo Carile (Milan: Cisalpino-Goliardica; Paris: Nizet, 1976).

Saint-Simon, Louis de Rouvroy, duc de, *Mémoires*, ed. by Arthur de Boislisle, 11 vols (Paris: Hachette, 1890–1930).

Sales, François de, *Œuvres completes de saint François de Sales, évêque et prince de Genève*, ed. by Henry-Joseph Crelier and Adolphe-Charles Peltier, 12 vols (Paris: Vivès, 1866).

Scaliger, Adam *dit* Chevalier de L'Escale, *La vertu resuscitée, ou la vie du Cardinal Albornoz, surnommé pere de l'Eglise* (Paris: Toussainct du Bray, 1629).

Séguier, Pierre, *Lettres et mémoires adressés au chancelier Séguier (1633–1649)*, ed. by Roland Mousnier, 2 vols (Paris: PUF, 1964).

Sirmond, Jean, *La Vie du cardinal d'Amboise, en suite de laquelle sont traités quelques points sur les affaires présentes* (Paris: Étienne Richer, 1631).

Soulas, Hilaire, *Anagrammes sur les noms du Roy, de la Reyne, de M' le Cardinal de Richelieu, de M' le Cardinal de Lyon, et de Monsieur l'Evesque de Poictiers* (Poitiers: Veuve d'Antoine Mesnier, 1633).

Stefanovska, Malina, 'Exemplary or Singular? The Anecdote in Historical Narrative', *Substance*, 118 (2009), 16–30.

Tallemant des Réaux, Gédéon, *Historiettes*, ed. by Antoine Adam, 2 vols (Paris: Gallimard, 1960–61).

—*Le Manuscrit 673*, ed. by Vincenette Maigne (Paris: Klincksieck, 1994).

Talon, Omer, *Mémoires d'Omer Talon*, in *Nouvelle Collection des Mémoires pour servir à l'histoire de France depuis le XIIIe siècle jusqu'à la fin du XVIIIe*, ed. by Joseph-François Michaud and John-Joseph-François Poujoulat, 10 vols (Paris: Didot, 1836–39).

Van Pasce, Eris, *Le roi et le cardinal dans une nef sur la Seine* (1628), BN, B12052/ Qb1 1628.

Vaugelas, Claude, *Remarques sur la langue françoise utiles a ceux qui veulent bien parler et bien escrire* (Paris: Jean Camusat and Pierre Le Petit, 1647).

Vialart, Charles, *Histoire du ministère d'Armand Jean du Plessis Cardinal Duc de Richelieu, sou le règne de Louis le Juste XIII. du nom. Roy de France et de Navarre* (Paris: Gervais Alyot et al, 1649).

Voiture, Vincent, *Lettres de Vincent Voiture*, ed. by Octave Uzanne (Paris: Librairie des Bibliophiles, 1880).

Voltaire, François-Marie Arouet de, *Correspondance and Related Documents*, ed. by Theodore Besterman, *The Complete Works of Voltaire*, LXXXV–CXXXV (Oxford: Voltaire Foundation, 1968–77).

C: SECONDARY WORKS

Abad, Reynald, 'Une première Fronde au temps de Richelieu? L'émeute parisienne des 3–4 février 1631 et ses suites', *DSS*, 218 (2003), 39–70.

Abraham, Claude, *Norman Satirists in the Age of Louis XIII*, Biblio 17, 8 (Tübingen: Narr, 1983).

Adam, Antoine, *Histoire de la littérature française au XVIIe siècle*, 5 vols (Paris: Domat, 1948–56).

Arnould, Colette, *La Satire, une histoire dans l'histoire* (Paris: PUF, 1996).

Auden, W. H., 'Notes on the Comic', *Thought*, 27 (1952), 57–71.

Audiat, Louis, *Un Fils d'Estienne Pasquier: Nicolas Pasquier, lieutenant général et maître des requêtes. Étude sur sa vie et sur ses écrits* (Paris: Didier, 1876).

Avezou, Laurent, 'La Légende de Richelieu: fortune posthume d'un rôle historique du XVIIe au XXe siècle' (unpublished doctoral thesis, Université Paris I, 2002).

–'Richelieu vu par Mathieu de Morgues et Paul Hay du Chastelet: le double miroir de Janus', *Travaux de Littérature*, 18 (2005), 167–78.

–'Le tombeau littéraire de Richelieu: genèse d'une héroïsation', *Hypothèses*, 1 (2001), 181–90.

Bailey, Donald Atholl, 'Les pamphlets de Mathieu de Morgues (1582–1670): bibliographie des ouvrages disponibles dans les bibliothèques parisiennes et certaines bibliothèques des États-Unis', *Revue Française d'Histoire du Livre*, 18 (1978), 3–48.

—'Writers Against the Cardinal: A Study of the Pamphlets which Attacked the Person and Policies of Cardinal Richelieu during the Decade 1630–1640' (unpublished PhD thesis, University of Minnesota, 1973).

Barbafieri, Carine, 'Hercule et Achille, héros français au XVIIe siècle: de la vraisemblance à l'âge classique', *L'Information littéraire*, 60.3 (2008), 43–54.

Barbier, Alexandre-Antoine, *Dictionnaire des ouvrages anonymes*, 2 vols (Paris: Daffis, 1874).

Bennini, Martine, *Les Conseillers à la Cour des Aides (1604–1697): étude sociale*, Histoire et Archives, 9 (Paris: Champion, 2010).

Bercé, Yves-Marie, 'Richelieu: la maîtrise de l'histoire et le conformisme historique', in *Idéologie et propagande en France*, ed. by Myriam Yardeni (Paris: Picard, 1987), pp. 99–106.

Bergin, Joseph, *Cardinal Richelieu: Power and the Pursuit of Wealth* (New Haven and London: Yale University Press, 1985).

—'Richelieu and His Bishops: Ministerial Power and Episcopal Patronage under Louis XIII', in *Richelieu and His Age*, ed. by Joseph Bergin and Laurence Brockliss (Oxford: Oxford University Press, 1992), pp. 175–202.

Bertière, Simone, *La Vie du cardinal de Retz* (Paris: Fallois, 1990).

Bireley, Robert, *The Jesuits and the Thirty Years War: Kings, Courts, and Confessors* (Cambridge: Cambridge University Press, 2003).

Blet, Pierre, *Richelieu et l'Église* (Versailles: Via Romana, 2007).

Bluche, François, *L'Ancien Régime: institutions et société* (Paris: Fallois, 1993).

—(ed), *Dictionnaire du Grand Siècle* (Paris: Fayard, 1990).

—*Richelieu: essai* (Paris: Perrin, 2003).

Boissier, Denis, *L'Affaire Molière: la grande supercherie littéraire* (Paris: Godefroy, 2004).

Bonnet, Marie-Jo, *Les Relations amoureuses entre les femmes du XVIe au XXe siècle: essai historique* (Paris: Jacob, 1995).

Bonney, Richard, *Political Change in France under Richelieu and Mazarin, 1624–1661* (Oxford: Oxford University Press, 1978).

—*Society and Government in France under Richelieu and Mazarin, 1624–61* (Basingstoke: Macmillan, 1988).

Bourgeois, Émile, and Louis André, *Les Sources de l'histoire de France, XVIIe siècle (1620–1715)*, 8 vols (Paris: Picard, 1913–35).

Bouteiller, Paul, 'Étienne Pasquier (1529–1615): sa vie et sa carrière' (unpublished doctoral thesis, Université de Lille III, 2001).

Braider, Christopher, *Indiscernible Counterparts: The Invention of the Text in French Classical Drama*, North Carolina Studies in the Romance Languages and Literatures, 275 (Chapel Hill: University of North Carolina Press, 2002).

Bredbeck, Gregory W., *Sodomy and Interpretation: Marlowe to Milton* (Ithaca: Cornell University Press, 1991).

Breiner, Laurence A., 'The Basilisk', in *Mythical and Fabulous Creatures: A Source Book and Research Guide*, ed. by Malcolm South (New York: Greenwood, 1987), pp. 113–22.

Brunet, Jacques-Charles, *Manuel du libraire et de l'amateur de livres*, 2 vols (Paris: Didot, 1861).

Burckhardt, Carl J. *Richelieu and His Age*, trans. Bernard Hoy, 3 vols (New York: Jovanovitch, 1970).

Butterworth, Emily, *Poisoned Words: Slander and Satire in Early Modern France*, Research Monographs in French Studies, 21 (Oxford: Legenda, 2007).

Carabin, Denise, 'Les Lettres de Nicolas Pasquier: la lettre de consolation', *Revue d'Histoire Littéraire de France*, 102 (2002), 15–31.

Carmona, Michel, *Richelieu: l'ambition et le pouvoir* (Paris: Seine, 1990).

Carrier, Hubert, *Les Muses guerrières: les Mazarinades et la vie littéraire au milieu du XVIIe siècle* (Paris: Klincksieck, 1996).

—*La Presse de la Fronde (1648–1653): les Mazarinades, la conquête de l'opinion* (Geneva: Droz, 1989).

Carroll, Stuart, *Blood and Violence in Early Modern France* (Oxford: Oxford University Press, 2006).

Catteeuw, Laurie, 'Censure, raison d'État et libelles diffamatoires à l'époque de Richelieu', *Papers on French Seventeenth-Century Literature*, 71 (2009), 363–75.

Castagnos, Pierre, *Richelieu face à la mer* (Rennes: Ouest-France, 1989).

Chartier, Roger, 'Pamphlets et gazettes', in *Histoire de l'édition française*, ed. by Henri-Jean Martin and Roger Chartier, 4 vols (Paris: PROMODIS, 1982–86).

Chaussinand-Nogaret, Guy, *Le Cardinal Dubois, 1656–1723* (Paris: Perrin, 2000).

Condeescu, N. N., 'Étlan contre Richelieu: à propos d'un pamphlet inédit "Le Passage de Somme" ou "Vers héroïques"', *Revue des Sciences Humaines*, 137 (1970), 15–26.

Constant, Jean-Marie, 'Le discours sur la guerre de l'opposition nobiliaire à Richelieu: amorce d'une autre vision politique et philosophique du monde', in *Armées, guerre et société dans la France du XVIIe siècle: actes du VIIIe Colloque du Centre international de rencontres sur le XVIIe siècle, Nantes, 18–20 mars 2004*, ed. by Jean Garapon, Biblio 17, 167 (Tübingen: Narr, 2006), pp. 25–35.

Courcelles, Jean-Baptiste de, *Histoire généalogique et héraldique des pairs de France, des grands dignitaires de la couronne, des principales familles nobles du royaume, et des maisons princières de l'Europe*, 12 vols (Paris: Bertrand, 1822–33).

Couton, Georges, *Richelieu et le théâtre* (Lyon: Presses Universitaires de Lyon, 1989).

Crawford, Katherine, *Perilous Performances: Gender and Regency in Early Modern Europe* (Cambridge, MA: Harvard University Press, 2004).

Csűrös, Klára, *Variétés et vicissitudes du genre épique de Ronsard à Voltaire*, Littérature Générale et Comparée, 21 (Paris: Champion, 1999).

Cummings, Mark L., 'The Long Robe and the Scepter: A Quantitive Study of the Parlement of Paris and the French Monarchy in the Early Seventeenth Century' (unpublished doctoral thesis, University of Colorado, 1969).

Dandrey, Patrick (ed.), *Dictionnaire des lettres françaises: le XVIIe siècle* (Paris: Fayard, 1996).

–*L'Éloge paradoxal de Georgias à Molière* (Paris: PUF, 1997).

Darnton, Robert, *The Devil in the Holy Water or the Art of Slander from Louis XIV to Napoleon* (Philadelphia: University of Pennsylvania Press, 2010).

Daston, Lorraine, and Katharine Park, 'The Hermaphrodite and the Orders of Nature: Sexual Ambiguity in Early Modern France', *GLQ: A Journal of Lesbian and Gay Studies*, 1 (1995), 419–38.

Desmaze, Charles, *Le Parlement de Paris: son organisation, ses premiers presidents et procureurs généraux* (Paris: Lévy, 1859).

Dubost, Jean-François, *Marie de Médicis: la reine dévoilée* (Paris: Payot, 2009).

Duccini, Hélène, *Faire voir, faire croire: l'opinion publique sous Louis XIII* (Seyssel: Champ Vallon, 2003).

Duggan, Anne E., 'Criminal Profiles, Diabolical Schemes, and Infernal Punishments: The Cases of Ravaillac and the Concinis', *Modern Language Review*, 105 (2010), 366–84.

Duprat, Annie, *Les Rois de papier: la caricacture de Henri III à Louis XVI* (Paris: Belin, 2002).

Elliott, J. H., *Richelieu and Olivares* (Cambridge: Cambridge University Press, 1991).

Faure, Gaëlle, 'How Plagiarism Software Finds a New Shakespeare Play', *Time*, 20 October 2009, <http://www.time.com/time/arts/article/0,8599,1930971,00.html>.

Fayard, Ennemond, *Aperçu historique sur le Parlement de Paris*, 3 vols (Paris: Picard, 1876–78).

Feinberg, Leonard, *Introduction to Satire* (Ames: Iowa State University Press, 1967).

Ferretti, Guiliano, 'Richelieu, le "Ministre-soleil" de la France, d'après une gravure d'Abraham Bosse', *Genèses*, 48 (2002), 136–53.

Ferreyolles, Gérard, 'Jansénius politique: le *Mars Gallicus*', in *Justice et force: Politiques au temps de Pascal. Actes du colloque "Droit et pensee politique autour de Pascal", Clermont-Ferrand, 20–23 septembre 1990*, ed. by Gérard Ferreyolles (Paris: Klincksieck, 1996), pp. 95–108.

Fumaroli, Marc, 'Richelieu, patron des arts', in *Richelieu: l'art et le pouvoir*, ed. by Hilliard Todd Goldfarb (Montreal: Musée de beaux-arts de Montréal, 2002), pp. 15–47.

Gatulle, Pierre, 'La grande cabale de Gaston d'Orléans aux Pays-Bas espagnols et en Lorraine', *DSS*, 231 (2006), 301–26.

Giesey, Ralph E., Lanny Haldy, and James Millhorn, 'Cardinal Le Bret and Lese Majesty', *Law and History Review*, 4 (1986), 23–54.

Gilby, Emma, 'Les textes qui nous restent de Tallemant de Réaux: mise au point bibliographique', *DSS*, 232 (2006), 513–21.

Glasson, Ernest, *Le Parlement de Paris: son rôle politique depuis le règne de Charles VII jusqu'à la Révolution*, 2 vols (Paris: Hachette, 1901).

Gonçalves, José, *Philippe de Champaigne: le patriarche de la peinture, 1602–1674* (Paris: ACR, 1995).

Griffin, Dustin, *Satire: A Critical Reintroduction* (Lexington: University Press of Kentucky, 1994).

Grosjean, A. N. L., 'Hepburn, John (*c.*1598–1636)', in *Oxford Dictionary of National Biography* (Oxford: Oxford University Press, 2004) <http://www.oxforddnb.com/view/article/13005>.

Haehl, Madeleine, *Les Affaires étrangères au temps de Richelieu: le secretariat d'État, les agents diplomatiques (1624–1642)* (Brussels: Lang, 2006).

Halperin, David M., 'How to Do the History of Male Homosexuality', *GLQ: A Journal of Lesbian and Gay Studies*, 6 (2000), 87–123.

Hildesheimer, Françoise, *Relectures de Richelieu* (Paris: Publisud, 2000).

–*Richelieu* (Paris: Flammarion, 2004).

–'Richelieu et Séguier ou l'invention d'une créature', in *Études sur l'ancienne France offertes en hommage à Michel Antoine*, ed. by Bernard Barbiche and Yves-Marie Bercé (Paris: École des Chartes, 2003), pp. 209–26.

James, Alan, 'L'évolution de la stratégie navale française du XVIe au XVIIe siècle: la guerre de trente ans en Méditerranée', *Cahiers de la Méditerranée*, 71.2 (2005), 1–25.

Joris, Freddy, *Mourir sur l'échafaud: sensibilité collective face à la mort et perception des executions capitals du Bas Moyen Âge à la fin de l'Ancien Régime* (Liege: Céfal, 2005).

Kadlec, Lauriane, *Quand le Parlement de Paris s'oppose à l'autorité royale: l'affaire de la chambre de l'Arsenal (14 juin 1631–mars 1632)*, Histoire et Archives, 7 (Paris: Champion, 2007).

Kearney, Patrick J., *A History of Erotic Literature* (London: Macmillan, 1982).

Keating, L. Clark, *Étienne Pasquier*, Twayne World Authors Series, 24 (New York: Twayne, 1972).

Kerviler, René Pocard du Cosquer de, *Le Chancelier Pierre Séguier, second protecteur de l'Académie française: études sur sa vie privée, politique et littéraire et sur le groupe académique de ses familiers et commensaux* (Paris: Didier, 1874).

Kettering, Sharon, 'Patronage and Kinship in Early Modern France', *French Historical Studies*, 16 (1989), 408–35.

Knecht, Robert, *Richelieu* (London: Longman, 1991).

Knox, Ronald A., 'On Humour and Satire', in *Satire: Modern Essays in Criticism*, ed. by Ronald Paulson (Englewood Cliffs: Prentice-Hall, 1971), pp. 52–65.

Koch, Erec R., *The Aesthetic Body: Passion, Sensibility, and Corporeality in Seventeenth-Century France* (Newark: University of Delaware Press, 2008).

Kociszewska, Ewa, 'The Sun King in the Realm of Eternal Winter: The Unknown Medal of Henri de Valois, King of Poland (1573)', *French Studies Bulletin*, 113 (2009), 78–82.

Koritz, L. S., *Scarron satirique* (Paris: Klincksieck, 1977).

Labatut, Pierre, 'Aspects de la fortune de Bullion', *DSS*, 60 (1963), 11–37.

Lacour, Léopold, *Richelieu dramaturge et ses collaborateurs: les imbroglios romanesques, les pièces politiques* (Paris: Ollendorff, 1926).

Lagny, Jean, *Le Poète Saint-Amant (1594–1661): essai sur sa vie et ses œuvres* (Paris: Nizet, 1964).

Larsen, Egon, *Wit as Weapon: The Political Joke in History* (London: Muller, 1980).

Laurentin, René, *Le Vœu de Louis XIII: passé ou avenir de France, 1638–1988, 350ᵉ anniversaire* (Paris: L'Œil, 1988).

Leber, Jean-Michel-Constant, *De l'état réel de la presse et des pamphlets depuis François Iᵉʳ jusqu'à Louis XIV* (Paris: Techener, 1834).

Leffler, Phyllis K., 'French Historians and the Challenge to Louis XIV's Absolutism', *French Historical Studies*, 14 (1985).

Le Guillou, Yves, *Les Bouthillier, de l'avocat au surintendant (vers 1540–1650): l'histoire d'une ascension sociale et formation d'une fortune* (Angoulême: Société Archéologique et Historique de la Charente, 1999).

Leoni, Edgar, *Nostradamus: Life and Literature* (New York: Exposition, 1961).

Lever, Maurice, *Les Bûchers de Sodome: histoire des "infames"* (Paris: Fayard, 1985).

Lim, Seung-Hwi, 'Mathieu de Morgues, Bon Français ou Bon Catholique?', *DSS*, 213 (2001), 655–72.

Levi, Anthony, *Cardinal Richelieu and the Making of France* (London: Robinson, 2000).

Loskoutoff, Yvan, *L'Armorial de Calliope: l'œuvre du Père Le Moyne S.J. (1602–1671). Littérature, héraldique, spiritualité*, Biblio 17, 125 (Tübingen: Narr, 2000).

Lüsebrink, Hans-Jürgen, and Rolf Reichardt, *The Bastille: A History of a Symbol of Despotism and Freedom*, trans. Norbert Schürer (Durham, NC: Duke University Press, 1997).

Magne, Émile, *Bourgeois et financiers du XVIIe siècle: la Fin troublée de Tallemant des Réaux d'après des documents inédits* (Paris: Émile-Paul, 1922).

Matei-Chesnoiu, Monica. *Early Modern Drama and the Eastern European Elsewhere: Representations of Liminal Locality in Shakespeare and his Contemporaries* (Madison: Fairleigh Dickinson University Press, 2009).

Mauzaize, Raoul J., 'La promotion cardinalice du Père Joseph de Paris et l'affaire des Custodes', *Études Franciscaines*, 16 (1966), 48–79.

Merle du Bourg, Alexis, *Peter Paul Rubens et la France* (Lille: Presses Universitaires du Septentrion, 2004).

Merrick, Jeffrey, 'The Cardinal and the Queen: Sexual and Political Disorders in the Mazarinades', *French Historical Studies*, 18 (1994), 667–99.

Minois, Georges, *Censure et culture sous l'Ancien Régime* (Paris: Fayard, 1995).

Mongrédien, Georges, *Isaac de Laffemas: le bourreau de Richelieu (documents inédits)* (Paris: Brossard, 1929).

–*La Vie littéraire au XVIIe siècle* (Paris: Tallandier, 1947).

Montbas, Hugues de, *Richelieu et l'opposition pendant la Guerre de Trente Ans (1635–1638)* (Paris: H. Champion, 1913).

Moote, A. Lloyd, *Louis XIII, the Just* (Berkeley: University of California Press, 1989).

Moreau, Célestin, *Bibliographie des Mazarinades publiée pour la Société de l'Histoire de France*, 3 vols (Paris: Renouard, 1850–51).

–*Choix de Mazarinades*, 2 vols (Paris: Renouard, 1853).

Mousnier, Roland, *Les Institutions de la France sous la monarchie absolue, 1589–1789*, 2 vols (Paris: PUF, 1974–80).

–*L'Homme rouge ou la vie du Cardinal de Richelieu (1585–1642)* (Paris: Laffont, 1992).

Murray, Timothy C., 'Richelieu's Theater: The Mirror of a Prince', *Renaissance Drama*, 8 (1977), 257–98.

Niderst, Alain, *Madeleine de Scudéry, Paul Pellisson et leur monde* (Paris: PUF, 1976).

Ó Gráda, Cormac, and Jean-Michel Chevet, 'Famine and Market in Ancien Régime France', *Journal of Economic History*, 62 (2002), 706–33.

Parrott, David, *Richelieu's Army: War, Government and Society in France, 1624–1642* (Cambridge: Cambridge University Press, 2001).

Phillips, Henry, *Church and Culture in Seventeenth-Century France* (Cambridge: Cambridge University Press, 1997).

–'Richelieu and the Edict of 1641', *Seventeenth-Century French Studies*, 15 (1993), 71–84.

Piat, Colette, *Le Père Joseph: le maître de Richelieu* (Paris: Grasset, 1988).

Pierre, Benoist, *Le Père Joseph: l'éminence grise de Richelieu* (Paris: Perrin, 2007).

Poulaille, Henry, *Corneille sous le masque de Molière* (Paris: Grasset, 1957).

Prévot, Jacques, *Cyrano de Bergerac, poète et dramaturge* (Paris: Belin, 1978).

Ranum, Orest A., 'Courtesy, Absolutism, and the Rise of the French State, 1630–1660', *Journal of Modern History*, 52 (1980), 426–51.

—*Richelieu and the Councillors of Louis XIII: A Study of the Secretaries of State and Superintendants of Finance in the Ministry of Richelieu 1635–1642* (Oxford: Clarendon Press, 1963).

—'Richelieu, guerrier héroïque?', in *Armées, guerre et société*, ed. Garapon, pp. 269–81.

Redfern, Walter, *Puns* (Oxford: Blackwell, 1984).

Russell, Daniel, 'M. de Montplaisir and His Emblems', *Neophilologus*, 67 (1983), 503–16.

Sauvy, Anne, *Livres saisis à Paris entre 1678 et 1701*, Archives Internationales d'Histoire des Idées, 50 (The Hague: Nijhoff, 1972).

Sawyer, Jeffrey K., *Printed Poison: Pamphlet Propaganda, Faction Politics, and the Public Sphere in Early Seventeenth-Century France* (Berkeley: University of California Press, 1990).

Scott, Paul, '"Ma force est trop petite": Authority and Kingship in *Le Cid*', *Forum for Modern Language Studies*, 45 (2009), 292–304.

—'Subversive Revisions in the Work of Charles de Beys', *French Studies*, 60 (2006), 177–90.

Seifert, Lewis, *Manning the Margins: Masculinity and Writing in Seventeenth-Century France* (Ann Arbor: University of Michigan Press, 2009).

—'Masculinity and Satires of "Sodomites" in France 1660–1715', in *Homosexuality in French History and Culture*, ed. by Jeffrey Merrick and Michael Sibalis (London: Routledge, 2002), pp. 37–52.

Sheehy, Philip Leo, 'The *Cour des Aides de Paris*: Perspectives on the Seventeenth-Century French Magistrature' (unpublished doctoral thesis, University of California, Los Angeles, 1977).

Shennan, J. H., *The Parlement of Paris*, 2nd edn (Stroud: Sutton, 1988).

Shoemaker, Peter W., *Powerful Connections: The Poetics of Patronage in the Age of Louis XIII* (Newark: University of Delaware Press, 2007).

Souleyreau, Marie-Catherine Vignal, *Richelieu et la Lorraine* (Paris: L'Harmattan, 2004).

—*Richelieu ou la quête d'Europe* (Paris: Pygmalion, 2008).

Test, George A., *Satire: Spirit and Art* (Tampa: University of South Florida Press, 1991).

Thomas, Jean-Pierre, *Le Régent et le cardinal Dubois: l'art de l'ambiguïté* (Paris: Payot, 2004).

Treasure, Geoffrey, *Mazarin: The Crisis of Absolutism in France* (London: Routledge, 1995).

Vance, Sylvia P., *The Memoirs of the Cardinal de Retz*, Biblio 17, 158 (Tübingen: Narr, 2005).

Vidal, Philippe, *Molière-Corneille: les mensonges d'une légende* (Paris: Lafon, 2003).

Watts, Derek A., 'Le sens des métaphores théâtrales chez le cardinal de Retz et quelques écrivains contemporains', *Travaux de Linguistique et de Littérature*, 13 (1975), 385–400.

Weigert, Roger-Armand, and Maxime Préaud, *Inventaire du Fonds français: graveurs du XVIIe siècle*, 17 vols (Paris: Bibliothèque Nationale, 1939–2008).

Wilson, Peter H., *The Thirty Years War: Europe's Tragedy* (London: Penguin, 2009).

Winegarten, Renee, 'A Neglected Critic of Malherbe: Jacques Favereau', *French Studies*, 6 (1952), 29–34.

MHRA Critical Texts

This series aims to provide affordable critical editions of lesser-known literary texts that are not in print or are difficult to obtain. The texts will be taken from the following languages: English, French, German, Italian, Portuguese, Russian, and Spanish. Titles will be selected by members of the distinguished Editorial Board and edited by leading academics. The aim is to produce scholarly editions rather than teaching texts, but the potential for crossover to undergraduate reading lists is recognized. The books will appeal both to academic libraries and individual scholars.

Malcolm Cook
Chairman, Editorial Board

Editorial Board
Professor Catherine Maxwell (English)
Professor Malcolm Cook (French) (*Chairman*)
Professor Ritchie Robertson (Germanic)
Professor Derek Flitter (Spanish)
Professor Brian Richardson (Italian)
Dr Stephen Parkinson (Portuguese)
Professor David Gillespie (Slavonic)

Published titles

1. *Odilon Redon, 'Écrits'* (edited by Claire Moran, 2005)
2. *Les Paraboles Maistre Alain en Françoys* (edited by Tony Hunt, 2005)
3. *Letzte Chancen: Vier Einakter von Marie von Ebner-Eschenbach* (edited by Susanne Kord, 2005)
4. *Macht des Weibes: Zwei historische Tragödien von Marie von Ebner-Eschenbach* (edited by Susanne Kord, 2005)
5. *A Critical Edition of 'La tribu indienne; ou, Édouard et Stellina' by Lucien Bonaparte* (edited by Cecilia Feilla, 2006)
6. *Dante Alighieri, 'Four Political Letters'* (translated and with a commentary by Claire E. Honess, 2007)
7. *'La Disme de Penitanche' by Jehan de Journi* (edited by Glynn Hesketh, 2006)
8. *'François II, roi de France' by Charles-Jean-François Hénault* (edited by Thomas Wynn, 2006)
9. *Istoire de la Chastelaine du Vergier et de Tristan le Chevalier* (edited by Jean-François Kosta-Théfaine, 2009)
10. *La Peyrouse dans l'Isle de Tahiti, ou le Danger des Présomptions: drame politique* (edited by John Dunmore, 2006)
11. *Casimir Britannicus. English Translations, Paraphrases, and Emulations of the Poetry of Maciej Kazimierz Sarbiewski* (edited by Krzysztof Fordoński and Piotr Urbański, 2008)

12. *'La Devineresse ou les faux enchantements'* by Jean Donneau de Visé and Thomas Corneille (edited by Julia Prest, 2007)
13. *'Phosphorus Hollunder'* und *'Der Posten der Frau'* von Louise von François (edited by Barbara Burns, 2008)
14. *Le Gouvernement present, ou éloge de son Eminence, satyre ou la Miliade* (edited by Paul Scott, 2010)
15. *Ovide du remede d'amours* (edited by Tony Hunt, 2008)
16. Angelo Beolco (il Ruzante), *'La prima oratione'* (edited by Linda L. Carroll, 2009)
17. Richard Robinson, *'The Rewarde of Wickednesse'* (edited by Allyna E. Ward, 2009)
18. Henry Crabb Robinson, *'Essays on Kant, Schelling, and German Aesthetics'* (edited by James Vigus, 2010)
20. Evariste-Désiré de Parny, *'Le Paradis perdu'* (edited by Ritchie Robertson and Catriona Seth, 2009)
21. Stéphanie de Genlis, *'Histoire de la duchesse de C***'* (edited by Mary S. Trouille, 2010)
22. Louis-Charles Fougeret de Monbron, *Le Cosmopolite, ou le citoyen du monde (1750)* (edited by Édouard Langille, 2010)
24. Narcisse Berchère, *Le Désert de Suez: cinq mois dans l'Isthme* (edited by Barbara Wright, 2010)
25. *Casimir Britannicus. English Translations, Paraphrases, and Emulations of the Poetry of Maciej Kazimierz Sarbiewski. Revised and Expanded Edition* (edited by Krzysztof Fordoński and Piotr Urbański, 2010)
27. *Aza ou le Nègre* (edited by Loïc Thommeret, 2010)

Forthcoming titles

19. *A Sixteenth-Century Arthurian Romance: 'L'Hystoire de Giglan filz de messire Gauvain qui fut roy de Galles. Et de Geoffroi de Maience son compaignon'* (edited by Caroline A. Jewers, 2010)
23. *La Chastelaine du Vergier. Livre d'amours du Chevalier et de la Dame Chastellaine du Vergier* (edited by Jean-François Kosta-Théfaine, 2011)
26. *'Eugénie et Mathilde'* by Madame de Souza (edited by Kirsty Carpenter, 2011)
28. Eliza Haywood, *'The Fortunate Foundlings'* (edited by Jan Herman and Beatrijs Vanacker, 2011)
29. Edward Kimber, *'The Happy Orphans'* (edited by Jan Herman and Beatrijs Vanacker, 2011)

For details of how to order please visit our website at www.criticaltexts.mhra.org.uk

www.ingramcontent.com/pod-product-compliance
Lightning Source LLC
Chambersburg PA
CBHW070547170426
43201CB00012B/1746